Teaching the Struggle
for Civil Rights,
1948–1976

Caroline R. Pryor, Jason Stacey, Erik Alexander,
Charlotte Johnson, and James Mitchell
General Editors

Vol. 1

The Teaching Critical Themes in American History
series is part of the Peter Lang Education list.
Every volume is peer reviewed and meets
the highest quality standards for content and production.

PETER LANG
New York • Bern • Berlin
Brussels • Vienna • Oxford • Warsaw

Teaching the Struggle for Civil Rights, 1948–1976

Edited by Whitney G. Blankenship

PETER LANG
New York • Bern • Berlin
Brussels • Vienna • Oxford • Warsaw

Library of Congress Cataloging-in-Publication Data

Names: Blankenship, Whitney G., editor.
Title: Teaching the struggle for civil rights, 1948–1976 /
edited by Whitney G. Blankenship.
Description: New York: Peter Lang, 2018.
Series: Teaching critical themes in American history; v. 1
ISSN 2576-0718 (print) | ISSN 2576-0726 (online)
Includes bibliographical references and index.
Identifiers: LCCN 2017060892 | ISBN 978-1-4331-4953-5 (hardback: alk. paper)
ISBN 978-1-4331-4366-3 (paperback: alk. paper)
ISBN 978-1-4331-5413-3 (ebook pdf) | ISBN 978-1-4331-5414-0 (epub)
ISBN 978-1-4331-5415-7 (mobi)
Subjects: LCSH: African Americans—Civil rights—
History—20th century—Study and teaching. | Minorities—Civil rights—
United States—History—20th century—Study and teaching.
Civil rights movements—United States—History—20th century—Study and teaching.
Civil rights—United States—History—20th century.
United States—Race relations—History—20th century—Study and teaching.
Classification: LCC E185.61.T255 2018 | DDC 305.896/0730904—dc23
LC record available at https://lccn.loc.gov/2017060892
DOI 10.3726/b13305

Bibliographic information published by **Die Deutsche Nationalbibliothek**.
Die Deutsche Nationalbibliothek lists this publication in the "Deutsche
Nationalbibliografie"; detailed bibliographic data are available
on the Internet at http://dnb.d-nb.de/.

Table of Contents

Tables

Preface to the Book Series Teaching Critical Themes in American History

The purpose of this book series is to provide teachers an examination of critical issues in American history and provide resources to teach these issues. The resources found in this series are: (a) historical content for exploring critical issues, (b) historical context for addressing the themes of civil rights and liberties, (c) examples of how to use national standards to augment lessons, and (d) primary and secondary source material to support the investigation of critical themes in American history.

In working with teachers who had developed lesson plans for our earlier publication on Abraham Lincoln, the theme that we (Pryor & Hansen, 2014) most often discussed was the nature and embodiment of civil rights and civil liberties. These teachers had, over the course of eight years, participated in a workshop titled *Abraham Lincoln and the Forging of Modern America,* funded by the National Endowment for the Humanities. This series of workshops prompted the development of Pryor and Hansen's 2014 book, *Teaching Lincoln: Legacies and Classroom Strategies,* a collection of essays and lesson plans written by historians, teachers and teacher educators.

We learned from these teachers that the challenges of teaching main events of the Lincoln era were many—however, the larger challenge was how to teach *critical issues* of this era. One of the themes of our workshop was slavery. A challenge for teachers had been how to address critical issues emanating from Lincoln's announcement of the Emancipation Proclamation. What role would newly free slaves have? Would they be citizens? If citizens, what rights would they have (e.g., the right to vote). From this awareness, we wondered what content and pedagogical resources teachers might need to more deeply address the critical issue of *all of American history—civil rights and civil liberties.*

The main theme of this book series emerged as the editorial team developed the topic of each volume and noticed the struggles and challenges of teaching each topic. These teaching challenges appeared to us as we explored how to provide students a more robust experience when learning about historical events. We drew from this pedagogical challenge the need to describe the political philosophies underlying the American historical narrative.

Book Series Organization

The series is initially composed of 10 separately titled books each examining a different significant problem/critical issue in American history. The target audiences of the series are middle and secondary school teachers and university professors of teacher education. Each volume will contain disciplinary content in American history, a discussion of disciplinary connectedness linking past and present thematic issues, a discussion of the pedagogical challenges in teaching that content, examples of lesson plans, and resources teachers could use in the classroom.

Each of the volumes can stand alone and each will directly address the Common Core Standards (CC) adopted by 46 states (http://www.core-standards.org), the C3 Framework (C3.ncss.org) and the National Curriculum Standards (NCS) of the National Council of the Social Studies (ncss.org). The *theme* (title) of each volume is supported by a series of *topics* (ideas/problems/questions) critical to understanding the theme. To connect the series' themes, topics within each theme may reappear in several volumes.

Each volume is accompanied by access to an electronic resource that will contain primary documents, secondary literature, and projects that the teacher can assign to the students based on and linked to the complementary foci of Common Core Standards, the C3 Framework, and the National Curriculum Standards of NCSS. The e-resource will be kept on a website designed and maintained by the editors and housed by the publisher of the series. Each book in the series and the accompanying e-resource can be used to supplement existing textbooks.

Caroline R. Pryor, Series Editor,
on behalf of the Editorial Team,
Jason Stacy, Erik Alexander,
Char Johnson and James Mitchell, 2017

Reference

Pryor, C. R., & Hansen, S. L. (2014). *Teaching Lincoln: Legacies and classroom strategies.* New York, NY: Peter Lang Publishers.

Acknowledgments

With appreciation and acknowledgement to the Series Editorial Advisory Board for their work, insights and dedication to teachers, students and the production of this series.

Whitney Blankenship, Laura Milsk Fowler, Brian Gibbs, Michael E. Karpyn, Julianna Kershen, Stephanie McAndrews, Jack Sevin, Mary Stockwell, and Dennis U. Urban Jr.

We also appreciate and acknowledge:

Stephen L. Hansen for his vision in bringing critical historical issues to the forefront of how teachers and students might discuss history.

Sarah Bode and Sara McBride, Peter Lang Publishing, for their flexibility and openness in testing new constructs and their helpful suggestions to bring these about.

To our respective universities for their support of our academic endeavors.

Introduction

WHITNEY G. BLANKENSHIP

The teaching of the modern Civil Rights movement has often focused on a narrow era roughly beginning with *Brown v. Board of Education of Topeka Kansas* and ending around 1968 with the assassination of Martin Luther King, Jr. Within this time frame the traditional textbook narrative often focuses on a few heroic individuals such as Rosa Parks and Martin Luther King, Jr., and key events including the Montgomery Bus Boycott, the lunch counter sit-ins, and the March on Washington. As a result, students gain an incomplete picture of the complexity of the African American civil rights movement, and a narrow understanding of the intersectionality of the many freedom movements of the period. This volume speaks to the missing voices of the traditional textbook narrative by focusing on the development of the modern civil rights movement in the period from 1947 to 1976.

The movements that emerged during this time frame can be understood to embrace two enduring themes: (1) the modern civil rights movement did not occur in a vacuum, but was shaped by the intersection of the foreign and domestic policy of the period; and (2) the strategies and tactics used by groups to achieve their aims evolved throughout the period in response to local, state, national, and international reactions to the freedom movements. These themes revolve around the quest for civil rights and civil liberties as they were experienced by participants in those movements. Recursive themes aid our understanding of why the modern civil rights movement exploded onto the scene in the mid-20th century even though organizations such as the National Association for the Advancement of Colored People, the Sleeping Car Porters Union, and the United Negro Improvement Association had been working towards greater economic, political, and social equality since the end of the 19th century.

Within the larger themes are sub-themes reflecting the role of lesser known individuals' contributions to the movement; the intersectionality between the African American, Women's Liberation, Chicano, and Asian American movements; and the absence of textbook narratives around controversial issues such as lynching. Through the investigation of these themes in the historical analysis chapters and the questions posed within the pedagogical challenges chapters, teachers can use the volume as a foundation for their own curricular planning.

The volumes' focus on this pivotal period in the evolution of the United States' understanding of civil rights and civil liberties offers deeper historical context that can enrich the narrative beyond the rather straightforward narrative of the freedom movements seen in textbooks and popular media. The emphasis on inquiry learning to address civil rights topics allows students to build their critical historical thinking skills while also giving teachers exemplars of inquiry projects to use as a starting point in their own curricular planning.

Pedagogical Content Knowledge and Teaching the Civil Rights Movement

One of the goals of this volume is to provide educators with a series of essays focused on historical and pedagogical issues related to the teaching of the Civil Rights Movement from 1948 to 1976. Lee Shulman (1987) described teacher practice as the confluence of an educators' content knowledge and pedagogical knowledge. He argued that each is a separate domain encompassing a deep understanding of disciplinary content and skills and an understanding of instructional best practices. These two discrete forms of knowledge come together as pedagogical content knowledge (PCK)—knowing *what* content to teach and *how* to teach it. Given that instructors may shy away from topics they do not feel prepared to teach, PCK provides a framework for the volume. The historical analysis essays are designed to strengthen teachers' content knowledge, while the pedagogical challenges essays alert teachers to potential areas of challenge and provide strategies to deal with those challenges. In short, the volume aims to deepen teachers' PCK.

The historical analysis essays that follow provide educators with rich historical content addressing people and events that are not typically covered in social studies textbooks. The authors provide insight into the overlapping goals of multiple civil rights movements as well as the tensions within and among movements.

The historical analysis section begins with Gary Homana's chapter focusing on the era of legal segregation in Baltimore, Maryland. Calling on oral history interviews completed as part of a larger documentary project, he highlights the unique experiences of students involved in the desegregation of Baltimore public schools. Homana's essay is followed by Kristen Duncan's "Education for Emancipation," which highlights the Mississippi Freedom schools established during the 1964 Freedom Summer. Duncan delves into the creation and implementation of the Freedom School curriculum by faculty and staff. As with the Homana essay, it offers insight into the unique reactions of communities to desegregation. The third essay by Chaddrick Gallaway is focused on Septima Clark. In much the same vein as Homana and Duncan, Gallaway illuminates the role of Clark's efforts as an educator, and illustrates the intersectionality of the African American civil rights movement and the Women's Movement. Taken together, these essays bring to light individuals whose experiences are integral to understanding the breadth of the Civil Rights movement.

The fourth essay moves the conversation away from local civil rights efforts, focusing instead on the role of Black athletes. In their essay, "They Never Lynched You, They Never Called You a N****," Christopher Busey and Paul Mencke use the frame of critical patriotism to underscore the role of these athletes in relation to the larger civil rights movement. Although athletes are occasionally brought into civil rights lesson via Muhammad Ali's anti-Vietnam position, or the integration of baseball by Jackie Robinson, the authors expand the list to include Wilma Rudolph, Kareem Abdul-Jabbar, and Jim Brown. Busey and Mencke also include contemporary athletes' political protests. The chapter provides a fresh perspective on the issue of race and athletics that is often missing from classroom lessons.

In addition to the essays addressing the African-American movement, the final essays in this section shed light onto other contemporaneous movements. "From the Margin to Center Stage: The Chicano Movement" identifies key people and events not commonly taught when discussing the Chicano Movement of the late 1960s and 1970s. The author, Ellen Bigler, calls for an expansion of the narrative beyond Cesar Chavez and the United Farm Workers (UFW), by emphasizing the work of women such as Delores Huerta and the connections between the UFW and the Filipino workers who started the Delano Grape Strike. In a similar fashion, Phonsia Nie and Noreen Naseem Rodriguez address the absence of Asian Americans in traditional civil rights narratives. Although the Chinese Exclusion Act and Japanese-American Internment are typically included in social studies curricula, the contributions of Asian Americans to 20th century civil rights groups are relatively absent. Nie and Naseem Rodriguez provide the reader with an introduction to the movement and give voice to the "Yellow Power" movement.

A limitation of this volume is the absence of Native American voices. This is problematic for a text seeking to widen the understanding of all civil rights movements of the period. Currently there are very few scholars within the social studies community doing work in this area and they are often stretched in their commitments to publish; as a result manuscripts covering Native American movements are scarce. Equally important is that social studies (as a whole) has not always done a good job of reaching out to Native American scholars to join in these conversations. It is hoped that as the number of scholars continues to increase and the social studies embraces the expansion of civil rights teaching to go beyond the traditional narrative that future volumes in the series will address Native American experiences.

The Pedagogical Challenges section begins with an essay by Aaron Bruewer and Jayne Beilke, "Teaching the Long Civil Rights Movement." The opening chapter addresses the problems of contextualization that are often missing from traditional civil rights curricula (which typically start with the 1954 Brown case and end with the 1965 Voting Rights Act). The authors stress the need for teachers to explicitly provide much-needed context to these events through the use of digital tools such as multimedia timelines and digital storytelling. They argue that these strategies help students to understand not only what came before and after a particular event, but also how any one event is situated within an era.

Controversial issues such as lynching are often ignored or glossed over in K–12 classrooms for a variety of reasons, including fear of losing control of the conversation and the possibility of criticism from parents or administrators. Bryan Gibbs suggests that having these difficult conversations is an important part of learning about civil rights movements. He incorporates specific suggestions for how lynching should be approached and makes clear connections to contemporary incidents of lynching to reinforce the need to include the topic in civil rights lessons.

"From the Bottom Up: Citizenship Education during the Civil Rights Movement," by authors LaGarrett King and John Moore, serves as a companion piece to Duncan's historical analysis essay on Freedom Schools. The authors argue that the master narrative of the civil rights movement most commonly taught in schools does not engage students in historical thinking, and provides only a very narrow picture of the movement as a whole. They posit that the narrative tends to show a movement that had a top-down structure—focusing on the heroic feats of a few key players while ignoring the massive bottom-up structure of the movement as it actually played out. They conclude with specific suggestions for teachers to consider when planning units of inquiry focused on a bottom-up narrative.

"It was never that simple" authored by ArCasia James is a companion piece to Gallaway's historical essay on Septima Clark. James argues that school segregation is consistently taught as being a positive for everyone involved. She draws upon the experiences of individuals from the mid-West who were the first to integrate their schools. The inclusion of narratives of African Americans involved in desegregation outside of the deep south provides a more complex understanding of the civil rights movement and the ordinary people who were involved.

The final piece in the pedagogical issues section focusses on the use of critical historical inquiry to understand the Latina/o Civil Rights Movement. In "The GI Forum, Felix Longoria, and *El Movimiento*" authors Cinthia Salinas, Amanda Vickery, and Noreen Naseem Rodriguez reveal the intersectionality of the Asian, Chicano, and African American movements, as well as the women's movement. It offers specific strategies for using critical historical inquiry to aid students understanding of civil rights movements across the era. The chapter provides a pedagogical companion piece to Bigler's historial analysis of *El Movimiento*, as well as Nie and Naseem Rodriguez's chapter on the Asian American civil rights movement.

Addressing the Common Core and Inquiry

In addition to addressing the pedagogical content knowledge needed to teach the civil rights movement, the volume also addresses the need for educators to include the Common Core State Standards (CCSS). The CCSS were introduced with the goal of boosting students' literacy and mathematics skills (National Governors' Association, 2010) and were implemented as an antidote to the patchwork of state standards that had come into existence in the early 1990s with the advent of the standards movement. The CCSS focus on literacy and mathematics led to the sublimation of the social studies under the literacy standards and only a passing reference to disciplinary literacy was included in the completed document. Social studies' answer to the CCSS was the creation of the College, Career, and Civic Life Framework (C3) emphasizing the use of inquiry in social studies classrooms. The C3 Framework continues to pose challenges for teachers preparing to teach social studies content and skills, as well as critical issues throughout United States history (National Council for the Social Studies [NCSS], 2016a) in a number of ways.

The CCSS pose a significant challenge for in-service teachers and for the pre-service training of teachers. Specifically, teachers using existing textbooks have difficultly preparing lessons that address the Common Core standards for social studies/history (Grant, 2014), when they are used as "stand-alone" standards. The C3 Framework expands on the CCSS requirement that students use textual evidence to support their analysis of primary and secondary sources, along with evaluating and integrating multiple perspectives into coherent narratives by focusing on the Inquiry Arc. Described as "a set of interlocking and mutually reinforcing elements that move from developing questions and planning inquiries to communicating conclusions and taking informed action" (Grant, Swan, & Lee, 2017, p. 3) the C3 Framework pushes beyond the CCSS by reinforcing the notion that content and disciplinary skills are important. Unlike the CCSS, the Inquiry Arc allows for content and skills to "become part of a curriculum and instructional whole" (p. 3). Even though inquiry has been included in social studies curricula in the past, its use has not been consistent. While the idea of including inquiry may be intriguing to teachers it can be an intimidating strategy to implement, particularly in an educational environment that places a premium on standardized testing. This can be especially difficult for preservice teachers who are still learning their craft. With these issues in mind the historical analysis and pedagogical issues essays are followed by a third section consisting of lesson plans developed using the Inquiry Design Model developed by S. G. Grant, Kathy Swan, and John Lee as part of C3 Teachers (2017). The lessons serve as a resource for teachers to engage in inquiry with their students as they become familiar with the inquiry design process. They are aligned to the topics addressed in the historical and pedagogical essays to capitalize on teachers' developing pedagogical content knowledge.

Educating for Citizenship: Common Core and the C3 Framework

Citizenship education has played a fundamental role in American education since the beginning of the public school system. Schools were expected to "Americanize" children from diverse immigrant communities into "model Americans" (Tyack, 1974; Tyack & Cuban, 1995). John Dewey's *Democracy and Education* (1916) imagined schools as the driving force behind preparing students for life in a democratic society and progressive educators followed his lead. Although other priorities also emerged during World War II and the Cold War, educators continued to view their primary task as one of preparing students for citizenship (Blankenship, 2008, 2015; Evans, 2004, 2007; Ugland, 1979).

More recently the National Council for the Social Studies (NCSS) argued for the inclusion of "powerful and authentic" social studies curricula designed to specifically prepare students for participation in democratic life (NCSS,

1992, 2016b). This complex task was included in the organization's call for increasing civic learning so that "we will instill civic competencies in America's youth to create a citizenry prepared to meet the demands of higher education, the challenges of a global society, the complexities of a highly skilled workforce, and the opportunities of a nuanced democratic society" (NCSS, 2013).

The teaching of civil rights necessitates the teaching of often controversial issues. Classroom discussion of controversial issues is necessary for the development of skills needed for active citizenship in a democracy (Gagon, 1989; Hess, 2005, 2009; Parker, 2008). Hess (2009) noted that given the current political climate teachers may choose to omit controversial issues from classroom discussions, further dampening even the most dedicated teachers' desire to go beyond the master narrative of the textbook. However, research has also shown that students who are able to make connections between the curriculum and their lived experiences gain a deeper and more nuanced understanding of the connections between the past and the present (Barton & Levstik, 2004; Downey & Levstik, 1991; Epstein, 2009; Salinas, Blevins, & Sullivan, 2012). This volume is presented as a resource for both in service and preservice teachers to strengthen their pedagogical content knowledge and provide exemplar inquiry lesson plans that may serve as models for the development of their own civil rights units. The inclusion of civil rights instruction that goes beyond the heroic and oversimplified narratives that became standard in many social studies classrooms is needed now more than ever.

References

Barton, K., & Levstik, L. (2004). *Teaching history for the common good.* Mahwah, NJ: Lawrence Erlbaum.

Blankenship, W. G. (2008). Education for victory: Pre-induction training at Austin High School, 1943–1945. *Curriculum History,* (2009), 16–30.

Blankenship, W. G. (2015). Social studies goes to war: An analysis of the pre-induction social studies curriculum of the Providence Public Schools. *American Educational History Journal, 42*(1), 65–78.

Dewey, J. (1916). *Democracy and education: An introduction to the philosophy of education.* New York, NY: The Macmillan Company.

Downey, M., & Levstik, L. S. (1991). Teaching and learning history. In J. P. Shaver (Ed.), *Handbook of research on social studies teaching and learning: A project of the National Council for the Social Studies* (pp. 400–410). New York, NY: Macmillan.

Epstein, T. (2009). *Interpreting national history: Race identity and pedagogy in classrooms and communities.* New York, NY: Routledge.

Evans, R. W. (2004). *The social studies wars: What should we teach the children?* New York, NY: Teachers College Press.

Evans, R. W. (2007). *This happened in America: Harold Rugg and the censure of social studies*. Charlotte, NC: Information Age Publishing, Inc.

Gagon, P. (1989). History's role in civic education: The precondition for political intelligence. In W. Parker (Ed.), *Educating the democratic mind* (Vol. 13, pp. 241–262). Albany, NY: State University of New York Press.

Grant, S. G. (2014). *History lessons: Teaching, learning, and testing in US high school classrooms*. Mahwah, NJ: Lawrence Erlbaum Associates.

Grant, S. G., Swan, K., & Lee, J. (2017). *Inquiry-based practice in social studies education: Understanding the inquiry design model*. New York, NY: Routledge and C3 Teachers.

Hess, D. E. (2005). Moving beyond celebration: Challenging curriculuar orthodoxy in the teaching of *Brown* and its legacies. *Teachers College Record, 107*(9), 2046–2067.

Hess, D. E. (2009). Controversial issues and democratic discourse. In L. Levstik & C. A. Tyson (Eds.), *Handbook of research in social studies education*. New York, NY: Routledge.

National Council for the Social Studies (NCSS). (1992). *A vision of powerful teaching and learning in the social studies: Building social understanding and civic efficacy* [Press release]. Retrieved from http://socialstudies.org/positions/powerful

National Council for the Social Studies (NCSS). (2013). *Revitalizing civic learning in our schools* [Press release]. Retrieved from http://www.socialstudies.org/positions/revitalizing_civic_learning

National Council for the Social Studies (NCSS). (2016a). *College, career, and Civic life (C3) framework for social studies state standards*. Retrieved from https://www.socialstudies.org/c3

National Council for the Social Studies (NCSS). (2016b). *A vision of powerful teaching and learning in the social studies*. *Social Education* (May/June), 180–182.

National Governors Association Center for Best Practices, & Council of Chief State School Officers. (2010). Common Core State Standards *Writing Anchor Standards*. Washington, DC.

Parker, W. C. (Ed.). Social Studies Today: Research and Practice. New York, NY: Routledge.

Salinas, C., Blevins, B., & Sullivan, C. C. (2012). Critical historical thinking: When official narratives collide with *other* narratives. *Multicultural Perspectives, 14*(1), 18–27.

Shulman, L. S. (1987). Knowledge and teaching: Foundations of the new reform. *Harvard Educational Review, 57*(1), 1–22.

Tyack, D., & Cuban, L. (1995). *Tinkering toward Utopia: A century of public school reform*. Cambridge, MA: Harvard University Press.

Tyack, D. B. (1974). *The one best system: A history of American urban education*. Cambridge, MA: Harvard University Press.

Ugland, R. M. (1979). Education for victory: The high school Victory Corps and curricular adaptation during World War II. *History of Education Quarterly, 19*(Winter 1979), 435–451.

Section 1

Historical Analysis

1. An American Dilemma: Contextualizing the Modern Civil Rights Movement, 1948–1976

ROBERT CVORNYEK AND WHITNEY G. BLANKENSHIP

The year of unrest and upheaval, 1968, symbolized the convergence of several freedom movements in the United States and throughout the world. The historical context for this eventful year and the freedom struggles it signified remain cast in a story that contemporary historians continue to reinterpret and refine. For some, the year represented the height of participatory protest. For others, it motioned the end of the modern Civil Rights era. Either way, disenfranchised Americans took to the streets to raise awareness of the discrepancies that existed between the ideals of democracy and the everyday realities of segregation, second-class citizenship, and economic injustice.

The origins, strategies, achievements, and disappointments that helped define the Civil Rights age are contested topics that generate academic debate and passionate discussion in the classroom. This is especially true for the African American freedom movement. The resistance to racial oppression that dramatically emerged during the 1960s exhibited characteristics of continuity and change relative to the long history of activism that preceded the decade.

By 1968, organizations including the National Association for the Advancement of Colored People, the Universal Negro Improvement Association, and the Brotherhood of Sleeping Car Porters established the earliest frameworks for racial equality (Levy, 1998). These organizations focused on a wide range of issues that included dismantling segregation, lobbying for anti-lynching legislation, guaranteeing fair housing and voting rights, and safeguarding educational and employment opportunities (Joseph, 2000; Levy, 1998; Lewis, 1998). These organizations shared a common cause, but the strategies to effect change and the principles that inspired their members differed broadly. The antecedents of the modern civil rights movements set a multi-dimensional stage for the dramatic developments that played out in newspapers and newscasts throughout the 1960s (Zangrando, 1969).

This era represents the mainstay in teaching about the Civil Rights Movement in classrooms across the country. Heroic figures such as Rosa Parks and Martin Luther King, Jr. capture the main focus of the schoolroom narrative that customarily begins with the *Brown* decision and ends with the rise of Black Power (Joseph, 2000; Loewen, 2007). What is often missing from the narrative is an understanding of the myriad individuals and groups that operated on the local level and resisted in spontaneous ways that escaped the historical record. Moreover, scholars pay inadequate attention to other civil rights movements of the period such as the Chicano movement, Black Power, Women's Liberation, and LGBTQ rights (Loewen, 2007; View, 2004). These omissions betray the complex interrelationships that existed among the groups and obscure the impact they had on each other. The absence of the lesser known figures, movements, and strategies paints an uneven and limited picture of the varieties of political, social, and economic reform.

Scholars frequently raise the question over the timing of the modern civil rights movement: why did it occur at this particular historical moment. One answer to this question reflects the recent scholarship by historians who place greater emphasis on the connection between domestic and foreign policy (Benziger & Cvornyek, 2004; Borstelmann, 2001; Dudziak, 2000; Gaines, 2007). This approach examines the transformative impact of World War II and the Cold War to further the freedom agenda. Advances in the struggle for equality became intimately linked with criticism by the nation's adversaries that America's political and economic institutions were neither inclusive nor responsive to the needs of all citizens (Dudziak, 2000; Gaines, 2007).

During World War II, African Americans in the factories and on the battlefield drew attention to the fact that they fought fascism and racism to help assure the survival of democracy; the same democracy that eluded them. This wartime experience encouraged African Americans to uncompromisingly claim their rights as first-class American citizens. Despite their sacrifices, African Americans encountered a post-war world that offered little hope for inclusion. Race relations remained stagnant (Benziger & Cvornyek, 2004).

What had changed was America's position in the global community. America assumed the mantel of leadership in the free world. America's ascension on the world stage created an opportunity for African Americans to exploit the nation's troubled racial past as leverage in the struggle to achieve a more just and equitable society. Could America's history of domestic racism undermine its moral leadership abroad? This, according to sociologist Gunnar

Myrdal, was the dilemma that confronted the United States. It should come as no surprise that the first successful efforts to desegregate public schools in the *Brown* case received the full support of the American State Department (Myrdal, 1962).

As the quest for Civil Rights transformed into the pursuit for liberation through Black Power, foreign policy concerns remained in play. African Americans employed a post-colonial critique to the police subjugation found in their communities and many supported Muhammad Ali's decision to evade the draft and label the Vietnam War as unjust (Benziger & Cvornyek, 2004). The escalation of the Vietnam War not only radicalized the Black freedom movement, it stimulated a militant shift within movements of liberation among women, Chicanos, American Indians, and the LGBTQ community. These movements questioned the legitimacy of American exceptionalism and challenged the belief that America's democratic institutions could deliver on the promise of freedom and equality (Benziger & Cvornyek, 2004; Zangrando, 1969).

An emphasis on the relationship between foreign and domestic policy does not reveal the whole story. Freedom movements adopted multiple strategies that evolved over time to address shifting domestic concerns. During the last half of the 20th century, specific strategies and tactics dominated at particular historical moments but never totally. New approaches were added and existing ones expanded as the situational context changed.

During the early years of the movement, for example, the NAACP looked to the courts for relief such as with school desegregation. This tactic dominated the reform program of the early period and remained a consistent and dependable force for change. The slow pace of change and the growing demand for direct action, however, led to the creation of mass, non-violent, and direct participatory efforts evidenced by the Southern Christian Leadership Conference and the Congress of Racial Equality. Protests organized by the SCLC and CORE were essentially top-down affairs with the leadership determining the agenda and organizing protests. Martin Luther King, Jr.'s leadership position within the SCLC, along with his ties to the national Democratic Party, drew criticism from local civil rights leaders who believed that the King-centered organizational style was out of touch with local concerns (Joseph, 2000; Lewis, 1998; Zangrando, 1969).

Although, non-violent direct participatory protest remained a central strategy, the needs of local, grassroots organizations called for different methods and approaches. In response, local leaders and neighborhood organizations sought to identify and challenge the power structure by training younger generations to be activists within their communities. Freedom Summer, and later the Delano Grape Boycott, capitalized on this strategy and laid a foundation for the community-based programs established by the Black Panthers. Grassroots activism eased the transition from civil rights to liberation and helped promote the benefits of self-identification, self-expression, and self-determination (Levy, 1998; View, 2004).

The following essays pose significant challenges to the traditional textbook narrative of the period by focusing on the range of tactics and strategies used by those engaged in the struggle for civil rights within national and international contexts. The authors establish connections between and among the various freedom movements and reveal the best strategies utilized to achieve their goals. The curricular materials highlight the agency exercised by minority communities to act on their own behalf and refresh the spirit of democracy through fresh ideas, tactics, and strategies.

References

Benziger, K. P., & Cvornyek, R. (2004). Redefining the narrative: The collision of American foreign and domestic policy in 1965, Vietnam and the civil rights movement. *International Journal of the Humanities, 2*(2), 1641–1650.

Borstelmann, T. (2001). *The cold war and the color line: American race relations in the Global Arena.* Cambridge: Harvard University Press.

Dudziak, M. L. (2000). *Cold war civil rights: Race and the image of American democracy.* Princeton, NJ: Princeton University Press.

Gaines, K. (2007). The civil rights movement in world perspective. *OAH Magazine of History, 21*(1), 57–64. doi:https://doi.org/10.1093/maghis/21.1.57

Joseph, P. E. (2000). Waiting till the midnight hour: Reconceptualizing the heroic period of the civil rights movement, 1954–1965. *Souls, Spring,* 6–17.

Levy, P. J. (1998). *The civil rights movement.* Westport, CT: Greenwood Press.

Lewis, J. (1998). *Walking with the wind: A memoir of the movement.* New York, NY: Simon and Schuster.

Loewen, J. (2007). *Lies my teacher told me: Everything your American history textbook got wrong.* New York, NY: Simon & Schuster.

Myrdal, G. (1962). *An American dilemma: The Negro problem and modern democracy.* New York, NY: Harper & Row.

View, J. L. (2004). Introduction. In D. Menkart, A. D. Murray, & J. L. View (Eds.), *Putting the movement back into civil rights teaching* (pp. 3–10). Upper Marlboro, MD: McArdle Printing.

Zangrando, R. L. (1969). From civil rights to black liberation: The unsettled 1960s. *Current History, 57*(339), 281.

2. Portraitures of Living in the Era of Legal Segregation: Baltimore, Maryland

GARY A. HOMANA

Voices of Baltimore: Life under Segregation (Homana, McDermott, & Campbell Jones, 2017) captures and preserves the rich oral histories of seven African Americans from the Mason-Dixon border area of Baltimore, Maryland who lived through the era of legal segregation (i.e., Jim Crow south). The project documents not just the stories, but something more—how the lived experiences intertwine and reflect both the individuals' personal integrity and moral imagination, as well as the ways that strong school and family supports, and cultural and religious institutions enabled them to maintain the resilience necessary to achieve equality and dignity in a historically oppressive society.

This film and accompanying curriculum guidebook will soon be available to pre-service and in-service teachers, schools and universities, and community members. Through these materials, people will learn more about Baltimore figures who never expected that their stories would become documentation of life in a historically oppressive society where the norms were in conflict with the very nature of democracy. As a teaching tool, the project is intended to engage students and adults in thoughtful discussion and critical analysis of the complex social, cultural, and political forces surrounding legal segregation and how they are reflected in schools and society today.

These narratives embody Goodson's notion of "critical incidents" that occur at various points across the life continuum creating "themes seen in a life perspective" (1992, p. 118). One feature of narrative construction focuses on the intersection of each life history with the history of society that "illuminate the choices, contingencies and options open to the individual" (p. 118). Critical incidents[1] shared by the film participants reveal much about the personal conflicts, role of family and community, high expectations for success, and the responsibility beyond oneself.

The dialogue from the unscripted interviews, which flowed from a discussion between the interviewee and film narrator, Dr. Franklin Campbell Jones, began with the initial open-ended prompt, "Share with us your experiences growing up during the era of legal segregation." A number of themes emerged from the responses to this question reflecting remarkable consistency across the conversations.

Although focused on Baltimore, reaction to the film by initial viewers suggest that the stories are representative of countless lives and experiences across the country, making the film both unique and shared. Noting that since perceptions of self, others, and the world are shaped by social and personal discourses, Grumet argues they do not lead to a fixed notion of voice (in Pinar, Reynolds, Slattery, & Taubman, 1995). Rather, she suggests that through these interactions "We have begun to hear our multiple voices within the contexts of our sustained collaboration, and thus recognized that 'finding voices' is not a definitive event but rather a continuous and relational process" (p. 525). Grumet, along with others (see for example, Barone, 1990; Ellis, 2004; Krizek, 2003; Pinar, 1998), supports the idea that autobiography, although inherently personal is not experienced or re-told in isolation but rather that the self is always in relationship to other persons across a range of unique contexts.

As we move forward as a country, especially in our current political and cultural environment, it is critical to understand and address the historical roots and contemporary relevance of the persistent inequality in our schools and society. This chapter is intended to help deconstruct the narrative of Jim Crow segregation relevant to black life in America during the mid-20th century. It explores four themes that emerged from the larger film narrative across the stories as presented in *Voices of Baltimore*. These themes include: (a) answering the call to civil rights; (b) the insular nature of segregated communities; (c) expectations and responsibilities greater than the self; and (d) reflections on desegregation and inequality within the context of society today.

Answering the Call to Civil Rights: "Making a Way Where There Ain't No Way"

Voices of Baltimore reveals that living through and breaking the barriers erected under Jim Crow America took on many forms in the lives of the participants. For example, according to Dr. Patricia Welch, just prior to the 1954 Brown v Board of Education Supreme Court ruling some of the film participants were "selected to attend the white schools—the girls would go to Eastern and the boys to City or Poly." Their parents were not consulted or asked whether the move to an all-white school would benefit their children. Rather, it appears that the decision was made by school administrators based on the students' ability to compete in the white schools. In other words, the students who were to integrate were high academic performers.

The film participants expressed the value of attending all-black schools during legal segregation. As Mrs. Frances N. Gill noted about her school, "I felt comfortable, I felt attractive. It was a school where there were people like me." According to our participants, black schools were places where students were supported and encouraged by their teachers to learn and succeed. The white schools, however, did not provide this type of encouragement—as shared by Dr. Welch regarding her experience at the all-white Eastern High School.

> And it was there that I was first introduced to another world, and it's different from my own comfortable world. And it's there that I met teachers who didn't think I should be smart and do well. I learned that it was just the opposite. You're not as smart as the rest of these children in this school.

Desegregation served as important junctures for how the participants viewed the world, the challenges that they would face, and how they would address those challenges. Similar to the above, school desegregation in Baltimore, as across the nation, also meant confrontation with angry protesters who wanted to maintain separate but equal. According to Dr. Walter A. H. Gill who was selected to integrate Poly Technic Institute:

> They were mostly white mothers because the men were at work. You know, it was get them out of our schools. The N-word was rarely used, it was get those Negros out, we don't want them in our schools, separate but equal. It was horrible.

Many white parents used religion to oppose desegregation. As a result, it was not uncommon for protest signs to read: Cursed is the Man Who Integrates, Holy Bible, Jeremiah 11:3–6; ½ Black + ½ White – ?; and God's Way is Not Integration. Others justified segregation based on individual "rights" for the "protection" of their children and families. A 1954 letter published by *The Baltimore Sun* from an individual opposing desegregated schools claimed the "right" to choose their child's classmates "One of our highest rights in this county is that of every man to dislike and avoid whom he pleases." It was an argument also made in the 1970s as justification for families "rights" against desegregation and for school choice (Baum, 2010, p. 219).

Despite the obstacles, legalized segregation were turning points for the participants leading them to become insistent that how they lived their lives made a difference for themselves, their communities, and society. With strong support from their families, teachers, and neighbors, they developed a resilience and determination to oppose inequality and injustice. As a 16 year-old student at Dunbar High School, one film participant, Robert Bell, was part of a movement organized by students at Morgan State University to challenge segregation by sitting at Hooper's Restaurant lunch counter—illegal in Maryland in 1960. The action resulted in the arrest and conviction of the twelve young students for criminal trespass. This led to the legal case, *Bell v. Maryland*, challenging racial discrimination based on violation of the Due Process and Equal Protection Clauses of the 14th Amendment of the United States Constitution, with Robert Bell as the lead plaintiff. The case was presented to the United States Supreme Court by Thurgood Marshall and Juanita Jackson Mitchel but was eventually overturned because by the time it was heard in 1964 both Maryland and Baltimore City had passed laws forbidding segregation of public facilities and all charges were dropped. Robert M. Bell would later attend Harvard Law School and become the first African American Chief Justice on the Maryland Court of Appeals.

There are countless stories shared by the *Voices of Baltimore* participants' civic engagement that reflect a deeply ingrained commitment to democracy, freedom, and the call for equal rights. For all of the participants, inequality would not be tolerated and the responsibility to stand up for human dignity and equal representation could not be ignored. In the words of Treopia Green Washington, another film participant, about the struggle and determination of living in legally segregated America, "All of the barriers that were there, [but] we were constantly able to find a way to either move them, go around them, or replace them in some sort of way."

Insulation/Isolation: The Insular Nature of Segregated Communities

Maryland was one of a handful of slave states that did not secede from the Union and join the Confederacy during the Civil War. The state's northern border is marked by the Mason-Dixon Line which symbolizes the "cultural boundary" between the north and south.

> Maryland is very much in the South, it's just up-South. There weren't signs like there were in Greenville, Mississippi, you know. And the Eastern shore was horrible. It was almost like Alabama and Mississippi. The last time there was a lynching was on the Eastern Shore. Central Maryland was split all the way back to the Civil War. (Gill, W.)

Yet, life under Jim Crow was different for African Americans living in Baltimore compared to African Americans living in the Deep South. As Chief Judge Robert Bell, whose family were rural southern sharecroppers shared,

> But when you went downtown on a Saturday, which was the day when everybody went downtown, they dealt with the same merchants, the same stores that everybody else dealt with. There was a difference. They went in the back doors. They were treated differently. There was a real deference that had to be paid to white people whether they were old or young. And I was never more embarrassed than when I saw my uncles being treated in a disrespectful way, and how they accepted that position.

While the first Jim Crow law in Maryland forbid marriages based on race (Maryland General Assembly, 1884) other laws in the early 20th century erected barriers for African Americans on railroad cars and steamboats. Perhaps the most influential, however, were the 1910–1913 Baltimore residential segregation ordinances prohibiting blacks and whites from living on the same street.[2] As a result, legalized segregation in Baltimore created geographical boundaries for African Americans—who were mostly confined to their black neighborhoods. For example, Chief Judge Bell disclosed "You were kept there in that neighborhood by, not necessarily because your parents kept you there, but because there was no place else to go—there was an obvious barrier." Other film participants described their experiences living in geographically segregated communities.

> My earliest awareness of Jim Crow was being in Baltimore County in an enclave in Overlea where we were surrounded by whites. You lived on two main blocks—the black people lived on two main streets, Beach Avenue where I grew up and Lindon Avenue. (Chatmon, E.)

> Schools were not integrated. There were black schools—schools only black children went. And so I only had black teachers. I never had the experience of white teachers. So everything was, you know—nothing was mixed. I know we might not have had a lot of things going on in school that maybe white schools had but we were all together. We went to the Y. The Y was, you know, for blacks. It was something we used to do. And we knew what we could and could not do. And go and could not go. (Gill, F.)

All of the Baltimore participants reported being denied access to segregated Baltimore sites such as Gwynn Oak Amusement Park, Read's Drugstore, the Cove Restaurant, White Castle Hamburger Shops, and Baltimore Junior College. Several participants explained how they couldn't even try on a hat or clothes in local department stores. Similar for people of color in America today, the film participants also shared experiences reflecting embedded hatred and racism.

Outside of our two streets it was scary. It could be very scary because you could be threatened at any moment. There were cross burnings and KKK might have been written at the end of the block—it could be very, very scary. (Chatmon, E.)

So I knew not far from where we lived, around the corner—which is now Guilford, I learned in Guilford—we used to walk through there, but you weren't welcome. You would move quickly because you really weren't supposed to be there. (Welch, P.)

I remember once I was stopped, and it was because I didn't go to school. I was out at Druid Hill Park. And this police officer, all he was going to do was to take me back to school, but he could've been—this particular case could have been even worse, if I defied him and looked him in the eye. And I've heard many of the older guys say, just don't look them in the eye, and feel that you have—I don't know what the word would be—but you've done what society wants you to do, don't argue with society, do what the whites say. (Diggs. L.)

Yet, legal segregation also had the effect of creating thriving and supportive communities among black Baltimoreans. For example, according to Dr. Gill, African Americans in black enclaves such as of Cross Keys "went to their own schools, families shopped at the same stores, people went to the same movie theaters and churches—all within the same neighborhoods." And, as Ms. Washington noted, the community afforded every opportunity to succeed in life.

Everything was separate. But the interesting thing—I think it was because my family, my family's friends, the community, church members, neighbors, made sure that we were able to do as many things as we possibly could. We never felt disenfranchised.

As throughout United States history, Jim Crow was another form of oppression that segregated African Americans into isolated communities with fewer resources. Yet, a critical theme shared by the participants was the resilience, determination, and the inherent belief instilled in them that they had a responsibility to stand up for equality. In this way, black communities not only served to buffer insidious and potentially dangerous outside forces, but also fostered expectations that not only would children succeed, but that they would bring others along after them (see Gill, 2016).

Expectations: The Responsibility Greater Than Yourself—the Obligation

A resonating theme shared by the participants was that black children had a responsibility to a whole group of people beyond themselves because they were expected to represent the race. Parents, neighbors, family members and teachers all understood the effects of segregation and were determined to ensure that children would become the "pioneers of possibility" (Homana et al., 2017). To achieve those possibilities, education was essential. The entire community insisted that children become the best they could, despite the legal restrictions placed on them. According to Treopia Washington, for example, "Mediocrity was not acceptable, only excellence. Our teachers and neighbors and families pushed, not to excess, but pushed us to do better and to excel." Other participants shared similar experiences.

> All the teachers instilled in us that we had to be twice as good. And you heard that mantra over and over again. You have to be twice as good. There was a great sense of pride in what we did, in who we were and people just motivated you. And you not only got it in school, you got in in the community. (Chatmon, E.)

> We knew to go back to our junior high school and talk to our teachers. And they propped us up, it was like you've got to stay there. No, you're not going to transfer and go to Douglas. You are going to stay at that school [Eastern High School], do your work, and you're going to be fine. So then it became even more critical that you do the best that you can and that you go to school each and every day, and no matter what's said to you, no matter how it's said to you, you stay there. (Welch, P.)

The demand for academic excellence of children living in Baltimore's African American enclaves such as Sandtown, Cherry Hill, Westport, Fairfield, Sugar Hill, and Hoe's Heights meant more than just ensuring individual success, however. There was an interrelationship and interconnectedness in these neighborhoods that promoted, recognized and celebrated achievement. As Chief Judge Bell shared, "If today you had a celebration of this person breaking a barrier, we could look at someone doing it again tomorrow. And it was not something that just the family celebrated, but everybody did."

Therefore, in Baltimore, life under Jim Crow was all about community. The messages instilled were those of high expectations, being the best that you could, staying in school and helping others.

> So that was what I grew up in. A neighborhood of people expecting that I would do the right thing, and that I would go to school, and that I would be smart. And I was going to be somebody. (Welch, P.)

> The teachers were determined that you are going to learn something because they knew when you finish those 12 years, that you're going to be out there in that world and you're going to be facing some problems that you're not prepared for. (Diggs, L.)

For each of the film participants, the support received from their community fostered the development of shared norms and values essential during these turning points in their lives. The communities served as a vital resource which enabled them to understand who they were, how they could lie in and address the oppressive world of Jim Crow, and ways to achieve their full potential as members of their schools, neighborhoods and society. From this perspective, the incidents could be viewed as opportunities where the film participants developed conceptions of individual and group rights with explicit recognition of and value to civic pluralism—leading to their continual engagement as contributing adults in the community itself.

Then and Now: Where We've Been, Where We're Going

Too many African Americans, and others living in Baltimore and across the country, face ongoing challenges because of highly segregated and under-resourced schools; limited access to quality housing and health care; the existence of barren food deserts; and alarmingly high rates of unemployment and poverty, among other issues. All of the film participants shared how different it was growing up during legal segregation and their concerns for where the black community is today—especially when viewed through the lens of desegregation.

> The problem was not so much integration, but how it was mismanaged. You don't make change like that. You get people ready for change, you do education for black people, for white people. You don't just throw people together who have historically believed that they were better than us and then expect a different result, you're not going to get a different result. So, I regret that integration occurred in the way it occurred because the way it occurred was so unhealthy and so wrong. And a great part of that had to do with the resentment. (Chatmon, E.)

> What happened unfortunately is, integration has had its own problems, so-called integration. I mean it was never complete, but once you've got to the point where [segregation] was no longer illegal, then there was no need to talk about the issues. So what happens? People start going back to doing the same things they did before. (Bell, R.)

These concerns are especially relevant when placed within the context of the challenges facing the black community in Baltimore today. As discussed by Baum (2010) the end of Jim Crow was not the end of segregation. Rather, what occurred was a transition from de jure to de facto segregation, which continues today. In other words, no longer is segregation defined by laws, but by institutional practices.[3] As such, the participants were very deeply concerned about the challenges facing society and the need to address those challenges, including the increasing rise of racism and bigotry across the country.

I see us on the same track as we were on then. While we have made a tremendous amount of progress—if you look at it we have a good ways to go. And a lot of it has to do with trying to beat back—once again—the same kinds of issues that we were facing back then. You know, you would have thought that you wouldn't have to fight certain battles again, but we are now looking at a situation where race, as a factor—a negative factor—is again raising its head. Racism in this country is becoming much more tolerant.

But the truth of the matter is, the only way you're really going to get to the bottom of it is by confronting it. And the reason the white teachers don't have to, is because of white privilege. That's it. So somebody's got to challenge it. (Bell, R.)

It is a very, very different world from the world I grew up in, where the community was behind you, where in your schools everybody looked like you and those teachers knew that in order for you to succeed in society you had to really be good. (Chatmon, E.)

Well, one reason that we were successful is because we had Negro, colored, African American teachers who cared about us. That's not the case today, eighty-four percent of elementary school teachers are white females. So we can't go back to that. (Gill, W.)

Yet, despite the challenges, there is an unwavering commitment among all of the film participants to continue to make a difference in society. Their ongoing actions, attitudes, and perceptions about the possibilities in life reflect a determination to do what they believe is right and just. For them, their experiences during the Civil Rights era were critical incidents which marked a beginning of lives dedicated to inspire, teach and serve—especially youth.

I've been doing this volunteer work for over 25 years now. I give bus tours trying to attract children to go through these communities—just share history. And this old church that I discovered that was falling down no bigger than a large log cabin—converted it to Diggs-Johnson Museum, where I could really share history with children. (Diggs, L.)

I still feel compelled and I am so serious. I still feel I have to make sure that students in schools learn from people who understand who they are. And, yes, I would love to be in a clean environment in a wonderful school where the roof doesn't leak and it's cool and it's clean and orderly, but I need to make sure that students are known to their teachers. (Welch, P.)

I think there is a great need to help young people feel that they are capable, that they do have what it takes to do whatever it is they want to do. I really feel we need to take a greater look at what we're doing with very young children to help them to get to the place where they need to be. (Washington, T.)

Conclusion

What stands out from the stories shared in *Voices of Baltimore* is not neces-sarily the struggles that the film participants endured as a result of legalized segregation—although they are critical aspects of the Civil Rights era because they demonstrate the resilience of the participants to overcome inequality. Rather, a central theme of the narratives was the role of the African American community—the commitment of parents, family members, teachers, religious institutions and others to ensure that children would have every opportunity to become successful and make a difference in a society structured to promote inequality.

It should not be surprising that the strength of the African American community has been all but ignored in the historical account of the Civil Rights Movement, especially in secondary education textbooks. These stories are personal and the participants who shared them made very clear that who they are, the choices they made, and how they live is a result of the support, encouragement, and expectations from all of the members of the community in which they grew up. Until this documentary, this aspect of the lived stories in the struggle for civil rights have mostly been overshadowed in textbooks, film and other media about the success of desegregating America resulting from protests, heroic figures, and legislative outcomes.

Voices of Baltimore brings to the forefront the largely unrecognized con-tributions of the members of the African American community upon which the Civil Rights Movement rested—the support and expectations of children for high academic achievement, maintaining certain moral and ethical stan-dards in the face of adverse circumstances, and the responsibility to break the barriers constructed by legal segregation. Underlying all of these expectations was the obligation instilled in children to think and act beyond themselves, to serve as role models, and to bring others behind them along.

The shared belief among the film participants that desegregation was not achieved, and the parallels of Jim Crow to society today are invaluable because it shatters the myth that the achievements accomplished during the Civil Rights Movement solved the issues of inequality based on color. The participants emphasized that even though desegregation has improved the lives of many African Americans and other people of color, inequality con-tinues across all spectrums of society. As noted by the participants, these are manifest through increasingly oppressive legislative policies and practices related to issues such as voting rights, employment and housing, health care, and the detention and incarceration of people of color. And, certainly central to this analysis is understanding and addressing the increased rise in hate crimes and hate groups across the country (see for example, Potok, 2017).

Voices of Baltimore offers multiple approaches to teaching the struggle for civil rights. Underlying all teaching should be a focus on developing tolerance, respect, cooperation and the ability to understand others points of views. The use of reflective journals are a valuable tool in the development of critical thinking and analysis in this process. Reflective journals provide students opportunities to record their understandings, beliefs, assumptions and interactions with others helping to foster thoughtful engagement as they grapple with the complexities of inequality and oppression in America.

Before watching the film, for example, students could write in their reflective journals responses to specific questions about democracy and equality. Questions could include: Why does democracy exist and what is its purpose? Describe the cornerstones of democracy. Who should democracy serve and why? What is equality? What is inequality? Are there people in the United States who are denied democratic rights? Who are these people and in what ways are they denied these rights? In small groups students could discuss their responses to these questions using a guiding question such as: Why is democracy important for all? (For more, see for example, Facing History, Facing Ourselves, 2017).

"Answering the Call: Making a Way Where There Ain't no Way" is the first section of the film watched by the entire class. After watching this part of the film, students could engage in an open classroom discussion exploring what stood out for them from the shared stories and why. The teacher would serve as the facilitator prompting students to examine their beliefs and assumptions about segregation. For example, students might want to discuss Dean Welch's experience integrating all-white Eastern High School and the message given that she "was not as smart as the other [white] children" Possible prompts might be: What does this say about how schools were integrated and the attitude and preparation of the teacher? What about the position of the school system? How might it affect student learning and motivation to succeed? How does it reflect broader racial prejudice and strategies to perpetuate racial discrimination? As part of their ongoing analysis, and in preparation for the next assignment, each student would spend 5–10 minutes critically reflecting in their journals on what they learned and how it challenged their thinking about segregations, equality, and democracy in the United States. These may be difficult conversations for students to have, and equally difficult for teachers to navigate, but they are of vital importance to enable students to deeply understand their own assumptions and biases about these issues.

The second segment, "Insolation/Isolation: The Insular Nature of Seg-regated Communities" provides an opportunity for in-depth teaching and learning about Jim Crow America. The entire class could watch this part of the film then engage in an all class discussion about the stories and underlying forces of oppression. Student responses using the earlier questions on democ-racy and inequality could be incorporated into this discussion. As homework, or in-class if time and resources are available, students could work in small groups engaging in research on Jim Crow, what it was, where it came from, how it differed in the Deep South and border states—and even how racial oppression existed in other areas of the country. Central to this work is exam-ination of de jure and de facto segregation as barriers to equality. Although students would be required to find their own resources, the teacher could model expectations for the assignment using, for example, *The Rise and Fall of Jim Crow* (Thirteen Online, 2002). Prior to watching the next section of the film the different groups could share their research and new understand-ings about life under Jim Crow.

"Expectations: The Responsibility Greater Than Yourself—the Obliga-tion" centers on the strengths of the African American community and the high standards expected by the members of the community for their young people under legalized segregation. The shared stories in this part of the film should challenge students' acceptance of the traditional narrative about the Civil Rights Movement. Teaching focused on moving beyond the traditional narrative should engage students in exploring how successful communities functioned, the characteristics of these communities, and the expectations they demanded from their members. The teaching should disrupt the tradi-tional narrative and students' assumptions about black communities, serving to reframe understandings regarding the realities of these stories and those who lived them.

The final segment "Then and Now: Where We've Been, Where We're Going" provides a strong reminder of the continual existence of inequality in the United States today. The stories in this part of the film can serve as learning opportunities for students to engage in critical discussion on a range of issues. For example, continuing the desegregation theme, students could engage in thoughtful dialogue on whether the approach to desegregation, especially for schools, was successful. Central to this process is the teacher's capacity to facilitate discussion around controversial issues that may emerge based on students' assumptions and biases. As follow-up, students could review current research comparing different types of schools and demographic populations examining drop-out, school attendance, test scores, and college attendance data. Equally important is investigation into the role of informal learning opportunities related to the arts, sports, museums, and other community-based organizations. Additional work could explore issues such as poverty, social movements, and other federal and local policies and practices.

The current rise of hate groups, bigotry, intolerance, and racial violence occurring across the country are vivid reminders of the embedded legacies of slavery and Jim Crow. It is important therefore to not only examine the historical context of the legal and political changes for African Americans after the Civil War, and the resistance of many whites opposing these efforts, but how they established the foundation for what is happening today.[4] At the same teaching and learning focused only on discussion and enhancing understanding is not enough to address these concerns. *Voices of Baltimore* can serve as the foundation for students to address inequality, segregation, and other forms of oppression by linking learning in the classroom to active, collaborative, and hands-on participation to improve their communities. Opportunities for students to actively engage in organizing and participating in peaceful protests and political rallies; addressing inadequate housing, food, and health care; challenging discriminatory voter suppression and incarceration policies; and working with local community and national action groups on other issues that strengthen democracy are extensions of teaching the struggle for civil rights.

Voices of Baltimore is a powerful film that raises questions about issues related to America prior to and during the Civil Rights era of the twentieth century, where we are today, how we got here, where we need to go, and the possibilities moving forward. There are numerous applications for the film and upcoming curriculum guidebook beyond documenting and preserving these stories. This work is intended to engage students, teachers, families, professionals and communities in ongoing dialogues that critically analyze the continuing struggles around issues of equity, power, privilege, and social justice faced by people across the nation. As our country becomes more ethnically and racially diverse it is important to recognize that inequities persist. It is hoped that *Voices of Baltimore* will contribute not only to students' moral and ethical responsibilities to become voices of change, but our nation's ability to understand, address, and engage in positive change, especially in high poverty and culturally linguistically diverse schools and neighborhoods, so that all children have an opportunity to achieve their dreams.

Notes

1. Meaning the identification and exploration of moments which were turning points in the lives of the participants; such moments are also critical in that they create empathetic intersections between the subjective (though different) lens of the viewer who

is now experiencing the moment with the participant, and perhaps forming a new way of understanding previous held assumptions and biases.

2. These residential ordinances also led to customary segregation of schools, theaters, and other businesses (see Powell, G. 1983).

3. Institutional racism is evident for people of color today through, for example, unlawful arrests, denial of voting rights, school desegregation, and disparities in home ownership and employment (see Alexander, 2012).

4. The 14th Amendment of the U.S. Constitution validating the citizenship rights of all persons born in the United States and the 15th Amendment granting voting rights to all black men were ratified by the U.S. Congress in 1868 and 1870, respectively. Maryland did not ratify either of the Amendments until 1959 and 1973 (see The Maryland State Archives and the University of Maryland College Park, 2007).

References

Alexander, M. (2012). *The new Jim Crow: Mass incarceration in the age of color blindness.* New York, NY: The New Press.

Barone, T. (1990). Using narrative text as an occasion for conspiracy. In E. Eisner & A. Peshkin (Eds.), *Qualitative inquiry in education: The continuing debate* (pp. 305–326). New York, NY: Teachers College Press.

Baum, H. (2010). *Brown in Baltimore: School desegregation and the limits of liberalism.* Ithaca, NY: Cornell University Press.

Ellis, C. (2004). *The ethnographic I: A methodological novel about autoethnography.* Walnut Creek, CA: AltaMira Press.

Facing History, Facing Ourselves. (2017). Retrieved from https://www.facinghistory.org/

Gill, W. A. H. (2016). *Yesterday's tomorrows.* Baltimore, MD: Dual Image Consultants.

Goodson, I. (1992). Sponsoring the teacher's voice: Teachers' lives and teacher development. In A. Hargreaves & M. Fullan (Eds.), *Understanding teacher development* (pp. 117–127). New York, NY: Teachers College Press.

Homana, G. (Executive Producer/Director), McDermott, M., & Campbell Jones, F. (Producers/Directors). (2017). *Voices of Baltimore: Life under segregation* [Documentary]. United States: Project Voice Productions/Towson University.

Krizek, R. (2003). Ethnography as the excavation of personal narrative. In R. P. Clair (Ed.), *Expression of ethnography: Novel approaches to qualitative methods* (pp. 141–152). New York, NY: SUNY Press.

Maryland General Assembly. (1884). *Session laws: January 2–March 31, 1884.* Retrieved from http://msa.maryland.gov/megafile/msa/speccol/sc2900/sc2908/000001/000424/html/am424--365.html

Pinar, W. (Ed.). (1998). *Curriculum: Towards new identities.* New York, NY: Garland.

Pinar, W., Reynolds, W., Slattery, P., & Taubman, P. (1995). *Understanding curriculum.* New York, NY: Peter Lang.

Potak, M. (2017, February). *The year in hate and extremism.* Retrieved from https://www.splcenter.org/fighting-hate/intelligence-report/2017/year-hate-and-extremism/

Powell, G. (1983). Apartheid Baltimore style: The residential segregation ordinances of 1910–1913. *Maryland Law Review, 42*, 289–330. Retrieved from http://digital-commons.law.umaryland.edu/mlr/vol42/iss2/4

The Maryland State Archives and the University of Maryland College Park. (2007). *A guide to the history of slavery in Maryland.* Retrieved from http://msa.maryland.gov/msa/intromsa/pdf/slavery_pamphlet.pdf

Thirteen Online. (2002). *The rise and fall of Jim Crow.* Retrieved from http://www.pbs.org/wnet/jimcrow/

United States Supreme Court. (1964). *Bell v Maryland,* 378 U.S 226. Retrieved from https://supreme.justia.com/cases/federal/us/378/226/case.html

3. Education for Emancipation: The Mississippi Freedom Schools

KRISTEN E. DUNCAN

As the 1960s began, Black college students began to increase their role in the Civil Rights Movement. In April 1960, with the help of civil rights activist Ella Baker, a group of students who had been active in nonviolent protests throughout the South convened and formed the Student Nonviolent Coordinating Committee (SNCC). Baker had worked with Dr. Martin Luther King and the Southern Christian Leadership Conference (SCLC), and she convinced the students to organize themselves and maintain their agency instead of leaning on well-known charismatic leaders to take the lead (Etienne, 2013). While SNCC's legacy grew to include sit-ins and other nonviolent protests, the organization's work went beyond that, as SNCC sought to implement community organizing along with its nonviolent protests.

Although the nonviolent protests that King and the SCLC led in Georgia and Alabama are well-known, the SCLC did not make many inroads in Mississippi. This was largely because the White power structure in Mississippi, the people who had the power to create and enforce laws, stood so firmly in its oppressive stance that it was even more dangerous than even Alabama or Georgia for Black people in pursuit of their civil rights (Etienne, 2013). While the Fourteenth Amendment had granted Black Americans the right to vote, Jim Crow laws passed throughout the South forbade Black Americans from exercising this right. SNCC understood that Blacks living in Mississippi would never be treated as first-class citizens without activism. While SNCC workers had initially gone to Mississippi in 1961, they did not make the progress they desired in helping Black Americans register to vote. Members of SNCC planned a Freedom Summer that was to take place in Mississippi during the summer of 1964. Freedom Summer was to include many different projects, and its ultimate goal was to register Black people to vote in Mississippi. The year before this was to take place, however, Mississippi NAACP leader Medgar Evers was murdered by members of the Ku Klux Klan. This and other acts of violence that had taken place throughout the state were fresh on the minds of civil rights activists and Black Mississippians as SNCC members embarked on Mississippi for Freedom Summer in 1964 (Etienne, 2013). Although danger certainly lurked around each corner, the civil rights workers who had come to Mississippi knew that they had a job to do.

Freedom Summer

The Freedom Summer project was designed to dramatically increase the number of Blacks who were registered to vote in Mississippi while simultaneously drawing the nation's attention to the violence that Blacks faced when attempting to exercise their constitutional right to vote. Over 1,000 volunteers came from different parts of the United States to work on SNCC's many Freedom Summer projects, which included canvassing urban and rural Black neighborhoods, the Mississippi Freedom Democratic Party (MFDP), and freedom schools. The ultimate goal of the Freedom Summer projects was not just to increase the number of Black voters in Mississippi, but also to increase Black activism in local, state, and national matters (Chilcoat & Ligon, 1999). SNCC workers and volunteers wanted to make a difference in Mississippi, but they also wanted to leave something that the people of Mississippi could carry on once the SNCC workers and volunteers had left the state.

As members of SNCC and other groups worked throughout the state, violence toward them and Black Mississippians appeared to continuously increase. The federal government did not offer any protection to those who were working to enfranchise Black people, and the rest of the country seemed to overlook what was going on in Mississippi. It is for this reason that SNCC members decided to invite outside workers to help them register Black voters in Mississippi. "We decided that in order to focus the country's attention on our situation we needed to bring the country's children down to help us, to face the kinds of risks we and the local people we were working with faced," writes Charles Cobb (2011, p. 108), who served as a field secretary for SNCC. Following a SNCC call for volunteers, over a thousand college students traveled to Mississippi in the summer of 1964, most of whom were White and from the northeast (Chilcoat & Ligon, 1995). It is primarily White volunteers that SNCC would utilize as teachers in the freedom schools. While most scholars report the freedom schools as taking place in the summer of 1964, Stephen Schneider (2006) writes that they existed in Mississippi as early as 1961, with the largest occurrence of freedom schools taking place during the

Freedom Summer project of 1964. The purpose of the freedom schools was to provide Mississippi's Black children with an education that would emancipate their minds from the oppressive, colonizing, segregated education they received in Mississippi's public schools. SNCC members also wanted to leave behind an infrastructure for activism that would remain present long after Freedom Summer was finished. Cobb, the SNCC member who proposed the freedom schools, explained that "we have to be concerned about building up our own institutions to replace the old, unjust, decadent ones which make up the existing power structure" (Chilcoat & Ligon, 1998b, p. 517; Rothschild, 1982, p. 403). Liz Fusco (1991), who served as the head of the Indianola Freedom School, notes that SNCC's decision to have freedom schools was a decision to enter into every phase of the lives of the people of Mississippi.

Freedom School Foundations

Education has long been something that people of African ancestry in the United States have sought to attain in an effort to improve their status in American society. As early as the 18th century, enslaved Africans were purposefully breaking laws in an attempt to learn to read. Enslaved people knew even then, that education had emancipatory power, just as the White lawmakers who made teaching literacy to enslaved people illegal knew that education held such power (Williams, 2005). White lawmakers knew that literate slaves would not want to continue in their places as subservient, owned property. One example of how they reacted to this belief follows the Nat Turner slave rebellion in Virginia. The governor of Virginia believed that Black churches were teaching slaves how to read, and he believed this literacy led Nat Turner and other slaves to rebel against their slave owners. For this reason, following the Nat Turner slave rebellion, the governor of Virginia made Black churches illegal in the state. This did not, however, keep slaves from attempting to gain literacy skills, as many slaves risked their lives to do so. Charles Cobb (2011) gives these slaves' attempts to educate themselves the distinction of being America's first freedom schools.

Just after the Civil War, newly freed slaves who were now citizens of the United States were steadfast in their attempts to attain education for themselves and their children. Just as they had during slavery, they held to the belief that education would allow them to improve their position in American society. They undoubtedly believed this would be the case for their children. While they had legally been emancipated from slavery, they knew that education had the power to liberate them from their social and economic standing and would allow them to be full participants in the democracy of the United States. Although the Freedmen's Bureau and northern mission-aries are commonly given credit for helping the freed men and women set up schools, the former slaves had already set up their own schools before the workers from the Freedmen's Bureau and the missionaries had even arrived in the South (Anderson, 1988). With the scant resources available to them, the United States' newest citizens had organized themselves in a manner that allowed those who held knowledge in some capacity to teach those who did not have said knowledge. Upon the arrival of the Freedmen's Bureau work-ers, African Americans were able to expand this schooling system, with our current tax-supported public schooling system serving as an outgrowth of former slaves' desire for education (Cobb, 2011).

Just north of Mississippi, in Tennessee, Myles Horton had begun an edu-cational center known as the Highlander Folk School. One of his goals for this school was not to simply organize labor, but to expose low-wage workers to ideas that would make them a danger to capitalism. After attending graduate school at the University of Chicago, Horton returned to Tennessee and estab-lished the school. The tenets of this school included: a commitment to social change, the use of problem-based education, education based on experience and dialogue, and the inclusion of students' cultures in learning activities. One of the Highlander Folk School's goals involved equipping adults with the tools to go back and teach what they learned to their neighbors and friends. It was hoped that those who were educated in the Highlander fashion would go on to take direct action and keep the movement going (Hale, 2007).

Myles Horton held a workshop for SNCC in 1962, wanting to help SNCC and their cause. Horton did not want to have SNCC members come to Highlander and have their teachers teach "at" them. Instead, Horton wanted Highlander teachers to learn from the students involved with SNCC and facilitate learning on their terms. Horton wanted to begin a program with SNCC that would be the brainchild of and executed by SNCC members. The Mississippi Freedom Schools were created from this relationship between Myles Horton and the Highlander Folk School and the Student Nonviolent Coordinating Committee (Hale, 2007).

Planning the Freedom Schools

Former SNCC field secretary Charles Cobb (2011) writes that after observing the horrifying educational disparities between what Black children received and what White children received in Mississippi, SNCC members decided to organize freedom schools as a part of their Freedom Summer of 1964. In places like Yazoo City, the school district spent $245 per White child each year, whereas they spent a meager $3 for each Black child attending school in the district (Street, 2004). Libraries in Black schools were understocked, and Black teachers were underpaid. In some places, Black families bore the responsibility of paying for the school's heating in the winter (Cobb, 2011). Throughout the South, Black people provided substantial financial contributions towards schools in addition to the taxes they were charged with paying. In the case of schools receiving money from the Rosenwald Fund, Black communities had to raise the same amount or more money than the fund was to contribute. All donations, including land, money, and other contributions, however, were to be deeded to the local school authorities. As Black citizens gave their resources and property and paid taxes, they were essentially doubly taxed while working to provide the children of their community with a quality education (Anderson, 1988). Issues like this resulted in the average White student in Mississippi attending school for eleven years, while the average Black student attended for only six years (Street, 2004). Members of SNCC felt that Black children were receiving a "sharecropper's education" (Cobb, 2011, p. 107), the sole intent of which was to keep Black people in their place—in subordinate status. Although a Black school in Mississippi may have had a new edifice, interior resources were anemically low. Cobb (2011), who was then a student at Howard University, wrote a proposal where he stated that freedom schools would be necessary to "fill an intellectual and creative vacuum in the lives of young Negro Mississippians" (p. 109) and to help Mississippi's Black students learn to question and critique. Chilcoat and Ligon (1999) note that Cobb wrote that the freedom school curriculum could supplement what Black students were already learning in their high schools, but this appears to paint a much rosier picture of how Cobb viewed the education that Black students received in Mississippi than the bleak picture Cobb painted with his own words. Chilcoat and Ligon (1999) later explain, however, that Cobb wanted the freedom schools to contrast the segregated, discriminatory, oppressive school system in Mississippi and create an engaged, youthful Black populace in Mississippi. Perlstein (1990) explains that the freedom schools would include an academic curriculum, a cultural program, and students would also study political and social matters. In addition to these curricular foci, freedom school students would create a newspaper and participate in civil rights organizing in their communities (Sturkey, 2010). The freedom schools would be yet another vessel through which SNCC workers could increase both practical and political literacy amongst Blacks in Mississippi.

The freedom schools were to take place as a six-week summer program. SNCC had initially planned to hold 36 freedom schools throughout the state of Mississippi that would serve 1,000 Black students. They had also planned for the students who attended the freedom schools to be about 15 years old, which according to Etienne (2013), illustrates SNCC's strong concern with adolescent development. Another important part of the plan included who would serve as the freedom school teachers. The SNCC members who were responsible for planning the freedom schools decided that the majority of the freedom school teachers would be the White volunteers who would come from different parts of the country, likely because they assigned the Black volunteers to other Freedom Summer projects such as voter registration and the Mississippi Freedom Democratic Party. After the volunteers attended a one-week training session in July 1964, SNCC ultimately ended up opening 41 freedom schools that served over 2,500 students.

After SNCC decided to take on the project of the freedom schools, they convened a curriculum conference in New York with other civil rights activists, educators, and clergy, including Ella Baker, Septima Clark, Myles Horton, and members of CORE, SCLC, and Students for a Democratic Society (SDS). The purpose of this conference was to come up with a freedom school curriculum that focused on civics and exploring new styles of democratic methodology and centered on questioning (Chilcoat & Ligon, 1999; Logue, 2008). Etienne (2013) believes that this focus on questioning came from the influence of Ella Baker. The co-coordinator of the Summer Educational Program Committee, Lois Chaffee, reminded the attendees that the curriculum they were writing needed to offer students the opportunity to remediate the academic work they did in their traditional schools. She also charged conference participants with including in their curriculum the opportunity for students to study matters that would be considered too controversial to discuss in a traditional Mississippi school. The attendees then divided into four groups and went about writing curriculum for the freedom schools. After two days, the large group reconvened, and each group reported on what they had written. The topics that would be included in the freedom school curriculum included a Black history curriculum that focused on positive changes that had taken place when Black people worked together for justice and equity and a citizenship curriculum that focused on three primary questions:

1. Why are we (teachers and students) in freedom schools?
2. What is the Freedom Movement?
3. What alternatives does the Freedom Movement offer us?

The citizenship curriculum also focused on three secondary questions, which Fusco (1991) considers to be even more important than the primary questions:

1. What does the majority culture have that we want?
2. What does the majority culture have that we don't want?
3. What do we have that we want to keep?

The freedom school volunteers who worked on this portion of the curriculum thought these questions were important, because they were open and essentially unanswerable. Freedom school curriculum writers also planned to help support students in traditional subjects in an effort to help them overcome the deficiencies students suffered in literacy, writing, and mathematics at the hands of Mississippi's public schools (Adickes, 2005; Chilcoat & Ligon, 1999; Fusco, 1991).[1]

Freedom Schools in Practice

Teachers and Students

As noted earlier, the majority of the teachers in the Mississippi Freedom Schools were White college students who had come from the North. Many of the volunteers who were not college students were professional educators (Adickes, 2005). Perlstein (1990) notes that Cobb wanted these volunteer teachers to implement the newest pedagogies, even though he was unfamiliar with them himself. Cobb spoke of having the nation's best and brightest minds involved in the freedom schools, and he felt that SNCC should recognize and take full advantage of their volunteers' value. The freedom schools' curriculum committee mailed curriculum materials to potential volunteer teachers in the spring of 1964, and Chilcoat and Ligon (1999) report that the materials were received well by both those who were professional educators and those who were not.

Although the curriculum conference resulted in a written curriculum and materials that freedom school teachers could use in their classrooms, those who volunteered to teach at the freedom schools were also encouraged to modify the written curriculum for their students or to create their own curriculum. Teachers taught classes in the areas that they were most familiar with, and classes like French and typing were incredibly popular with the freedom school students.

For the Black students of Mississippi, the freedom schools represented the first time school (both the teachers and the curriculum) took them seriously. Freedom schools allowed them to express themselves without being rejected in the process. While SNCC originally planned for students who were about 15 years old, those who attended the freedom schools were as young as preschoolers and as old as 70. Additionally, Fusco (1991) writes that when many Black students began their freedom school experience, they talked about leaving Mississippi for the North or the West when they were old enough to do so. By the time they had finished their freedom school classes, many of these students had turned their focus to staying in Mississippi to continue working in the Movement.

Learning the Freedom School Way

Although the programs were called freedom schools, very few of them took place in actual school buildings. The location of the freedom schools varied between communities. According to Etienne (2013), some freedom school classes took place in parks and residential homes, but the majority of them were held in churches. The physical location of the freedom schools allowed them to remain free of the curricular and pedagogical restraints of Mississippi's segregated public schools.

The curriculum of the freedom schools focused on asking critical questions. The goal of the teachers, directors, and planners was to have students learn to question why things existed in their current manner throughout society. Students began each day by singing freedom songs, and teachers used a curriculum that was heavily based in civics and Black history, in addition to classes like typing, drama, speech, and foreign language (Adickes, 2005; Chilcoat & Ligon, 1998b; Etienne, 2013; Street, 2004). Photographs taken by Herbert Randall (1964) show students engaging with folk singers and reading *Ebony* magazine, which teachers used as text alongside the writings of Langston Hughes, Carter G. Woodson, and James Baldwin (Street, 2004). Fusco (1991) writes that studying the history of their own people allowed Black students to see themselves as part of a group who could produce heroes. This was a much different narrative than what students received in many of their schools and in their day-to-day lives, as one SNCC member referred to Black history as America's blind spot (Street, 2004). While studying Black history, students made connections between Joseph Cinque of the Amistad and their own story of fighting for freedom in Mississippi (Fusco, 1991).

A Pedagogy of Discussion

The main pedagogical method that freedom school teachers used in teaching their students to question was discussion. These teachers required that their students actively participate in discussions, because students needed to learn how to share their thoughts and ideas, and because freedom school teachers thought discussion would help students develop their thoughts (Chilcoat & Ligon, 1998a). Freedom school discussions usually began with three questions, the first of which involved the teacher asking students, "How do you feel about …?" Once students expressed their feelings about the topic at hand, a topic that usually related to their lives somehow, the teacher asked, "Why do you feel this way?" As the class got deeply involved in the discussion, the teacher would ask students to analyze each other's opinions, asking, "How do you feel about her idea?"

In his speech classes, Stokely Carmichael used discussions to teach his freedom school students about the use of language in power and resistance. In Carmichael's class, students came to realize that those with power spoke a certain way and imposed their values on the majority of society (Schneider, 2006). In a Black history class, students debated the principles of Booker T. Washington and W. E. B. DuBois and questioned why they were familiar with Booker T. Washington but had not learned about W. E. B. DuBois until they attended freedom schools (Fusco, 1991).

Expressing Thoughts and Emotion through Drama
While discussion was the primary method used to encourage students to form questions, freedom school teachers also used drama to help students express their thoughts and emotions. Students used drama to think and process problems, utilizing drama to create solutions for their problems. Teachers hoped that students would take the process they learned in their drama classes and use it to solve problems in their lives. The students used drama classes to tackle problems that were close to them, including the murder of Medger Evers, the need for increased Black community involvement, and White violence towards Blacks (Chilcoat & Ligon, 1998b). Freedom school students also created their own newspapers, the first of which was titled *The Freedom News* (Sturkey, 2010). Because the traditional schooling context was heavily censored, the freedom school newspapers allowed students to report on issues that were important to them. The freedom schools had twelve newspapers that were regularly published, each of which was almost completely student run. The newspapers featured articles written by students, as well as poetry and other forms of expression.[2] The students saw the newspapers as a means of reaching out to the community and getting the word of freedom out (Sturkey, 2010).

Legacy of the Freedom Schools

The most obvious legacy of the Mississippi Freedom Schools lies in the activism the schools sparked in the hearts of students. Many Black children and their parents likely would have remained passive objects in the Black struggle for freedom in Mississippi, but the freedom schools encouraged these students to go back to their communities and work to create change. This is exactly what Cobb and the other SNCC members envisioned when they decided to host the freedom schools in the summer of 1964. Some of the freedom school students continued to be active in pursuit of social justice, with some even going on to hold political office. They credit their freedom school experience with encouraging them to be active in local, state, and national civic issues (Etienne, 2013).

The Mississippi Freedom Schools did not simply teach their students about civics. They allowed their students to participate in and witness civics in action. Embodying the notion of citizenship as shared fate (Williams, 2003), the young SNCC activists who created and executed the Mississippi Freedom Schools understood that their fates were entangled with the fates of Black people who lived under the consistent threat of violence and oppression in Mississippi. This is why they took their activism to Mississippi and persisted in it, despite the violence that targeted them regularly. Freedom school teachers then passed on this notion of citizenship as shared fate to their students, helping them understand how their fates were intertwined with other people in their community. This is what kept many students who had dreamed of leaving Mississippi to stay and advocate for their communities. Simply put, SNCC activists and the students they taught understood that none of them were free from oppression until everyone was free from oppression.

Jon Hale (2011) explains that the freedom schools could be taught as part of an entire middle or high school social studies course that revolves around the Black fight for democracy in the 20th century. He argues that the content of the civil rights struggle meets state content standards, and the culturally relevant, student-centered pedagogies implemented by freedom school teachers could be used by teachers in contemporary schools. Additionally, the work of the freedom schools lives on today, as the Children's Defense Fund holds a summer enrichment program where young students of color are encouraged to engage in reflection and inquiry (Smith, 2010). Former SNCC field secretary Charles Cobb (2011) also expressed his belief that curriculum and pedagogy like that implemented in the freedom schools could help to eliminate the school-to-prison pipeline, which involves school discipline policies that push students out of schools and ultimately into the prison system. Freedom school curriculum and pedagogy would engage students in new ways and could ultimately create an entirely different educational experience for Black students in particular, opening up an entire world of opportunities.

Conclusion

Unfortunately, of all of the events and projects that were part of Freedom Summer, the freedom schools are the project that has likely received the least historiographical attention. Charles Payne suggests that this is likely because the voter registration position received more prestige within SNCC's organization, and it is also likely because the teaching roles within freedom schools were frequently given to women (Street, 2004). It appears that the freedom schools may have had a greater impact than even some of the projects like the Mississippi Freedom Democratic Party, which garnered much more attention. This is because the freedom schools trained up a new set of activists and encouraged a new generation of thinkers. The freedom schools have many valuable lessons that educators cannot afford to ignore.

Both teachers and students should learn about the Mississippi Freedom Schools, as the Freedom Summer program teaches students how to participate in democracy, and it teaches teachers how to help students go about this. Students need to learn how to hold discussions, ask critical questions, and develop their ideas, and the freedom schools give us a template to follow. Their curriculum was simultaneously student-centered, democratic, and culturally relevant, all of which teacher educators frequently espouse in our own classrooms. Studying the Mississippi Freedom Schools and implementing their practices would provide students with the ultimate lesson in democracy.

Notes

1. For access to Mississippi Freedom School planning documents, please visit the Civil Rights Digital Library at crdl.usg.edu.
2. For newspapers articles, poems, stories, and other works created by Mississippi Freedom School Students, please see *To Write in the Light of Freedom: The Newspapers of the 1964 Mississippi Freedom Schools* by William Sturkey and Jon N. Hale (Eds.)

References

Adickes, S. E. (2005). *The legacy of a Freedom School*. New York, NY: Palgrave Macmillan.

Anderson, J. D. (1988). *The education of Blacks in the South 1860–1935*. Chapel Hill, NC: The University of North Carolina Press.

Chilcoat, G., & Ligon, J. (1995). "We will teach what democracy really means by living democratically within our own schools." Lessons from the personal experience of teachers who taught in the Mississippi Freedom Schools. *Education and Culture, 12*(1), 24–42.

Chilcoat, G., & Ligon, J. (1998a). "We talk here. This is a school for talking." Participatory democracy from the classroom out into the community: How discussion was used in the Mississippi Freedom Schools. *Curriculum Inquiry, 28*(2), 165–193.

Chilcoat, G., & Ligon, J. (1998b). Theatre as an emancipatory tool: Classroom drama in the Mississippi Freedom Schools. *Journal of Curriculm Studies, 30*(5), 515–543.

Chilcoat, G., & Ligon, J. (1999). "Helping to make democracy a living reality": The curriculum conference of the Mississippi Freedom Schools. *Journal of Curriculum and Supervision, 15*(1), 43–68.

Cobb, C. (2011). Freedom's struggle and Freedom Schools. *Monthly Review: An Independent Socialist Magazine, 63*(3), 104–113.

Etienne, L. (2013). A different type of summer camp: SNCC, Freedom Summer, Freedom Schools, and the development of African American males in Mississippi. *Peabody Journal of Education, 88*(4), 449–463.

Fusco, L. (1991). Freedom Schools in Mississippi. *Radical Teacher, 40*, 37–40.

Hale, J. N. (2007). Early pedagogical influences on the Mississippi Freedom Schools: Myles Horton and critical education in the deep South. *American Education History Journal, 34*(2), 315–329.

Hale, J. N. (2011). The Freedom Schools, the Civil Rights Movement, and refocusing the goals of American education. *The Journal of Social Studies Research, 35*(2), 259–276.

Logue, J. (2008). Mississippi Freedom Schools' radical conception of pedagogy, citizenship, and power. *Philosophical Studies in Education, 39*, 57–65.

Perlstein, D. (1990). Teaching freedom: SNCC and the creation of Mississippi Freedom Schools. *History of Education Society, 30*(3), 297–324.

Randall, H. (1964). *Freedom Summer photographs, 1964 (Collection M351)*. McCain Lib. & Archives, University of Southern Mississippi, Hattiesburg, MS.

Rothschild, M. A. (1982). The volunteers and the Freedom Schools: Education for social change in Mississippi. *History of Education Quarterly, 22*(4), 401–420.

Schneider, S. (2006). Freedom schooling: Stokely Carmichael and critical rhetorical education. *College Composition and Communication, 58*(1), 46–69.

Smith, K. (2010). Fostering regimes of truth: Understanding and reflecting on the Freedom School way. *Pedagogy, Culture, and Society, 18*(2), 191–209.

Street, J. (2004). Reconstructing education from the bottom up: SNCC's 1964 Mississippi summer project and African American culture. *Journal of American Studies, 38*(2), 273–296.

Sturkey, W. (2010). "I want to become a part of history": Freedom Summer, Freedom Schools, and the Freedom News. *Journal of African American History, 95*(3/4), 348–368.

Williams, H. A. (2005). *Self-taught: African American education in slavery and freedom*. Chapel Hill, NC: University of North Carolina Press.

Williams, M. (2003). Citizenship as identity, citizenship as shared fate, and the functions of multicultural education. In K. McDonough & W. Feinberg (Eds.), *Education and citizenship in liberal democratic societies: Teaching for cosmopolitan values and collective identities* (pp. 208–247). New York, NY: Oxford University Press.

4. *Invisible Leader: Septima Poinsette Clark's Covert Contributions to the Civil Rights Movement*

Chaddrick Gallaway

The canon of quintessential civil rights leaders is largely male-dominated. However, when considering those that are women, Fannie Lou Hamer, Diane Nash, Dorothy Height, Ella Baker, and most conventionally known Rosa Parks, are generally names that come to mind. While these Black women and many others have a rightful place in the history of the Civil Rights Movement, some names like Rosa Parks have been pushed to the front of the movement. According to James Loewen (1995), women tend to be pushed to the back or side-barred in textbooks in comparison to men. Because of this, students often learn about men's contributions in movements in lieu of women's contributions. It is essential that educators begin to teach the full history the Civil Rights Movement and truly showcase all of the men and women involved in order to highlight the impact of each group. With the exception of Rosa Parks, the Civil Rights Movement is set within a narrative that only displays the work of heterosexual Black men. To complicate this history, I argue that Septima Clark is one of many who should be well known within this literature and tradition; however, her name and contributions remain in the background.

In this chapter, I highlight the life and work of Septima Clark to bring forth her important role in the Civil Rights Movement. Relegated to the shadows of the Civil Rights Movement her work was has been overlooked by historians, teachers and textbooks. To shine a light on the work of Septima Clark, as well as how she was made invisible during the Civil Rights Movement, I will first speak on the early beginnings of her activism. Then I will show how, if not for Clark, the Civil Rights Movement as well as voter registration, and the literacy rates of African Americans in the South would have come to a standstill. I will showcase how she and many other Black women were made invisible by Black men in the Civil Rights Movement due to a maternal frame of reference, as well as underscore Ms. Clark's on perceptions of Black women's invisibility in the movement. Though Black women were made invisible by Black men in the civil rights movement, historians, teachers and textbooks have also privileged Black men by underscoring their stories over those of Black women. This led to the hyper-invisibility of Black women in the Civil Rights Movement.

Although Ms. Clark was an instrumental figure in the Civil Rights Movement, she has routinely gone unnoticed in textbooks because she did not garner national media attention achieved by male activists in the movement (Charron, 2009; Loewen, 1995; Stokes-Brown, 1990). This chapter underscores the risk in continuing to relegate this matriarch of the Civil Rights Movement behind her Black male counterparts.

There is no one central figure in the Civil Rights Movement. The movement and its success was due to a compilation of Black individuals of different intersecting races, classes, and gender identities. Although many individuals were focused on gaining civil rights for African Americans, men mainly took over the movement as leaders by overshadowing Black women through their sexist beliefs and practices (Aldridge, 2006; Charron, 2009; Dixson, 2003; Kuumba, 2001; Robnett, 2000). Though the Civil Rights Movement's success was based on the work and leadership of men and women, lesser-known Black women and their contributions have been erased, ignored and made invisible by essentially everyone because of the social construction of gender during this time (Barnett, 1993; Charron, 2009; Gyant & Atwater, 1996). Black Women in the civil rights movement were ignored for their intellectual ability, and also faced rampant sexual harassment and discrimination due to their gender which led many to joining the Feminist movement during the 1970s (Civil Rights History Project, n.d.). These positive and negative experiences need to be included in the history of the Civil Rights Movement in order to showcase the resistance Black women faced not only from a racist white society, but Black men as well. Gender roles and patriarchy were enforced by Black men on most, if not all, Black women in the Civil Rights Movement, including Ms. Clark; however, she and others did their best to resist this patriarchy and sexism[1] (Bryan, 1988; Gyant & Atwater, 1996).

I have chosen Ms. Clark as a starting place in hopes of using her story to not only show Black heroism in the Civil Rights Movement, but also to model and advocate for the inclusion and celebration of more stories about Black women. The overarching goal of this chapter is to show an exemplar

Black woman's integral impact on the Civil Rights Movement through Ms. Clark's story; a secondary goal is to explain why Ms. Clark's and so many other Black women's work remains invisible.

Septima Clark's Work: Construction of an Activist

Ms. Clark's first teaching job began in 1916 on Johns Island, a place where Ms. Clark noted most of the population was illiterate and unaware of their civil rights (Jordan-McFadden, 1990; Stokes-Brown, 1990). Due to the dire conditions in which the residents of Johns Island were living, Ms. Clark took it upon herself to empower the community through literacy. Ms. Clark was convinced that the only way for African Americans on Johns Island to improve their quality of life was through gaining first class citizenship (Charron, 2009; Clark, 1962; Gyant & Atwater, 1996). This belief led her to teach men of the community to read and write. She helped them write speeches using the same methods she used to teach her middle school students reading and writing skills. Through the community's commitment to learning how to read and write, Ms. Clark was living her life's dream—teaching poor and underserved communities how to empower themselves through literacy (Charron, 2009; Clark, 1962; Gyant & Atwater, 1996; Jordan-McFadden, 1990; Stokes-Brown, 1990).

After working on Johns Island and neighboring island communities in South Carolina, Ms. Clark furthered her teaching and activism by joining the National Association for the Advancement of Colored People (NCAACP). Through the NAACP she pursued legal action to enable Black teachers to teach at Black public schools rather than at Black private schools. Her activism paid off, and this law was changed in 1919 (Charron, 2009; Rouse, 2001; Stokes-Brown, 1990). Although this was a victory for the NAACP and Ms. Clark, there remained much to accomplish in subsequent years. Next, Ms. Clark worked with the NAACP to equalize the pay of Black and white teachers (Charron, 2009; Rouse, 2001; Stokes-Brown, 1990). Again, her resolve and activism paid off. By 1942 Ms. Clark's pay increased from $780 a year to $4,000 (Clark, 1962; Hall, Walker, Charron, & Cline, 2010; Gyant & Atwater 1996; Rouse, 2001). This action was significant because it permitted Black teachers to gain economic stability by teaching in a public school and earning a livable wage.

Ms. Clark's impact on Johns Island and other local communities was truly life altering for its residents. During the early 1900s, fewer than 100 Black people were registered to vote in this region (Gyant & Atwater, 1996). However, by the end of the Civil Rights Movement that number had sky-rocketed to 600. Many Black residents returned to school and proceeded to matriculate and graduate from college. Of this number a few went on to successfully pursue political office (Gyant & Atwater, 1996). This change is undeniably connected to Ms. Clark's work as a teacher while living on Johns Island (Gyant & Atwater, 1996; Jordan-McFadden, 1990).

Septima Clark: The Highlander Folk School and Citizenship Schools

In the summer of 1954, Ms. Clark made her way to The Highlander Folk School (hereafter, HFS) for the first time. In May of that year, the Supreme Court of The United States of America (hereafter, SCOTUS) ruled segregation unconstitutional (Stokes-Brown, 1990). While staying at the HFS, Ms. Clark was unsure if HFS was the right place for her work (Roth, personal communication, May 23, 1973; Walker, personal communication, July 30, 1976). Fortunately for Ms. Clark, HFS and the Civil Rights Movement, she was not given much of a choice. When SCOTUS ruled for schools to be desegregated in 1954, the state of South Carolina required teachers to reveal their organizational affiliations and memberships. Ms. Clark noted that many Black teachers did not want to cite the NAACP as an organization of which they were part; however, Ms. Clark did not hesitate. A year later, the state of South Carolina passed a law that would outlaw any state employee to be a part of the NAACP. The passage of this law would allow states to fire any teacher associated with the NAACP in the South, a strategy designed to "wipe out" the NAACP (Charron, 2009; Stokes-Brown, 1990).

Because of Ms. Clark's membership in the NAACP, she was dismissed from her job as a Charleston teacher in 1957 (Charron, 2009; Jordan-McFadden, 1990; Stokes-Brown, 1990). After spending two summers participating in HFS workshops, Ms. Clark became the director of workshops (Charron, 2009; Roth, Personal communication, May 23, 1973; Stokes-Brown, 1990). The goals of HFS were to break down barriers between Blacks and whites to produce leaders focused on improving social conditions for all people, while seeking to expand democratic principles in their everyday lives (Charron, 2009; Clark, personal communication, May 23, 1973; Gyant & Atwater, 1996; Horton, 1971; Rouse, 2001; Tjerandesen, 1980). To reach a real democracy, workshop participants learned that racial barriers must be eliminated. At HFS, Blacks and whites did all daily tasks together, including eating, sleeping, working and other daily life activities, with the intention of providing the experience of living in a world with no racial barriers; a world where real democracy and the rights of all people, regardless of race, would be equal (Charron, 2009; Clark, 1962; Gyant & Atwater, 1996; Horton, 1971; Rouse, 2001). Clark worked for 15 years as the director of workshops and eventually she became the director of education.

Along with her work at HFS, Ms. Clark was also a founding member of and a participant in Citizenship Schools (Brown-Nagin, 1999; Charron, 2009; Clark, 1962; Gyant & Atwater, 1996; Hall et al., 2010; Horton, 1971; Rouse, 2001; Stokes-Brown, 1990). The first Citizenship School began in 1959 on Johns Island, the place of Ms. Clark's first teaching job (Charron, 2009; Hall et al., 2010; Stokes-Brown, 1990). The Citizenship schools and the students revealed the hunger for freedom of Black people throughout the South.

The basis of the Citizenship School was to teach illiterate members of Black communities throughout the South how to read and write so that Black Americans could gain first class citizenship rights (Brown-Nagin, 1999; Charron, 2009; Hall et al., 2010; Gyant & Atwater, 1996; Rouse, 2001; Stokes-Brown, 1990). With the ability to read and write, southern Black people would be able to not only understand their rights by reading the laws of their state and country, but also register to vote (Charron, 2009; Hall et al., 2010; Gyant & Atwater, 1996; Rouse, 2001; Stokes-Brown, 1990). Ms. Clark, with the help of Bernice Robinson and members of HFS, created a curriculum that would help give illiterate Black people the opportunity to develop reading and writing skills. Near the end of the movement for civil rights, Septima Clark's Citizenship Schools had educated more than 10,000 teachers, and by extension 25,000 students and upwards of 700,000 registered voters by the late 1960s (Brown-Nagin, 1999, p. 95).

Ms. Clark's activism began a decade before Dr. King was born, and her work in Citizenship Schools should be considered just as important as Dr. King's peaceful protest and captivating speeches. Had it not been for Ms. Clark, Dr. King, and the Civil Rights Movement would have lacked a force of socially conscious Black citizens willing to confront the rampant racism and physical violence that was imposed upon Blacks when protesting for Civil Rights (Brown-Nagin, 1999).

Black Women's Invisibility in the Civil Rights Movement

Though Ms. Clark and many other Black women impacted the Civil Rights Movement in a plethora of ways, they were still invisible within the movement. According to Barnett (1993), Black southern women performed several roles in the Civil Rights Movement, roles that were comparable to their male counterparts. Many Black women had leadership roles in creating strategies, protests, and communicating across networks. These women did not come from any one class or career background. Rather they were "Sisters in Struggle, sharecroppers, domestic and service workers, school teachers, college professors, housewives, beauticians, students, and office secretaries" that made tremendous physical, and mental sacrifices for the Civil Rights Movement (Barnett, 1993, p. 1993). Though many of the Black women in the Civil Rights Movement came from different occupational backgrounds, one constant remained true—their goal was to work towards and fight for the civil rights of African Americans, present and future, no matter the cost.

Barnett's (1993) study of Black women's leadership roles in the Civil Rights Movement shows that Black women were not highly cited in relation to men in the movement. In Barnett's study, 36 former civil rights activists (23 men and 13 women), whose work took place during the 1950s and 1960s cited Black male activists over Black women as leaders in the Civil Rights Movement at a rate of 739 to 38 (pp. 172). Interview participants answers suggested that male leaders of the Civil Rights Movement had a larger impact and performed roles that were considered the more important than female leaders. An even more telling sign of Black women's invisibility in the Civil Rights Movement in Barnett's study is that participants cited women generally as a group in the category "Roles Most Important", whereas many men, like Martin Luther King Jr., Ralph David Abernathy and Charles Sherrod, were named individually (pp. 172). When the participants in the study were asked to name influential women in the Civil Rights Movement from 1955 to 1968, out of 30 respondents, not one Black woman was named more than six times, and Rosa Parks was cited most often.

Black women of the civil rights era and their impact have largely been erased because of societal constraints placed on them due to their gender (Barnett, 1993). Patriarchy was rampant in the South and structured all women's lived experiences regardless of race (Brown-Nagin, 1999; Gyant & Atwater, 1996; Hall et al., 2010). Because of this, traditional gender roles were established by Black men within the Civil Rights Movement, which placed men in leadership positions with speaking roles, inevitably making Black women voiceless and invisible (Barnett, 1993).

Men of the Civil Rights Movement imposed a maternal frame of reference on Black women, which subjugated women into stereotypical roles as mothers, child bearers and homemakers, instead of leaders (Aldridge, 2006). When women could participate in the Civil Rights Movement, it was often in secondary roles to men (Aldridge, 2006; Kuumba, 2001). Because of the maternal frame of reference imposed upon Black women by society, many Black women like Septima Clark pushed back against the norms that limited Black women to being gendered stereotypes. One important note is that the Civil Rights Movement was not a movement without error. The maternal frame of reference, as well as the sexism that Black women endured at the hands of Black male leaders, shows that the Civil Rights Movement was not a movement for the rights of all Black people, but a movement that centered on the wants and needs of Black men. Black women had to create a space for themselves within the Civil Rights Movement because Black men did not. They navigated the Civil Rights Movement by working with Black men as an act of selflessness and sacrifice that went unacknowledged.

Septima Clark's View on Black Women's Impact in the Civil Rights Movement

In her first-person narrative (Stokes-Brown, 1990), there is an entire chapter that centers on Ms. Clark's interactions with men in the Civil Rights Movement, highlighting her experience combating a maternal frame of reference. Ms. Clark was an executive staff member of the Southern Christian Leadership Conference (SCLC), Ms. Clark states,

> I was on the executive staff of SCLC, but the men on it didn't listen to me too well. They liked to send me into many places, because I could always make a path in to get people to listen to what I have to say. But those men didn't have any faith in women, none whatsoever they just thought that women were sex symbols and had no contribution to make. (Stokes-Brown, 1990, p. 77).

Ms. Clark also notes that Black men in the Civil Rights Movement had no faith in Black women to accomplish tasks and goals despite the many efforts of Black women that sustained and energized the movement (Brown-Nagin, 1999; Charron, 2009; Gyant & Atwater, 1996; Hall et al., 2010; Stokes-Brown, 1990). Despite all the work that Ms. Clark had done at the HFS and Citizenship School helping southern Black people gain access to voter identification cards through the means of literacy, Ms. Clark's seat at the SCLC table was questioned and challenged by men. Reverend Abernathy, a notable civil rights leader, co-founder and executive board member of SCLC constantly asked Dr. Martin Luther King, "Why is Mrs. Clark on this staff?" (Stokes-Brown, 1990, p. 77). Dr. King would come to her defense and speak on how Ms. Clark progressed the SCLC's agenda in many southern states (Aldridge, 2006; Clark, personal communication, May 23, 1973; Hall et al., 2010; Jordan-McFadden, 1990; Kuumba, 2001).

Though Dr. King often defended Ms. Clark, he did not follow her advice on numerous occasions. Ms. Clark stated,

> I sent a letter to Dr. King asking him not to lead all the marches himself, but instead to develop leaders who could lead their own marchers. Dr. King read the letter before the staff. It just tickled them; they just laughed. (Stokes-Brown, 1990, p. 78).

Instead of heeding her advice Dr. King shared Ms. Clark's letter in a way that seemed to belittle and demean her own intentions.

Ms. Clark felt multiple leaders, versus one leader, was a better system because the movement would not be halted if something happened to Dr. King (Stokes-Brown, 1990). However, he did not listen to her advice. Ms. Clark perceived Dr. King to be hungry for power, which led him to seek recognition for himself (Stokes-Brown, 1990). This is evident when she states,

> I think that there is something among the Kings that makes them feel that they are the kings, and so you don't have a right to speak. You can work behind the scenes all you want. That's all right. But don't come forth and try to lead. That's not the kind of thing they want. (p. 78)

Ms. Clark, like many others in the Civil Rights Movement had a strong affinity for Dr. King. However, she challenges and complicates our view of Dr. King by highlighting his faults which are rarely critiqued.

According to Aldridge (2006), multiple Black women in the Civil Rights Movement criticized Dr. King for his sexist and chauvinistic actions, as well as his lack of focus on promoting Black women as leaders of the movement, despite their impact. Ms. Clark's accounts of Dr. King show him as a sexist and patriarchal figure; she states,

> Like other Black ministers, Dr. King didn't think too much of the way women could contribute (to the civil rights movement). But working in a movement he changed the lives of so many people that I was getting to the place where he would have to see that women are more than sex symbols. (Stokes-Brown, 1990, p. 79).

This illustrates that Dr. King did not see a need for women in the Civil Rights Movement outside of being sexual objects. Coretta Scott King, Dr. King's wife, was no exception and was also subjected to the maternal frame of reference which placed her and many other women into subsidiary gendered roles (Stokes-Brown, 1990).

Ms. Clark, a mother herself, notes that Coretta Scott King had to give up her own career and work in civil rights because many men, including Dr. King, felt her place was at home (Aldridge, 2006; Brown-Nagin, 1999; Clark, 1962; Gyant & Atwater, 1996; Hall et al., 2010; Kuumba, 2001; Stokes-Brown, 1990). This may be unsettling to many that view Dr. King as a largely positive historical figure, but Ms. Clark's accounts reveal a glaring blind spot toward gender equity and inclusivity from Dr. King and other Black men in the Civil Rights Movement. Even though Ms. Clark's experiences with Dr. King may garner a negative perception of him, her story also shows the perseverance and commitment to Civil Rights of Black women.

They remained in the movement and worked in a male dominated spaces that upheld patriarchal and sexist norms.

Ms. Clark describes the treatment of Black women by Dr. King and other Black men in the Civil Rights Movement as a "weakness." This weakness was not completely of Black men's doing, but men as a larger collective that socialized women to be docile (Stokes-Brown, 1990). Ms. Clark, however, escaped the grasp of patriarchy because of her atypical mother, who was "the boss of her house" and did not submit to her husband (p. 79). Ms. Clark's experiences traveling around the South showed her that she too was atypical in her behavior. She noted,

> I found all over the South that whatever the man said had to be right. They had the whole say. The women couldn't say a thing. Whatever the men said would be right and the women would have to accept it. (pp. 79–80).

A man's word was taken as law by women. Ms. Clark admitted that her own views on women were determined by the way her father treated women, as docile creatures, that could not even carry the groceries into their home. Ms. Clark's father often stated that women should be silent and that their role was in the house, an interesting belief considering whom he married (Stokes-Brown, 1990).

Nonetheless, Ms. Clark's father socialized her into a maternal frame of reference which made her believe women should remain silent, and so Ms. Clark was silent in her early adult years (Stokes-Brown, 1990). Eventually Ms. Clark learned that women have important contributions to make, and her silence led to her own oppression as a woman. As a result of this revelation, she decided to break her silence and speak her opinions. Ms. Clark recalled that in her twenties, women (white and Black) were silent, meager, and never stood up to men, even when wrongdoing was present (Stokes-Brown, 1990). But in the 1960s, women of both races began to speak out against men for their sexism (Stokes-Brown, 1990). Even though this was the case, women were still not valued intellectually by men, and Black women dealt with a double edge sword of inequality because of their race and gender.

Ms. Clark noted that Black women themselves had been erased from the history books on the Civil Rights Movement when she stated "Until recently black women have just been ignored in the history books. Now books are coming out that show the impact that black women have had on the shaping of America" (Stokes-Brown, 1990, p. 83). Black women played a major role in the organization of the Montgomery bus boycott, as well as its execution (Stokes-Brown, 1990). After the victory of Montgomery bus boycott, southern Black women joined together once again to organize a march on Washington D.C. known as the "The Prayer Pilgrimage." At the time, the Prayer Pilgrimage was the largest civil rights demonstration created by African Americans. Ms. Clark ended her discussion on women's role in the Civil Rights Movement by stating the true impact of Black women,

> In stories about the civil rights movement you hear mostly about the black ministers. But if you talk to the women who were there, you'll hear another story. I think the civil rights movement would never have taken off if some women hadn't started to speak up. A lot more are just getting to the place now where they can speak out. (Stokes-Brown, 1990, p. 83).

This quote from Ms. Clark illustrates that if it were not for Black women speaking up, despite Black men's beliefs on a woman's place, the Civil Rights Movement would not have been successful. However, due to these beliefs Black women were kept in the background of the Civil Rights Movement, and they have seldom had the same opportunity to be celebrated as Black male leaders of the movement.

The Importance of Septima Poinsette Clark's Story

The story and life work of Septima Clark is one of great sacrifice, love, perseverance and dedication to a movement, and to people, who did not always reciprocate those values. While Ms. Clark was focused on the freedom and civil rights of all people, especially African Americans, she was challenged, perhaps most viscerally, by Black men in the Civil Rights Movement. It is important for those teaching and learning about the Civil Rights Movement and its leaders to know that sexism and patriarchy are one of its greatest faults. A movement that was focused on liberating Black Americans from White systemic racism and oppression also played a major role in the oppression of Black women. Ms. Clark's account complicates the notion that the Civil Rights Movement was built for the liberation of Black people; instead, her experiences show it was built on the liberation of Black men. Ms. Clark's experiences showcase the major role and impact that she had on the Civil Rights Movement. It is important to continue tracing the history of the Civil Rights Movement and its leaders to seek out other Black women leaders who had an impact on the movement. We must interrogate why we have failed to learn about and celebrate their work in the same way and manner as we have Black men.

Centering Black men in the Civil Rights Movement, without including the work and sacrifices of Black women, shows a one-sided history where men are the heroes of an entire group of people and the women had little value. The Civil Rights movement, on the contrary, would not have been as successful without Ms. Clark, and the essential work of many other Black women. Though Black women may not have stood in front of many microphones, they still found a way to exist, and persist in a movement and a world that placed little value on them. Showcasing Black women in the Civil Rights Movement will highlight and make visible the true intellectual value and hard work of Black women. By failing to teach and study the history of Black women in the Civil Rights Movement, we will continue to fall into the same cycle of erasing Black women and their accomplishments in this movement, and others that follow.

Conclusion

I have illustrated the life and work of Septima Poinsette Clark, a civil rights leader, who men have made invisible in the Civil Rights Movement. As a Black woman, Ms. Clark, as well as other women in the Civil Rights Movement, not only had to deal with being second class citizens because of her race but also because of her gender. Even though Ms. Clark spent a large portion of her life devoted to educating southern Black people formally and informally as a teacher, Ms. Clark's motive was to empower those with whom she crossed paths. Although she accomplished these tasks to support the Civil Rights Movement, sexism in a patriarchal society hindered her and other Black women from not only receiving proper credit for their impact, but also from receiving respect in the Civil Rights Movement from her male peers.

Ms. Clark's life mission was to improve the lives of her people—African American people. Even though Ms. Clark and many other women have been overshadowed by men in the Civil Rights Movement, Ms. Clark's impact is clear. From her early start as a teacher on Johns Island, to working with HFS and the Citizenship school, Ms. Clark showed that literacy is powerful. Without her work to increase the literacy of southern Blacks, the Civil Rights Movement would not have been the same. It is important to tell and retell her story and work to push her and other Black women to the front of the success of the Civil Rights Movement.

Note

1. In this chapter, when speaking on sexism and patriarchy of the Civil Rights movement, I am not talking about how we view sexist and patriarchal actions in 2017, but how Ms. Clark and many other Black women viewed sexism and patriarchy as they experienced it during the mid-1900s. There is certainly overlap, and unfortunately many of the sexist issues we face today are like those of the past, however this chapter aims to discuss sexist issues based on existing historical evidence.

References

Alridge, D. P. 2006. The limits of master narratives in history textbooks: An analysis of representations of Martin Luther King, Jr. *Teachers College Record* 108(4): 662–686.

Barnett, B. M. (1993). Invisible southern black women leaders in the civil rights movement: The triple constraints of gender, race, and class. *Gender & Society, 7*(2), 162–182.

Brown-Nagin, T. (1999). The transformation of a social movement into law? The SCLC and NAACP's campaigns for civil rights reconsidered in light of the educational activism of Septima Clark. *Women's History Review, 8*(1), 81–137.

Bryan, P. G. (1988). Her story unsilenced: Black female activists in the civil rights movement. *Sage, 2*, 60–63.

Charron, K. M. (2009). *Freedom's teacher: The life of Septima Clark.* Chapel Hill, NC: University of North Carolina Press.

Civil Rights History Project. (n.d.). *Women in the civil rights movement.* Retrieved October 12, 2017 from https://www.loc.gov/collections/civil-rights-history-project/articles-and-essays/women-in-the-civil-rights-movement/

Clark, S. P. (1962). *Echo in my soul.* New York, NY: E. P. Dutton.

Dixson, A. D. (2003). "Let's do this!" black women teachers' politics and pedagogy. *Urban Education, 38*(2), 217–235.

Gyant, L., & Atwater, D. F. (1996). Septima Clark's rhetorical and ethnic legacy: Her message of citizenship in the civil rights movement. *Journal of Black Studies, 26*(5), 577–592.

Hall, J. D., Walker, E. P., Charron, K. M., & Cline, D. P. (2010). "I train the people to do their own talking": Septima Clark and Women in the Civil Rights Movement. *Southern Cultures, 16*(2), 31–52.

Horton, A. I. (1971). *The Highlander Folk School: A history of the development of its major programs related to social movements in the South; 1932–1961* (Doctoral dissertation). School of Education, University of Chicago.

Kuumba, M. B. (2001). *Gender and social movements.* Walnut Creek, CA: AltaMira Press.

Loewen, J. K. (1995). *Lies my teacher told me.* New York, NY: The New Press.

McFadden, G. J. (1990). Septima P. Clark and the struggle for human rights. In *Women in the Civil Rights Movement: Trailblazers and Torchbearers, 1941–1965*, ed. Vicki L. Crawford, Jacqueline A. Rouse, and Barabara Woods, 85–98. Brooklyn, NY: Carlson Publishing Inc.

Robnett, B. (2000). *How long? How long?: African-American women in the struggle for civil rights.* Oxford: Oxford University Press.

Roth, J. (1973). *Interview of Septima Clark, May 23, 1973; Audio 525* [Interview]. Retrieved September 23, 2017 from https://snccdigital.org/people/septima-clark/

Rouse, J. A. (2001). "We seek to know … in order to speak the truth": Nurturing the seeds of discontent-Septima P. Clark and participatory leadership. *Sisters in the Struggle: African American Women in the Civil Rights-Black Power Movement*, 95–120.

Stokes-Brown, C. (1990). *Ready from within: Septima Clark and the civil rights movement.* Trenton, NJ: Africa World Press.

Tjerandsen, C. (1980). Education for citizenship: A foundation's experience. Santa Cruz, CA: Emil Schwarzhaupt.

Walker, E. (1976). *Oral History Interview with Septima Poinsette Clark, July 30, 1976* [Interview G-0017]. Retrieved September 23, 2017 from https://snccdigital.org/people/septima-clark/

5. "They Never Lynched You, They Never Called You a N*****": Black Athletes, Black Critical Patriotism, and the Mid-20th Century Freedom Movement

CHRISTOPHER L. BUSEY AND PAUL D. MENCKE

Introduction

Regardless of whether an individual came to know him as Cassius Clay the Olympian, Ali the heavyweight champion, or the final torch lighter for the 1996 Olympic games in Atlanta, Georgia, the death of Muhammad Ali on June 3, 2016 sparked memories for many throughout the U.S. and the world. Ali, considered by TIME Magazine to be one of the most influential people of the 20th century, was not just respected for his physical acumen in the boxing ring, but also for his socio-political stance on race, racism, and U.S. foreign policy throughout the 1960s and 1970s. Despite whether one's views aligned with Ali's, of note is how he utilized his platform to contest systemic racism and racial oppression in the U.S. Unapologetically critical, Ali's social contestations were unique yet part of a larger movement by mid-20th century Black athletes who collectively challenged racist apparatuses (Wiggins, 2014). Professional running back Jim Brown of the NFL's Cleveland Browns, Kareem Abdul-Jabbar (formerly recognized as Lew Alcindor) of the NBA's Milwaukee Bucks, and Olympic track and field stars Wilma Rudolph, Tommie Smith, and John Carlos, would use their position as athletes to speak out against racism on national and international stages (Edwards, 1969; Hall, 2011; Henderson, 2009).

Although contemporarily celebrated, activism on behalf of Black athletes was not embraced, which is one of several contradictions underlying sports in general (Leonard & King, 2009; Wiggins, 2014). For one, sports provide avenues for immense economic gain, but also contributes to the larger commodification of Black bodies (Griffin, 2012; Van Rheenen, 2013). When examining the landscape of sports, the double standard is evident when white owners of professional franchises as well as pre-dominantly white institutions (PWI's) of higher learning economically benefit from Black athletes. Resultantly, athletes—in particular Black athletes—who speak out on social issues are neither commonplace nor universally accepted as it potentially disrupts the financial gain for majority white beneficiaries. Henceforth Black athletes—and athletes in general—are expected to simply play ball for the leisurely enjoyment of interested parties. Again, this is what made Ali, Abdul-Jabbar, Brown, Rudolph, Smith, and Carlos among many others unique; they dared challenge the commodification and subjugation of their Black bodies with political and intellectual demonstrations of their unbridled opinions on racism in the U.S.

In this chapter we draw from Black critical patriotism (Busey & Walker, 2017) as a theoretical framework and curricular starting point for examining Black athletes' agency and activism during the mid-20th century freedom movement. We use the phrase *mid-20th century freedom movement* to represent a more historically inclusive time period that stretched before and beyond what is commonly referred to as the Civil Rights Movement (Davis, 2016). First we provide a summary of Black critical patriotism. Then we use the principles of Black critical patriotism to offer curricular considerations for social studies teachers to address Black athletes' agency throughout the mid-20th century freedom movement—more specifically the 1950s thru 1970s—to speak on anti-Black racism. We conclude with a call for further exploration of historical and contemporary Black athlete agency in the social studies classroom. Lastly, we offer suggestions for students and teachers to explore Black athletes' critical patriotism to address contemporary matters of race and racism.

Black Athletes, Black Critical Patriotism and the Mid-20th Century Freedom Movement

Building upon Tillet's (2012) conceptualization of critical patriotism, Busey and Walker (2017) offer Black critical patriotism as a theoretical framework rooted in a multifaceted resistance to efforts to ontologically position Black people to sub-personhood status (Mills, 1997). Busey and Walker (2017) argue that extant conceptualizations of patriotism in civic education, even those that are critical in nature, fail to capture Black motives for resistance.

Those extant conceptions of patriotism in civic education situate ideals such as liberty, democracy, and freedom as patriotic principles for either obedience or dissent (Westheimer, 2009). Meanwhile "Black critical patriotism centralizes the person first before a set of ideals" (Busey & Walker, 2017, p. 5) therefore constituting a version of racialized citizenship (Ladson-Billings, 2004). Subsequently, a Black theorization of patriotism challenges hegemonic discourses of citizenship that promote White men as purveyors of American patriotism. Three tenets underscore Black critical patriotism: physical resistance, political thought, and Black intellectualism. These tenets are explicated in the proceeding sections.

Exploring Black athletes of the mid-20th century highlights the intersection of their activism among all three tenets of Black critical patriotism. Classroom analyses of Ali, Brown, Abdul-Jabbar, Rudolph, Smith, and Carlos' stance against injustice should not be limited to specific silos of physical resistance, political thought, or critical intellectualism. Instead teachers should highlight the complexity of their positions while simultaneously acknowledging certain stances can be located within multiple spheres. Furthermore, focus must be placed on the dislike, hate, and threats made toward these individuals for their activism thus acknowledging that these athletes were not celebrated as they are today (Ratchford, 2012). Moreover, this approach connects civil rights related curriculum to current social justice movements.

Physical Resistance

The first tenet of Black critical patriotism, physical resistance, refers to the self-positioning of Black bodies as sites for dissent, resistance, and activism. Furthermore, it counters traditional social studies curriculum which contextualizes the Black body as an object acted upon rather than a subject in active resistance to often violent manifestations of white supremacy (Brown & Brown, 2010; Busey & Walker, 2017). Through the lens of physical resistance, it is important to focus on the difficulty in being the "first" Black athlete in any sport. Concurrently, due to the overt visual dislocation of seeing a Black body in a White-intended or White-normalized space, physical resistance as a tenet of Black critical patriotism can theoretically be used to explore the desegregation of professional leagues and university sporting teams during the mid-20th century. Jackie Robinson might be the most visible example, yet an intersectional lens can be used to explore the experiences of Althea Gibson, the first Black woman to win a major international tennis tournament. Additionally, physical resistance can be used as a framework to collectively examine lesser known Black collegiate athletes who desegregated university athletic teams despite threats, hostile racial environments, and a myriad of institutionally racist barriers.

However, while acknowledging the vital role of "firsts," curriculum must move into more nuanced areas of study in regards to physical resistance. Black athletes not only positioned themselves in particular spaces, but they also used their national and global platforms to physically demonstrate their resistance to racial apparatuses in the U.S. (Edwards, 2017; Gaines, 2007). One poignant example of physical resistance includes John Carlos and Tommie Smith's 1968 Mexico City Olympic medal ceremony protest in which both Olympic sprinters held up a Black Power fist in addition to wearing no shoes in solidarity with the maltreatment of poor communities of color. Carlos and Smith did so during the playing of the United States' national anthem eliciting racial backlash on-air and in news periodicals; now-famed television commentator Brent Musburger referred to them as "black-skinned storm troopers" (Musburger, 1968). Facing death threats, and eventually never being able to compete for the Olympic team again, these undeterred athletes are the epitome of physical resistance and Black critical patriotism.

Political Thought

The next tenet, political thought, underscores efforts by Black athletes to change or enact policy, place Black perspectives into historical socio-political movements dominated by White perspectives (i.e., labor, populist, women's movement), or trouble mythical narratives of socio-political equality (Busey & Walker, 2017). Muhammad Ali was a prominent example of this tenet by refusing to serve in the Vietnam War after being drafted by the U.S. government. By underscoring Black people's collective suffering in the U.S. in addition to the imperialist goals inherent in the fight against communist countries, Ali's profound statements highlighted the United States' contradiction to ideals of freedom and equality. Ali further rationalized his refusal to fight in Vietnam in a 1970 interview with the journal *The Black Scholar* (Ali, 1970) in which he directed his disdain for anti-Black racism and racial violence in the U.S. stating:

> I met two black soldiers a while back in an airport. They said: "Champ, it takes a lot of guts to do what you're doing." I told them: Brothers, you just don't know. If you knew where you were going now, if you knew your chances of coming out with no arm or no eye, fighting those people in their own land, fighting Asian brothers, you got to shoot them, they never lynched you, never called you nigger, never put dogs on you, never shot your leaders. You've got to shoot your "enemies" (they call them) and as soon as you get home you won't be able to find a job. (p. 30)

Olympic track star Wilma Rudolph is another example of how Black athletes of the mid-20th century used political thought and activism as a demonstration of Black critical patriotism. Rudolph participated in the desegregation of a public restaurant in her hometown and is collectively remembered for insisting that her Olympic celebration parade be integrated. While a parade might seem insignificant, of importance is that Wilma Rudolph is from Clarksville, Tennessee, a locale geographically and symbolically representative of the Jim Crow South. Moreover, parades—be they local or national—often "engage with and promote existing racial structures" (Liberti & Smith, 2015, p. 26) while simultaneously displaying everyday life. In her hometown of Clarksville, Tennessee an integrated parade celebrating her 1960 Olympic accomplishments was projected by local press as a sign of racial progress, but closer examination of Rudolph's insistence and efforts to ensure that the parade was integrated demonstrate her political activism against racial structures (Liberti & Smith, 2015). Finally, in 1969, baseball star Curt Flood both challenged and changed policy by refusing to be traded to the racially unwelcoming Philadelphia Phillies. His resistance led to the implementation of a new rule allowing extended rights for veteran players. These three examples challenge U.S. policy as well as liberal movements commonly viewed as beyond the scope of Black citizenship, both nationally and globally.

Critical Intellectualism

Resistance to racism in U.S. history curriculum is often limited to stories of slave revolts, abolitionism, and messianic master narratives of the Civil Rights Movement (Aldridge, 2006: Woodson, 2016). What is often unacknowledged is how Black people intellectually challenged Black sub-personhood in the U.S. (Grant, Brown, & Brown, 2016; King, 2014). For centuries, Black people used their intellect and intellectual spaces to challenge racism and racially oppressive structures. What was not expected however was that Black athletes would be so vocal in challenging racial structures that disproportionately and intentionally affected Black people for centuries in the US. The use of critical intellectual agency to describe Black athletes' racial activism during the mid-20th century freedom movement presents athletes as intellectuals. More specifically, the final tenet of Black critical patriotism—Black intellectualism—illustrates the contributions made by increasing Black collective conscience.

Black tennis player, Arthur Ashe not only demonstrates Black intellectualism, but his exploits are also indicative of the interrelated nature of Black critical patriotism. That is, the tenets of Black critical patriotism operate symbiotically. Arthur Ashe used his platform as a successful tennis star to critique American racism as well as apartheid South Africa (Hall, 2011). Although admittedly not as separatist in stance as other Black athletes during the mid-20th century freedom movement, Ashe, a "militant integration-ist" (Hall, 2011, p. 476) like Martin Luther King Jr., aligned himself with the causes of Black liberation. Over time however Ashe grew increasingly more militant in stance as he spoke for Black power and equal rights across the globe (Hall, 2011).

Conclusion

Racial oppression and systemic racism are rooted in the social, physical, and psychological fabric of the United States and consequently, as an institution, sports are not excluded from these racist structures. Racial consciousness among Black athletes of the mid-20th century freedom movement implicated the nexus of race and sports, and more specifically the ways in which sport operates as a racial apparatus in the U.S. Of further note is that mid-20th cen-tury Black athletes grounded their efforts within global discourses of racism by connecting their efforts with international Black liberation movements (Gaines, 2007; Henderson, 2009).

The channeling of a Black athlete's agency on social issues remains salient today as the Black Lives Matters (BLM) movement, the increased visibility of anti-Black racism, and the homicides of Black men and women have led many to question whether or not Black athletes should use their platforms as social pulpits (Edwards, 2010; Gil, 2016; Grano, 2009; Wright, 2016). Some may consider this a longing for the athlete's heroic voice to intervene in current socio-political crises (Grano, 2009; Leonard & King, 2009). Its acceptance by the general public can also depend on the manner by which Black athletes demonstrate their agency. The issue of Black athlete agency and activism is embedded in decades of civic debate. Because this longstanding issue remains open, and many would consider at its "tipping point", Black criti-cal patriotism among Black athletes warrants discussion in secondary social studies classrooms.

References

Aldridge, D. P. (2006). The limits of master narratives in history textbooks: An analysis of representations of Martin Luther King, Jr. *Teachers College Record, 108*(4), 662–686. doi:10.1111/j.1467-9620.2006.00664.x

Ali, M. (1970). Interviews: Muhammad Ali. *The Black Scholar, 1*(8), 32–39. doi:10.1080/00064246.1970.11430684

Brown, A. L., & Brown, K. D. (2010). Strange fruit indeed: Interrogating contemporary textbook representations of racial violence toward African Americans. *Teachers College Record, 112*(1), 31–67.

Busey, C. L., & Walker, I. (2017). A dream and a bus: Black critical patriotism in elementary social studies standards. *Theory & Research in Social Education.* Advance online publication. doi:10.1080/00933104.2017.1320251

Davis, A. Y. (2016). *Freedom is a constant struggle: Ferguson, Palestine, and the foundations of a movement.* Chicago, IL: Haymarket.

Edwards, H. (1969). *Revolt of the black athlete.* New York, NY: Free Press.

Edwards, H. (2010). Social change and popular culture: Seminal developments at the interface of race, sport and society. *Sport in Society, 13*(1), 59–71.

Edwards, H. (2017). *Revolt of the black athlete* (Anniversary Ed.). Urbana-Champaign, IL. University of Illinois Press.

Gaines, K. (2007). The Civil Rights Movement in world perspective. *OAH Magazine of History, 27*(1), 57–64.

Gill, E. L., Jr. (2016). "Hands up, don't shoot" or shut up and play ball? Fan-generated media views of the Ferguson Five. *Journal of Human Behavior in the Social Environment, 26*(3–4), 400–412. doi:10.1080/10911359.2016.1139990

Grano, D. A. (2009). Muhammad Ali versus the "modern athlete": On voice in mediated sports culture. *Critical Studies in Media Communication, 26*(3), 191–211.

Grant, C. A., Brown, K. D., & Brown, A. L. (2016). *Black intellectual thought in education: The missing traditions of Anna Julia Cooper, Carter G. Woodson, and Alain LeRoy Locke.* New York, NY: Routledge.

Griffin, R. A. (2012). The disgrace of commodification and shameful convenience: A critical race critique of the NBA. *Journal of Black Studies, 43*(2), 161–185.

Hall, E. A. (2011). "I guess I'm becoming more and more militant": Arthur Ashe and the Black Freedom Movement, 1961–1968. *The Journal of African American History, 96*(4), 474–502.

Henderson, S. (2009). Crossing the line: Sport and the limit of civil rights protest. *International Journal of the History of Sport, 26*(1), 101–121. doi:10.1080/09523360 802500576

King, L. J. (2014). More than slaves: Black founders, Benjamin Banneker, and critical intellectual agency. *Social Studies Research and Practice, 9*(3), 88–105.

Ladson-Billings, G. (2004). Culture versus citizenship: The challenge of racialized citizenship in the United States. In J. A. Banks (Ed.), *Diversity in citizenship education* (pp. 99–126). San Francisco, CA: Jossey-Bass.

Leonard, D., & King, C. (2009). Revolting black athletes. *Journal for the Study of Sports and Athletes in Education, 3*(2), 215–232. doi:10.1179/ssa.2009.3.2.215

Liberti, R., & Smith, M. M. (2015). *(Re)Presenting Wilma Rudolph.* Syracuse, NY: Syracuse University Press.

Mills, C. W. (1997). *The racial contract.* Ithaca, NY: Cornell University Press.

Musburger, B. (1968, October 17). Bizarre protest by Smith, Carlos tarnishes medals. *Chicago American*, p. 4.

Ratchford, J. L. (2012). "Black fists and fool's gold": The 1960s Black athlete revolt reconsidered, the Lebron James decision and self-determination in post-racial America. *The Black Scholar, 42*(1), 49–59.

Tillet, S. (2012). *Sites of slavery: Citizenship and racial democracy in the post-civil rights imagination.* Durham, NC: Duke University Press.

Van Rheenen, D. (2013). Exploitation in college sports: Race, revenue, and educational reward. *International Review for the Sociology of Sport, 48*(5), 550–571. doi:10.1177/1012690212450218

Westheimer, J. (2009). Should social studies be patriotic? *Social Education, 73*(7), 316–320.

Wiggins, D. K. (2014). "Black athletes in white men's games": Race, sport, and American national pastimes. *The International Journal of the History of Sport, 31*(1–2), 181–202. doi:10.1080/09523367.2013.857313

Woodson, A. N. (2016). We're just ordinary people: Messianic master narratives and Black youths' civic agency. *Theory & Research in Social Education, 44*(2), 184–211. doi:10.1080/00933104.2016.1170645

Wright, J. (2016). Be like Mike? The Black athlete's dilemma. *Spectrum: A Journal on Black Men, 4*(2), 1–19.

6. *From the Margins to Center Stage: The Chicano Movement*

Ellen Bigler

It may come as a surprise to many of the nation's social studies teachers to learn that they have omitted a significant civil rights movement in their teaching of the Civil Rights era. It certainly did to this author back in 1985, when as a teacher I began to take graduate courses on Latin America in anticipation of an upcoming curriculum change in New York State schools, and encountered the Chicano Movement: *El Movimiento*. It was not for lack of interest in the struggles of oppressed groups that we weren't acquainted; I had interned in inner city schools, taught American Studies regents classes, and developed electives in minority studies courses as a teacher in upstate New York. But somehow, growing up in Ohio and then completing an education program in New York, *El Movimiento* never crossed my path until I returned for coursework in Puerto Rican, Latin American and Caribbean Studies.

As a teacher educator in Rhode Island over the past 20 years, I have asked education majors if anything has changed: Did they learn of *El Movimiento* in their high schools? The response is almost always one of puzzlement. Perhaps César Chávez and the United Farm Workers struggle, but most assuredly not the larger context of *El Movimiento*. Nor have I found that the teachers I work with, some of the best in the field, are likely to incorporate it into their teaching.

Studies of texts and curricula across the country underline that this lack of attention to issues around race and class is a phenomenon by no means restricted to Rhode Island and the Northeast. Rather, it represents a consistent pattern of omissions in the teaching of social studies (Bigler, Willox, & Shiller, 2013; Loewen, 2007). Additionally, teaching about the Civil Rights era in social studies classrooms is oftentimes done in "black and white" (Stavans, 2016), when it should embrace the struggles of all groups who organized for their rights, including Chicanos, Puerto Ricans, Filipinos and other Asian Americans, Native Americans, LGBTQ activists, and women of all ethnic backgrounds. This essay intends to lay out the case as it relates to the Chicano Movement for remedying that inequity, and provides some tools to begin the process.

Resistance to Chicano Studies

Chicano Studies, including the Chicano Movement—the struggle for civil rights for the Mexican American community that was in its heyday from the mid-1960s to the mid-1970s—began to make its way into universities in California and subsequently elsewhere by the early 1970s. The *Plan de Santa Barbara*, authored by Chicano activists in 1969, had called for the creation of Chicano Studies at the university level (Chicano Coordinating Council on Higher Education, 1969). Chicano professors and students, inspired by the political activism around them, demanded college courses that focused on the Chicano experience and that addressed the widespread social and economic inequalities their communities confronted.

But the call for inclusive curricula in the nation's public schools made little substantive headway.[1] Nationally, contentious debates over curriculum were underway, with conservatives arguing that ethnic "particularism" that addressed oppressed groups' histories and struggles was divisive (e.g., Ravitch, 1990). By the mid-1980s, the conservative 1987 California Framework for History and the Social Sciences, co-authored by Diane Ravitch, was in place. The California State Board of Education, which included Ronald Reagan appointees, threw their support behind the Framework and texts that focused on an *e pluribus unum* vision of U.S. history (Ravitch, 1990). As the California State Board of Education approves textbooks for use in the schools, and California had the largest student population in the country, textbook editors were happy to comply (Campbell, 2016).

Chicano studies in the academy did continue to evolve and become more inclusive of diverse voices, including women and the LGBTQ community, by the 1980s and 1990s. At the secondary level though, the integration of the Chicano experience and the Movement made little headway. In May of 2010 that began to shift, at least in the Southwest. Arizona made national headlines when the legislature passed Bill 2281, prohibiting a school district (or charter school) from offering courses that did any of the following: promoted the overthrow of the U.S. government; created resentment toward any race or class; advocated ethnic solidarity; or were designed for a particular ethnicity (Campbell, 2016). The new law was quickly applied to a Mexican-American studies program taught in the Tucson Unified School District, and rather than lose state funding the school board chose to disband it. Ironically, it had the opposite effect of what was intended, at least regionally. As news spread, California and Texas classroom teachers began to examine their own offerings, and to implement ethnic studies and Chicano studies classes. People organized to challenge the ban in Arizona, and *"librotraficantes"* raised money to bring books banned from school districts to community sites in Texas and Arizona (Campbell, 2016).

In 2016, Texas activists pushed back against a move to approve a book on Mexican American history that was deemed racist, and succeeded in turning down its adoption by the Texas Board of Education (Diaz, 2017). California, meanwhile, approved a new History-Social Science Framework, adopted in 2016, that specifically addresses many aspects of Chicano history and the Chicano Movement. All students in California will now require an ethnic studies course for graduation as of 2019 (Lynch, 2016).[2] Arizona, meanwhile, continues the ban; yet a bill to extend that ban to the university level failed in 2017.

Interest in integrating ethnic studies classes and greater incorporation of the histories and experiences of oppressed groups appears to be on the rise. How then do social studies educators who recognize the value of such content make room for "one more thing," at a time when hours devoted to social studies teaching have declined precipitously as the role of standardized tests has grown? Reduced time for social studies teaching is all the more troubling given that these curricular changes are disproportionally affecting poor and minority students who are forced to spend time preparing for standardized tests in math and English at the expense of classes like art, music, science, and social studies (Kaladis, 2013). This, despite the fact that researchers have documented the positive effects of courses like Chicano Studies on student retention, graduation rate, and college attendance (Diaz, 2015).

On one level, as social studies educators we can commit to becoming more proactive in advocating for increased quality time spent in the social studies classroom. We can develop electives that promote critical thinking skills and encourage students to become engaged citizens in the democratic process. And we can examine what and how we currently teach in light of the C3 Framework for the Social Studies that puts inquiry at the center of our teaching. The Chicano Movement is a topic well served by this inquiry model, and integrating it using C3 would accomplish multiple objectives simultaneously: A more accurate and inclusive history for all students at a time when the harassment of oppressed groups is on the rise again (Costello, 2016); culturally responsive instruction that speaks to students left out of the picture and who are now in the majority in many districts; and development of the "three Cs", critical thinking skills, communication skills, and citizenship in a democratic society.

So What Is the Chicano Movement?

Perhaps it makes sense to start first with the question "What is a Chicano?" for those unfamiliar with the term. It may have arisen as a shorthand for the Spanish word "Mexicano," derived from the indigenous name "Mexica" (Aztecs) for the people of central Mexico, where the "xi" is pronounced like "shee." Whatever its origins, it became a disparaging term for Mexican Americans in the Southwest until the mid-1960s, when politically active Mexican Americans, taking a page from the black Civil Rights movement, began to use it to affirm a sense of unity, empowerment, and pride. It captured their indigenous and Mexican roots and their uniqueness as a community, and it was one they themselves chose—unlike the government-imposed term "Hispanic" or the troubling label of hyphenated Mexican-Americans.

The Chicano Movement, or in Spanish *El Movimiento*, "that upheaval that sought to reconfigure, during the Civil Rights era, their place in the tapestry that is the United States" (Stavans, 2016, p. ix), takes its name then from the term's widespread use in the Southwest. *El Movimiento* "galvanized the Mexican American community, from laborers to student activists, giving them not only a political voice to combat prejudice and inequality, but also a new sense of cultural awareness and ethnic pride" (Montoya, 2016, p. xiii), and produced "a paradoxical agenda of civil rights and equal opportunity demands, on the one hand, and a more separatist ethnic nationalist rebellion, on the other" (García, 1997, p. 2). Diverse leaders, agendas, organizational strategies, tactics—all came together under the banner of *El Movimiento*.

It would be impossible to do the Movement justice in this limited space, but I intend to outline the general parameters and to point to some excellent resources. The earlier events that I reference here contributed to the demands for change that became the Chicano Movement and are readily integrated into the U.S. history/social studies classroom at the appropriate juncture, setting up students to understand the rise of the Chicano Movement when covered as part of the Civil Rights era. Appropriate resources can be found in the endnote references.

Mexico Loses Almost Half Its Territory to the U.S.

While the treaties signed following the Mexican War promised to respect the rights of Mexicans in these lands, they were routinely violated (Grady, 2016).[3]

Economic Marginalization

Mexican-descent Americans, seen by many as an inferior "race," encounter social, political, and economic discrimination throughout the Southwest and elsewhere.[4] Migrant workers were exempted from federal legislation benefiting industrial workers in the 1930s (McKay, 2010).

Depression and World War II-Era Abuses of Civil Rights

The Great Depression increased tensions between Anglos and Mexican Americans, and over one half million people of Mexican descent, including U.S. citizens, were rounded up and sent back to Mexico without benefit of legal counsel[5] (Florido, 2015). Mexican Americans served in the military fighting "to make the world safe for democracy" (Wilson, 1917),[6] but the home front environment for Mexican Americans did not change appreciably in response to the war effort. Two events in particular, the Sleepy Lagoon Murder Trial (Citizens' Committee, 1942) and the Zoot Suit Riots, left lasting scars on the psyches of Mexican Americans[7] (Pagan, 2003).

Confronting Educational Inequities

On the educational front, Mexican Americans in the Southwest were typically placed in substandard schools and often segregated, where they learned nothing of their historical presence in the U.S. and faced stiff punishments for speaking Spanish. Mexican American parents challenged these practices through the courts.[8]

Post-War Discriminatory Treatment Continues

The post-war boom that the country as a whole experienced did not extend to the Mexican American community, and they had little representation politically. In 1960, a third of Mexican American families were living below the poverty level, with unemployment double that of Euro-Americans. The 1960s mark the beginning of a period of sustained activism among oppressed groups in the U.S., and Mexican Americans were no exception. Federal actions in response to pressures for change also provided Mexican Americans new means to fight for their rights. In 1964, President Johnson supported the Civil Rights Act of 1964 that desegregated public accommodations throughout the country, and in 1965 the Voting Rights Act ended the poll tax and provided Mexican Americans and other oppressed groups legal tools to fight against discriminatory voting practices (Montoya, 2016).

Organizing the Migrant Farmworkers

While the majority of Mexican Americans by 1965 were no longer working in the fields, they felt a strong affinity with those who were. It was César Chávez who would gain national recognition for his leadership of the United Farm Workers (UFW), inspiring Mexican Americans across the U.S. to join in the struggle for their civil rights and launching the peak years of the Chicano Movement. Less recognized until recently (Puig, 2017) was Dolores Huerta, who like Chávez began her organizing work with the Mexican American advocacy group named the Community Service Organization (CSO). Both left to found the National Farm Workers Association (NFWA) and focus on organizing exploited farmworkers. In 1965 they led their first successful strike, but failed to gain union recognition from the growers.

Meanwhile another farmworker union, the Agricultural Workers Organizing Committee (AWOC) under the leadership of Filipino American Larry Itliong, was also struggling for recognition. It was Itliong who approached Chávez about joining their strike and ultimately convinced him to join forces with his group.[9] The rest of course is history: The struggle to be recognized gained traction; Senator Robert F. Kennedy became an ardent supporter of the cause; AWOC and NFWA merged into the United Farm Workers (UFW) Organizing Committee; the 21-day march from Delano to the California state capitol in 1966 captured the nation's attention; a call for boycotting non-union grapes and lettuce put pressure on growers; and young Mexican Americans joined *La Huelga* in force.

Beyond the UFW and Farmworker Issues

Chávez then was the first Mexican American leader to capture the national spotlight in the 1960s, and would ultimately be labeled as the first of the "Four Horsemen," men leading and representing the distinct and diverse strands of what would become known as the Chicano Movement. The other three were Reies López Tijerina, leader of the land grant movement; Corky Gonzales, the author of "I am Joaquín" and founder of the "Crusade for Justice"; and José Angel Gutiérrez, organizer of La Raza Unida Party (Busto, 2005; Meier & Rivera, 1972).[10] Teaching the Chicano Movement should not end with Chavez and the farmworkers; it has other equally significant players and agendas, allowing students to better understand the depth and breadth of the Movement, its origins, its similarities and differences with other civil rights movements, and its successes and ongoing challenges. Thanks to the proliferation of online resources and the work of Chicano scholars and others over the ensuing decades to document and analyze *El Movimiento*, there are valuable resources readily available even when textbooks (or book bans) fail to comprehensively address such matters. Topics that can be pursued include the struggle to take back lands lost to Euro Americans; use of the courts to address unequal treatment; voter registration initiatives and the fight to remove common barriers like poll taxes, literacy tests and intimidation; the youth movements; the struggle for inclusion and representation in schools and universities; ending educational injustices in public schools; anti(Vietnam) war protests; use of the arts to foster identity and political awareness; alliances with other oppressed groups; and the emergence of Chicana voices. I address some of these aspects below.

Reclaiming Land
In the early 1960s, Reies López Tijerina, the second "horseman" of the Chicano Movement, organized the *Alianza Federál de Mercedes Reales* to work to reclaim communal land grants that Hispanos in New Mexico had been awarded by Spain and Mexico. Tijerina documented how Hispanos had been systematically disenfranchised. He acquired a following, but his efforts were largely derailed after a failed 1967 courthouse raid led to his imprisonment (Kamerick, 2016). While his leadership role was thus fairly brief, "(i)t's the moment that the Chicano movement became an important part of the civil rights movement," according to David Correia, professor at the University of New Mexico (Colker, 2015).[11] It is also a cautionary tale of how government forces allied against his message; like Martin Luther King and others, he was targeted by the FBI program COINTELPRO.[12]

Political Activism
The third of the "four horsemen" was Rodolfo "Corky" Gonzales, who first gained fame for his 1967 epic poem *Yo Soy Joaquín/I am Joaquín*. The poem spoke to the many who would ultimately choose to claim an identity as "Chicanos." It captured vividly and poetically the history of an "imagined" people (Anderson, 1983) whose roots on this continent could be traced back to pre-Columbian times, and going forward embraced both conquerors and the conquered. "Joaquín" could trace his descent from the despot Cortes as well as the great Aztec civilization and all those proud Mexicanos who came after and struggled against oppression—including among them Emiliano Zapata, Benito Juarez, and Father Hidalgo. Yes, he now dwells in a country that has wiped out his history and stifled his pride. Yes, his land has been lost and stolen, his culture has been raped. But whatever names he goes by—La raza, Méjicano, Español, Latino, Chicano—he survives and refuses to be absorbed. All are one, and Joaquín proclaims that he will endure. When playwright Luis Valdez and his group Teatro Campesino turned the poem into a film,

the imagery of the Chicano past riveted audiences who knew nothing of the murals of Mexico, Mesoamerican sculptures, and their ancestors' resistance to oppression. "Through this poem ... Mexican Americans were transformed into Chicanos" (Hartley, 2017).

Gonzalez had begun his political activism in the fold of assimilationist politics and as a supporter of the Democrats' Viva Kennedy movement, but as he became more aware of the brutal treatment of Mexican Americans at the hands of law enforcement and came to doubt the willingness of the Democratic party to take action to make meaningful change, his approach shifted. He resigned to organize the Crusade for Justice, emphasizing self-determination and community control along with ethnic pride and rejection of domination by Anglo cultural and economic norms. With Tijerina, he participated in the 1968 Poor People's Campaign in Washington, D.C. Together they argued for a larger role for Chicanos in the 1968 Poor People's Campaign and jointly presented several major initiatives with African American and Native American groups. The Chicano contingent working with Gonzales also produced their own declaration, *El Plan del Barrio*, focused on Mexican American-specific demands such as bilingual education and restitution of community land grants (Montoya, 2016).

In 1969 the Crusade for Justice organized the influential Chicano Youth and Liberation Conference in Denver. Here, Chicano leaders from across the Southwest and the country articulated a vision for their community in the founding document of Chicano nationalism, *El Plan Espiritual de Aztlán* (Montoya, 2016). *El Plan* was a political manifesto and guide for future Chicano activism (Montoya, 2016). It also drew heavily upon the concept of Aztlán as articulated by the radical Chicano poet Alurista. Aztlán, according to Aztec legend, was the mythical homeland of the Aztecs that they were forced to leave because of a long drought. They migrated southeast to settle in the valley of central Mexico, but prophecy was that they would one day return to Aztlán—which it was argued was the region of northern Mexico and the American Southwest. The belief that it was their spiritual homeland, if not their actual one, proved to be a powerful one as it provided a sense of legitimacy to Chicanos' presence in the Southwest.

El Plan Espiritual de Aztlán was above all else a call to action:

> Nationalism was the unifying force, defined by pride in culture and history and by the quest for self-determination, an independent and self-reliant Mexican American community. (Goals were that) "all should be committed to the liberation of La Raza." Other goals included autonomous institutions and community control over the economy, education, and self-defense ... to "drive the exploiter out of our communities" and set up a system that rejected materialism

and embraced humanistic values of cooperation and distribution of wealth and resources. Similarly in education, the document advocated community control and a curriculum relevant to Chicanos (Montoya, 2016, p. 96).

A third political party was also called for, as the two-party system had failed to meet their needs. This call for change would resonate with a new generation of ethnically aware, politically energized Mexican Americans.

On campuses across the Southwest activist Chicano organizations sprang up—MAYA, MAYO, MASO, UMAS, MASA,[13] focused initially on encouraging education as the key to success and involvement in electoral politics. Here too the shift toward a cultural nationalist perspective and more confrontational actions came out of a widely shared sense of frustration that the traditional Mexican American assimilationist stance failed to address the plethora of problems facing the Mexican American community (Movimiento Estuidantil Chicanx de Azatlán, 2017).

The "Blowouts"

In 1968 a student walkout at an East Los Angeles high school quickly drew support from other high school and college students; 10,000 ultimately joined in. Their concerns were longstanding ones: High dropout rates near 50%; discriminatory school policies and racist faculty; a curriculum that ignored their history and presence; and few Mexican American faculty and administrators. When police from the LAPD were caught on tape beating student demonstrators, many parents and community members also joined in the demands for a just educational system. Ultimately school strikes, known as "blowouts," spread to other areas of the Southwest, most notably Crystal City Texas (Montoya, 2016). As Montoya notes (2016, p. 112), the aggressive responses to calls for reform had the effect of increasingly radicalizing youth as they encountered the unwillingness of the system to change. The Brown Berets, a paramilitary group who followed strict codes of behavior, organized and gained visibility at this time acting as a self-defense group to protect young students. Groups soon spread across the country (Estrada, 2017; University of Washington, 2017).[14]

The Crystal City Strike and the Raza Unida Party

In 1969, José Angel Gutiérrez, the "fourth horseman" of the Chicano Movement, returned to his hometown of Crystal City Texas with Mario Compean to take on issues facing Mexican American students. Almost 90% of the high school students were Mexican American, but the school board and teachers were overwhelmingly white. Whites controlled access to important positions, including selection of candidates for school board elections. Spanish was prohibited; students reported being punished for even speaking Spanish. Mexicans and Mexican Americans were invisible in the curriculum, and many of the students spoke of being disparaged for being Mexican and called names. Even the cheerleading squad allowed only one token Mexican American on the team.[15]

The strikers achieved some of their demands. The following spring, the newly formed Raza Unida Party put forward a slate of candidates who won control of the school board and initiated additional changes, inspiring many in the Mexican American community to believe that exercising their right to vote could make a difference. The Raza Unida Party would ultimately spread to other areas, but like other third parties their successes were limited (Palazzol, 2013).

The Chicano Moratorium. The Chicano Movement coincided with growing resistance across the U.S. to the Vietnam War. While Mexican American communities were initially supportive of the war effort, as more young men returned home in body bags (deaths were twice those of the larger population of the Southwest) and the war dragged on with no end in sight, Mexican Americans too began to question why they were involved in it (García, 2010). The resistance culminated in the largest antiwar effort by any U.S. minority group, the Chicano Moratorium of August 29, 1970, where perhaps 30,000 people took part. What began as a peaceful, even festive event with many families and children in attendance turned violent however when Los Angeles police, massed and fully armed, responded to a disturbance at a liquor store where local youth had stolen drinks. Arriving in full riot gear, they began forcing participants to leave. Participants threw objects at the police, who then escalated the conflict by throwing tear gas containers directly into the crowd as the officers crossed the field in military formation (García, 2010).

Ultimately 60 demonstrators were wounded. Two Chicano teens were killed, and Ruben Salazar, a respected *Los Angeles Times* journalist covering the event, died when a tear gas projectile thrown into a bar where he sought shelter hit him in the head. Because he had been already warned by LA police to censor what he was writing about police violence and other related events and was perceived by entrenched powers as a threat to the status quo, his death was considered highly suspicious; he ultimately became seen as a martyr for the cause.[16]

Aftermath. The Chicano Moratorium is often seen as the high point of the Movement. Subsequent rallies to address and protest police brutality were organized, but police responded with more violence and attendance at rallies declined (Montoya, 2016, p. 126). Like other activist minority groups and leaders, including the Young Lords Party and the Black Panthers, the Brown Berets and the National Chicano Moratorium Committee were infiltrated with the intention of undermining their work. By the mid to late 1970s students in general were less involved politically and more focused on their individual wellbeing; the national mood had shifted (Montoya, 2016).

Most of the goals driving the militancy of the Chicano Movement were very basic ones: The right to a quality education and inclusion in the curriculum; fair treatment in the justice system and an end to police brutality; an end to an unpopular war that weighed disproportionately on minority communities across the U.S.; and an end to social and economic discrimination.

Educational access and access to the ballot box were recognized as critically important. At the university level, Chicano studies programs were established at most California institutions of higher education, and subsequently spread to other regions with large Mexican American populations. Mexican American faculty were hired; Mexican American students gained greater access. Some programs remained rooted in the local communities as called for in the original Plan—though given the realities of the academy many would chose to focus on more traditional scholarly paths. Much of the scholarship and research on Mexican Americans and the Chicano Movement available today resulted from the institutionalization of Chicano Studies.

Chicana Feminism

While Chicanas played a vital role in the Chicano nationalist struggles, many had come to feel that they were struggling against not only the racism and inequality of the larger society, but also entrenched sexism and male domination within their own communities and political organizations.

Chicana feminists, like their African American counterparts, largely rejected the white feminist movement for ignoring the salience of race and class, and identified with other feminists of color. Chicana feminist thought emerged out of their struggle to identify and work to counter the intersecting race, gender and social class oppressions they confronted; feminists who were lesbians experienced and wrote about yet another form of oppression. Their work began to appear in various journals and newspapers, and they established many of their own. The Chicana feminist movement yielded a rich trove of literature and provided a means to examine how oppression within the cultural nationalist movement and the larger Chicano culture, as well as the larger society, acted to constrain their lives and potential (García, 1997).

The Chicano Cultural Renaissance

Finally, the Chicano Movement produced an immense outpouring of works in the visual arts, literature, drama, film, and other forms that was coined the "Chicano Renaissance" in 1971 by Felipe Ortego de Gasca (Candelaria, 2017). Artists and their works, emphasizing Chicano themes, would become key players in the political activities of the day.

> Having embraced the symbolism of Aztlán and the concept of la raza as central to Chicano identity, visual artists, authors, poets, and playwrights explored these ideas in various formats. Playwright Luis Valdez's play Zoot Suit (1978) presented to audiences El Teatro Campesino's vivid dramatization of the Zoot Suit Riots of the 1940s ... (A)uthors ... used Chicano cultural themes and integrated the Spanish language into their prose. Visual artists ... integrated Chicano imagery into their pieces. ... Chicano identity took a tangible form that illustrated the history, imagery, and pride embraced by the Chicano movement. (Candelaria, 2017)

Chicana feminists inserted their presence here too, confronting the "machismo" of the male artists and exploring woman-related themes. Some would take a more global perspective, weaving the Chicana/o story into the histories, cultures and experiences of other groups. Judy Baca, for example, spearheaded the Great Wall of Los Angeles, a half-mile long mural depicting the histories of diverse groups of Californians (Baca, 2017). The wall continues to grow as young artists work to incorporate the last four decades of the 20th century.[17] For her, as for many who participated in the Chicano Renaissance, their artistic endeavors are intended to educate. "I want to use public space to create a public voice, and a public consciousness about the presence of people who are, in fact, the majority of the population but who are not represented in any visual way" (Baca, 2017).

Judy Baca's contention that "(b)y telling their stories we are giving voice to the voiceless and visualizing the whole of the American story" (Baca, 2017) could as easily apply to us as social studies educators. By telling the stories of groups who were once voiceless, we too contribute to helping to visualize "the whole of the American story" for our own social studies students.[18]

Notes

1. This is certainly not a new phenomenon. In the early 1900s W. E. B. Dubois was calling for black history in schools, albeit to also better educate whites, and the 1960s Freedom Schools developed curricula to teach what was being left out (Anderson, 2016). Such victories, it is worth noting, begin small; the impetus in part arose from one such course that started in a San Francisco school in 2008.

2. For educators interested in exploring this era in depth, an excellent bi-national project that analyzes the tensions between the two young nations, their differing perspectives, and the war's aftermath can be found online (PBS/KERA, 2006) with the film available on YouTube.

3. Labor strikes periodically occurred despite the obvious risks. Emma Tenayuca and the 1938 pecan shellers' strikes (San Antonio, Texas) provide windows into their experiences and link to the U.S. labor movement (American Postal Workers Union, 2012). Today agricultural workers still lack many of the protections of the NLRA or the FLSA at the national level. These government actions disproportionately affected workers of color, including Mexican Americans (Kelkar, 2016).

4. Labor strikes periodically occurred despite the obvious risks. Emma Tenayuca and the 1938 pecan shellers' strikes (San Antonio Texas) provide windows into their experiences and link to the U.S. labor movement (American Postal Workers Union, 2012). Today agricultural workers still lack many of the protections of the NLRA or the FLSA at the national level. These government actions disproportionately affected workers of color, including Mexican Americans (Kelkar, 2016).

5. The current threat of mass deportations of undocumented immigrants can be examined in light of this historical precedent.

6. See National Park Service (2015) for an overview of the service and post-war experiences of Mexican Americans and Puerto Ricans.

7. Excellent materials built around the films Zoot Suit (by Luis Valdez) and Zoot Suit Riots (PBS American Experience), including primary documents, photos, active learning strategies, firsthand accounts and the like can be found online (Pomona College Department of Theatre & Dance, 2017). The PBS film Zoot Suit Riots is available on YouTube.

8. Mexican American parents in 1931 challenged the Lemon Grove School District's attempt to create a separate school for their children, leading to the first successful desegregation court decision in the U.S. (Alvarez, 1986). A film based on research by Robert Alvarez, whose father was one of those children, is available free online (Espinosa & KPBS, 1985) and depicts both the local and national context of the incident. Also noteworthy on the educational front is the 1946 court case *Mendez v. Westminster* which provided the legal argument that prevailed eight years later in *Brown v. Bd. of Education* (United States Courts, 2017): Segregation leads to feelings of inferiority. A re-enactment is available at the U.S. government courts site above, and Sylvia Mendez' reminiscence of her experiences in segregated California and the school system is available from NPR online (Echavarri & Bishop, 2016).

9. The film *The Delano Manongs: Forgotten Heroes of the United Farm Workers*, documents the struggles of Filipino workers in the U.S. both before the formation of the UFW and subsequently within it, and is available online (PBS/WGBH, 2014).

10. Matt Meier and Feliciano Rivera, in *The Chicanos: A History of Mexican Americans* (1972), framed *El Movimiento*'s diverse and distinct strands as unified under the leadership of the "Four Horsemen." See Busto (2005) for an analysis of this construction of the Movement.

11. Tijerina's story, including interviews with him and his followers, is available online (see Kamerick, 2016).

12. See Gordon (2006) for a thoughtful discussion of the role of government in domestic spying and potential for abuse.

13. The names are acronyms for Mexican American Youth Association, Mexican American Youth Organization, Mexican American Student Organization, United Mexican American Students, Mexican American Student Association; in 1969 most such organizations were merged under the umbrella association *Movimiento Estudiantil Chicano de Aztlan*, which still exists.

14. An interactive map maintained by the University of Washington (2017) shows their eventual distribution across the U.S., as well as the proliferation of UFW chapters, the umbrella student organization MeChA, LULAC, and the Raza Unida political party, giving a visual sense of the spread of the Movement.

15. An overview of the grievances and demands, and how the high school students' actions unfolded (Palazzol, 2013), is available on the interactive Global Nonviolent Action Database site. The data base, combined with a *Teaching Tolerance* article on the same event (Barrios, 2009), is an excellent vehicle for exploring how entrenched powers hold onto that power and assessing what strategies for change are effective.

16. A film contextualizing his life work and his death during this turbulent area, *Ruben Salazar: Man in the Middle*, is available to PBS members (PBS, 2014). A collection of all his articles published in the Los Angeles Times and elsewhere, including his powerful and often-cited "Who is a Chicano? And What Is It the Chicanos Want" (Salazar, 1970, pp. 235–237) is available online.

17. The Great Wall, an excellent educational resource for teachers, is historically contextualized online (SPARC, 2017). For teachers considering a mural project, perhaps in conjunction with the art department, or exploring the significance of local murals, it is particularly instructive. Similarly, Chicano Park in San Diego and its murals have been designated a national landmark (Warth, 2017). The movie *Chicano Park*, available on YouTube, depicts the struggles of the local community of Barrio Logan to resist the takeover of their neighborhoods and to establish a park with murals under the Coronado Bridge.

18. For those who have little knowledge of the Movement, I recommend the book *Chicano Movement for Beginners* (Montoya, 2016) for its entertaining and useful framework. It is an accessible and easily consumed text that will give you/ students the background to move on to other resources. The film series *Latino USA* and *Chicano!*, available online, provide background, visual impact, and an overview of this important era, and bring in the current status of our growing Latino communities. The Teaching Tolerance website (www.tolerance.org) offers a free standards-based resource kit for educators (among many other valuable resources), Viva La Causa: The Story of César Chávez and a Great Movement for Social Justice that is appropriate for grades 6–12.

References

Alvarez, R. (1986, Spring). The Lemon Grove incident. *Journal of San Diego History, 32*(2). Retrieved from http://www.sandiegohistory.org/journal/1986/april/lemongrove/

American Postal Workers Union. (2012). Pecan shellers' strike sparked Hispanic workers' movement. *American Postal Workers Union, AFL-CIO*. Retrieved from http://www.apwu.org/labor-history-articles/pecan-shellers%E2%80%99-strike-sparked-hispanic-workers%E2%80%99-movement

Anderson, B. (1983). *Imagined communities: Reflections on the origin and spread of nationalism*. London: Verso.

Anderson, M. D. (2016, March 7). The ongoing battle over ethnic studies. *The Atlantic*. Retrieved from https://www.theatlantic.com/education/archive/2016/03/the-ongoing-battle-over-ethnic-studies/472422/

Baca, J. (2017). *Booking Judy Baca*. Retrieved from http://www.judybaca.com/artist/contact/contact-template/

Barrios, G. (2009, Spring). Walkout in Crystal City. *Teaching Tolerance*. Retrieved from http://www.tolerance.org/magazine/number-35-spring-2009/feature/walkout-crystal-city

Bigler, E., Willox, L., & Shiller, J. (2013). The teaching of race and class in American social studies classrooms. In J. Passe & P. Fitchett (Eds.), *The status of social studies: Views from the field* (pp. 153–168). Charlotte, NC: Information Age Publishers.

Busto, R. V. (2005). *King tiger: The religious vision of Reies López Tijerina*. Albuquerque, NM: University of New Mexico Press.

Campbell, D. (2016, July 20). Writing Chicano/Latino history into California textbooks. *Democratic Socialists of America*. Retrieved from http://www.dsausa.org/writing_chicano_latino_history_into_california_textbooks

Candelaria, C. C. (2017). Chicano renaissance (entry ID: 1829702). *ABC-CLIO*. Retrieved from http://freecontent.abc-clio.com/ContentPages/contentpage.aspx?entryid=1829702&currentSection=1829268&productid=1829269

Chicano Coordinating Council on Higher Education. (1969). *El Plan de Santa Barbara*. Oakland, CA: La Causa Publications.

Citizens' Committee for the Defense of Mexican-American Youth (1942). Sleep Lagoon. *Digital History*. Retrieved from http://www.digitalhistory.uh.edu/disp_textbook) print.sfm?smtid=3&pside=605

Colker, D. (2015, January 22). Reies Lopez Tijerina dies at 88; Chicano rights movement leader. *Los Angeles Times*. Retrieved from http://www.latimes.com/local/obituaries/la-me-reies-lopez-tijerina-20150123-story.html

Costello, M. B. (2016, November 28). The Trump effect: The impact of the 2016 presidential election on our nation's schools. *Southern Poverty Law Center*. Retrieved from https://www.splcenter.org/20161128/trump-effect-impact-2016-presidential-election-our-nations-schools

Diaz, T. (2015, April 24). Diaz: Mexican-American studies are path to success. *Houston Chronicle*. Retrieved from http://www.houstonchronicle.com/opinion/outlook/article/DiazMexican-American-studies-are-path-to-success-6222889.php

Diaz, T. (2017, June 13). Arizona wants to ban your culture. *Huffington Post*. Retrieved from http://www.huffingtonpost.com/entry/arizona-wants-to-ban-your-culture_us_593e680ae4b094fa859f19ff

Echavarri, F., & Bishop, M. (2016, March 11). "No Mexicans allowed": School segregation in the southwest. *NPR: Latino USA*. Retrieved from http://latinousa.org/2016/03/11/no-mexicans-allowed-school-segregation-in-the-southwest/

Espinosa, P., & KPBS. (1985). *The lemon grove incident* (film). Retrieved from http://espinosaproductions.com/project/the-lemon-grove-incident/

Estrada, J. (2017). *Chicano movements: A geographic history*. Retrieved from http://depts.washington.edu/moves/Chicano_geography.shtml

Florido, A. (2015, September 8). Mass deportation may sound unlikely, but it's happened before. *NPR Morning Edition*. Retrieved from http://www.npr.org/sections/codeswitch/2015/09/08/437579834/mass-deportation-may-sound-unlikely-but-its-happened-before

García, A. M. (Ed.). (1997). *Chicana feminist thought: The basic historical writings*. New York, NY: Routledge.

García, M. T. (2010, August 30). Lessons from the Chicano anti-war movement. *National Catholic Reporter*. Retrieved from https://www.ncronline.org/blogs/ncr-today/lessons-chicano-anti-war-movement

Gonzales, R. (1967). *I Am Joaquín*. Denver, CO: Crusade for Justice.

Gordon, E. (2006, January 18). COINTELPRO and the history of domestic spying. *NPR Rhode Island Public Radio*. Retrieved from http://www.npr.org/templates/story/story.php?storyId=5161811

Grady, T. (2016). *The treaty of Guadalupe Hidalgo*. Retrieved from https://www.archives.gov/education/lessons/guadalupe-hidalgo

Hartley, G. (2017, September). *I Am Joaquín*: Rodolfo "Corky" Gonzales and the retroactive construction of Chicanismo. Electronic Poetry Center, SUNY-Buffalo. Retrieved from http://epc.buffalo.edu/authors/hartley/pubs/corky.html

House Bill 2281: An Act Amending Title 15, Chapter 1, Article 1, Arizona Revised Statutes, Title 15 CFR (2010).

Kaladis, J. (2013, September 23). Bring back social studies. *The Atlantic*. Retrieved from https://www.theatlantic.com/education/archive/2013/09/bring-back-social-studies/279891

Kamerick, M. (2016). This land is my land: The story of Reies López Tijerina. *National Public Radio* (podcast). Retrieved from http://latinousa.org/2016/03/11/this-land-is-my-land-the-story-of-reies-lopez-tijerina/

Kelkar, K. (2016, September 18). When labor laws left farm workers behind – and vulnerable to abuse. *PBS Newshour*. Retrieved from http://www.pbs.org/newshour/updates/labor-laws-left-farm-workers-behind-vulnerable-abuse/

Loewen, J. (2007). *Lies my teacher told me: Everything your American history textbook got wrong*. New York, NY: Touchstone.

Lynch, G. H. (2016, December 6). California will soon provide ethnic studies classes for all high schoolers. Here's why. *Global Nation PRI's the World*. Retrieved from https://www.pri.org/stories/2016-12-06/california-will-soon-provide-ethnic-studies-classes-all-high-schoolers-heres-why

McKay, R. R. (2010). Mexican Americans and repatriation. *Handbook of Texas*. Retrieved from https://tshaonline.org/handbook/online/articles/pgmyk

Meier, M., & Rivera, F. (1972). *The Chicanos: A history of Mexican Americans.* New York, NY: Hill and Wang.

Montoya, M. (2016). *Chicano movement for beginners.* Danbury, CT: For Beginners LLC.

Movimiento Estuidantil Chicanx de Azatlán. (2017). *UMAS: United Mexican American Students.* Retrieved from http://www.chicanxdeaztlan.org/p/history.html

National Archives (Producer). (2017, November 26). *Record of rights: The Zoot Suit Riots, 1943* [Exhibit]. Retrieved from http://recordsofrights.org/events/62/zoot-suit-riots

National Park Service. (2015). *Latinos in World War II: Fighting on Two Fronts.* Retrieved from https://www.nps.gov/articles/latinoww2.htm

Pagan, E. O. (2003). *Murder at the Sleepy Lagoon: Zoot suits, race, and riot in wartime L. A.* Chapel Hill, NC: University of North Carolina Press.

Palazzol, N. (2013, May 16). Chicano students strike for equality of education in Crystal City, Texas, 1969–1970. *Global Non-Violent Action Data Base.* Retrieved from http://nvdatabase.swarthmore.edu/content/chicano-students-strike-equality-education-crystal-city-texas-1969–1970

PBS. (2014). *Ruben Salazar: Man in the middle* (film). Retrieved from http://www.pbs.org/video/2365231799/

PBS/KERA. (2006). *U.S.-Mexican War: 1846–1848* (for educators, also available in Spanish). PBS. Retrieved from http://www.pbs.org/kera/usmexicanwar/educators/

PBS/WGBH (2014, May 14). *The Delano Manongs: Forgotten heroes of the United Farm Workers.* Retrieved from http://www.pbs.org/video/2365815392/

Pomona College Department of Theatre & Dance. (2017). *Zoot suit discovery guide.* Retrieved from http://research.pomona.edu/zootsuit/

Puig, C. (2017). Dolores' Sundance review: activist Dolores Huerta gets her props in stirring doc. *The Wrap.* Retrieved from http://www.thewrap.com/dolores-sundance-review-dolores-huerta-documentary-ufw/

Ravitch, D. (1990, Spring). Diversity and democracy: Multicultural education in America. *American Educator: The Professional Journal of the American Federation of Teachers, 14*(1), 16–20 and 46–48.

Salazar, R. (1995, published 1970). Who is a Chicano? And what is it the Chicanos want? In R. Salazar & M. Garcia (Eds.), *Ruben Salazar, Border correspondent: Selected writings, 1955–1970.* Berkeley, CA: University of California Press (out of print). Retrieved from http://publishing.cdlib.org/ucpressebooks/view?docId=ft058002v2&chunk.id=d0e7791&toc.depth=1&toc.id=d0e6486&brand=ucpress

SPARC. (2017). *The Great Wall of Los Angeles.* Social and Public Resource Center – SPARC. Retrieved from http://sparcinla.org/programs/the-great-wall-mural-los-angeles/

Stavans, I. (2016). Foreword by Ilan Stavans. In M. Montoya (Ed.), *Chicano movement for beginners.* Danbury, CT: For Beginners LLC.

United States Courts. (2017). *Mendez v. Westminster re-enactment.* Retrieved from http://www.uscourts.gov/educational-resources/educational-activities/mendez-v-westminster-re-enactment

University of Washington. (2017). *Chicano/Latino movements history and geography.* Retrieved from http://depts.washington.edu/moves/Chicano_intro.shtml

Warth, G. (2017, January 11). Chicano Park named national historic landmark. *San Diego Union-Tribune.* Retrieved from http://www.sandiegouniontribune.com/news/politics/sd-me-chicano-historic-20170111-story.html

Wilson, W. (1917). War Message. Sixty-Fifth Congress, 1 Session, Senate Document No. 5.

7. The Asian American Movement and Civil Rights

PHONSIA NIE AND NOREEN NASEEM RODRIGUEZ

The Civil Rights Movement helped inspire Americans of Asian ancestry across the country to join together to create a politicized and multiethnic Asian American movement and identity during the 1960s and 1970s. Americans of disparate Asian ancestries including Japanese Americans, Chinese Americans, and Filipino Americans recognized commonalities in their 20th century histories of migration and experiences of racial discrimination and prejudice in the United States. This historical overview addresses how Asian American identity was created by politically engaged Asian American leaders and organizations with suggestions for primary sources and instructional resources. It will also address how the history of the Asian American movement encouraged an interracial vision of political organizing against racial discrimination and protest for inclusion in educational curriculum and American identity.

The term "*Asian American*" was first coined by historian and activist Yuji Ichioka in 1968 when he and Emma Gee founded the Asian American Political Alliance (AAPA) at the University of California, Berkeley (Maeda, 2015). AAPA encouraged solidarity among Americans of Asian descent and "Third World" people, a common term used to describe politically left communities of color in the United States, to protest against racism, imperialism, and the Vietnam War (Maeda, 2015). Americans of Asian ancestry like Ichioka recognized the problem of racial discrimination facing Asians of all backgrounds in the United States (Maeda, 2015; Wei, 1993). They sought to organize groups of Asian Americans to protest against the mistreatment of Americans of Asian ancestry in labor and housing practices, immigration laws, and citizenship requirements. The Asian American movement as it grew into the 1970s did not coalesce into one organization or around one political goal, but was instead comprised of several diverse organizations across the country that supported a variety of causes including anti-war in Vietnam, free speech, feminism, Black Power, anti-imperialism, student rights, and many others. Despite this diversity and breadth, the Asian American movement began to create and support a collective solidarity among Americans of Asian descent to increase political impact and action. Many primary sources from the AAPA and other early organizations in the Asian American movement can be found in the anthologies *Asian Americans: The Movement and the Moment* (Louie & Omatsu, 2001) and *Roots: An Asian American Studies Reader* (Tachiki, 1971) and through the University of California at Berkeley's Asian American Studies collection at the Ethnic Studies Library.

A Shared Asian American History

The origins of the pan ethnic term "Asian American" and the Asian American movement relied on Asian Americans identifying commonality in their experiences and history in the United States. As historian Daryl Maeda (2009) explains in his study of the Asian American movement,

> although they confronted the United States in separate ways and at different times, Asian immigrants were exploited and excluded in remarkably similar fashion and were legally and socially discriminated against in ways that differ significantly from the treatment of white European immigrants. (p. 23)

The Asian American movement of the late 1960s and 1970s articulated for the first time a shared history of Americans of Asian ancestry. Disparate groups such as Filipino Americans and Japanese Americans with different cultural practices and traditions began to identify as Asian Americans with similar experiences and legacies of racial discrimination in the United States. Several facets of American history demonstrated an Asian American shared history of exclusion, exploitation, and discrimination.

Immigration and Naturalization

Beginning in 1882 with the *Chinese Exclusion Act* that prohibited immigration of Chinese laborers to the United States, Asian Americans became the first group to be excluded from the United States based on their race and class; notably, this act only excluded laborers while allowing immigration by Chinese diplomats, teachers, students, and merchants. United States immigration laws then extended immigration and citizenship restrictions against most Asian immigrants throughout the early twentieth-century (Lee, 2003). The *1917 Immigration Act*, also known as the Asiatic Barred Zone Act, prohibited immigration from any persons in the Asia-Pacific zone including South Asians, Japanese, and Koreans (Lee, 2003).

Naturalization laws, or the federal policies that define who qualifies for United States citizenship, restricted Asian immigrants from claiming citizenship and enjoying its associated rights and privileges. Many Asian Americans turned to the courts to challenge legal restrictions regarding citizenship. After being denied re-entry into the United States and told he was not a citizen after visiting family abroad in China, San Francisco-born Wong Kim Ark fought for his birthright citizenship in the Supreme Court case *U.S. v. Wong Kim Ark* (1898). He successfully argued that the United States could not deny his birthright citizenship because of his ethnicity, as the citizenship clause of the 14th Amendment granted citizenship to any person born on United States soil.

For Asian immigrants, two Supreme Court cases, *Ozawa v. U.S.* (1922) and *U.S v. Thind* (1923), clarified Asian legal racial status as "nonwhite," and, thus, ineligible for United States citizenship according to naturalization law at the time. Takao Ozawa lived in the United States for 20 years, though he had been born in Japan and immigrated to California as a teenager. He spoke fluent English, practiced Christianity, attended University of California, Berkeley, married an American-educated Japanese American woman, and worked for an American company. He believed both his light skin and cultural assimilation qualified him for United States citizenship. The Supreme Court ruled Ozawa "ineligible for citizenship" based on his race in *Ozawa v. U.S.* (1922). The courts made the same argument against Bhagat Singh Thind, who was born in India, immigrated to the United States as a student to attend the University of California, Berkeley, and served in the United States Army as an Acting Sergeant during World War I. Despite Thind's military service and ethnic background as a high caste Indian anthropologically classified as "Caucasian," the Supreme Court ruled in *U.S v. Thind* (1923) that Indian immigrants were racially ineligible for United States citizenship (Kuo, 1998).

Though legislation after World War II effectively repealed most immigration and citizenship policies against Asian immigrants, Asian Americans during the 1960s recognized the shared history of racial prejudice against Asians and Americans of Asian ancestry that informed United States immigration and naturalization policies.

Unfair Labor Practices

The Asian American movement and its organizations and leaders also shed light on the shared history of labor exploitation and discrimination against

Americans of Asian descent. Racial prejudice against Americans of Asian descent often translated into labor practices that treated Asian Americans as outsiders and disposable in the workforce. The history of Japanese, Korean, and Chinese sugarcane workers in Hawaii, Chinese railroad workers and laundries in California, Punjabi farmers in California's Central and Imperial Valleys, and Filipino farmers in California demonstrated unfair treatment toward Asian American workers in United States history.

The most prominent example of Asian American dissent against unfair labor practices was the *Delano Grape Strike* in 1965 that brought together over 2,000 Filipino and Mexican American farm workers together in protest against unfair wages (Scharlin & Villanueva, 2000). The Agricultural Workers Organizing Committee (AWOC), comprised of mostly Filipino American farm workers and led by Philip Vera Cruz and Larry Itliong, collectively walked off grape-growing farms, refusing to work until paid the federal minimum wage for their labor (Scharlin & Villanueva, 2000). The predominantly Mexican American National Farmworkers Association led by Cesar Chavez joined the strike, and the joint effort resulted in the formation of the United Farm Workers of America (UFW) in 1966 (Scharlin & Villanueva, 2000). The Delano Grape Strike revealed the potential in political action through interracial alliance among and between communities of color, and many primary sources featuring AWOC and the UFW are available through the digital archives at Wayne State University's Walter Reuther Library. The documentaries *Viva La Causa* (2008) and *Delano Manongs* (2014) highlight the interracial alliances between Filipino and Mexican farmworkers in the UFW.

Japanese American Incarceration

The history of Japanese American incarceration during World War II motivated many Japanese Americans to become perhaps the most vocal Asian American activists during the late 1960s and beyond. During World War II when the United States was at war with Japan, President Franklin D. Roosevelt signed *Executive Order 9066* (Roosevelt, 1942), a presidential executive order that authorized the relocation of Americans of Japanese ancestry to American concentration camps. Targeting all Japanese Americans, both citizens (who made up 62% of the incarcerated population) and non-citizens, the United States defended the relocation and incarceration of thousands of Japanese Americans as a wartime necessity (Hayashi, 2004). Beginning in 1942, thousands of Japanese Americans across the country were forced to leave their homes with few personal belongings and moved to military-guarded concentration camps located far from populated areas in the interior of the United States. Beyond the property and material loss in their forced relocation, Japanese American families experienced extreme emotional hardship being racially targeted as a national enemy (Gordon & Okihiro, 2006; Houston, 1973).

While Japanese American removal and incarceration have been well documented by many organizations and individuals, from the Densho Project and Korematsu Institute to photography collections by Ansel Adams and Dorothea Lange, the emotional and economic repercussions of incarceration on Japanese American communities receive far less attention. Although this falls beyond the scope of the modern Civil Rights Movement, it is important to note that the Japanese American activism which began in the 1960s culminated in the Redress Movement of the late 1970s and 1980s. The Redress Movement successfully lobbied for the creation of a federal commission to investigate the causes and consequences of Japanese American internment, resulting in the Commission on the Wartime Internment and Relocation of Civilians (CWRIC) and its subsequent recommendation for national apologies issued by Congress and the President as well as financial compensation to surviving detainees (Daniels, 1971, 2004; US CWRIC, 1997). For Asian American movement and civil rights activists, Japanese American incarceration during World War II served as evidence of federal policies supporting blatant racial discrimination, mistreatment, and the denial of citizenship rights to Asian Americans.

Notable Figures in the Asian American Movement

Despite being a loosely connected network of various Asian American organizations and causes, the Asian American movement and its associated pan-ethnic identity and activism produced key figures in Asian American history who advocated for collective solidarity and Asian American equality and rights. These included Fred Korematsu, who challenged the constitutionality of Executive Order 9066; Chris Ijima, folk music singer, law professor, and activist; Grace Lee Boggs, civil rights and labor activist; Richard Aoki, an early member of the Black Panther Party; and Frank Chin, critically acclaimed playwright who challenged Asian American stereotypes.

A notable leader in Asian American activism was Yuri Kochiyama (see accompanying lesson plan in Section III). Best known for advocating government reparations to Japanese American internees in the 1980s, Kochiyama was an activist for a variety of civil rights causes throughout her lifetime and served as a mentor for Asian American movement organizations. As a teenager, Kochiyama had been a model student and citizen in support of the United States government even as she and her family were relocated and incarcerated at a Japanese American camp in Jerome, Arkansas during World War II. She met her husband, Bill, at a USO-sponsored Japanese American social during World War II in Arkansas while he was stationed there briefly as part of the highly decorated Japanese American 442nd Regimental Combat Team. Years after the war, they began a lifetime of political activism when they moved to Harlem, New York in 1960 and joined the Congress of Racial Equality (CORE), one of the major African American organizations during the Civil Rights Movement (Fujino, 2005).

Joining working-class activists and pan-Africanist organizations during the early 1960s, Kochiyama began to see the parallels of her own family history—being incarcerated during World War II in Jerome, Arkansas—and that of other minorities experiencing racial discrimination and exploitation. Kochiyama became politically linked to Malcolm X in the early 1960s and joined revolutionary organizations on the more radical end of the political spectrum. Kochiyama drew much of her experience and intellectual thought from pan-Africanist and black nationalist organizations and encouraged other Asian American organizations and leaders to support and participate in interracial coalitions (Fujino, 2005). Kochiyama's personal journey to Asian American activism, involvement with African American organizations, and support for interracial coalitions throughout her lifetime demonstrate the trajectory of the Asian American movement and evolution of Asian American identity.

Asian American and Interracial Coalitions

The Asian American movement in the late 1960s and 1970s was comprised of diverse groups of Asian American and Asian ethnic-specific organizations across the United States. On the East Coast, Asian Americans for Action (AAA) organized in 1969, and on the West Coast along with Ichioka's Asian American Political Alliance (AAPA), many Asian American student organizations formed to protest and advocate for Asian American issues on campus.

Asian American movement organizations and activists received the most visibility in their organizing with the *Third World Liberation Front (TWLF)* in 1968 at San Francisco State University (SFSU). An interracial coalition including AAPA, the Black Students Union, the Latin American Students Organization, the Pilipino Collegiate Endeavor (PACE), the Filipino-American Students Organization, and El Renacimiento, a Mexican American student organization (Maeda, 2009; Pulido, 2006). TWLF called for collective solidarity among Asian Americans, Mexican Americans, African Americans, and other marginalized groups in the United States. Identifying themselves through a shared history of oppression and disenfranchisement, TWLF demanded that

SFSU alter its hiring practices, campus culture, and educational curriculum to value non-white students and faculty and establish Ethnic Studies courses on campus (Maeda, 2009; Pulido, 2006). The five-month TWLF protest and strike effectively shut down campus for a week due to the increased numbers of protestors and student-police confrontations. The SFSU strike inspired a TWLF to form at the University of California, Berkeley in 1969 and successfully demand the establishment of minority-led Ethnic Studies programs and courses (Maeda, 2009; Pulido, 2006). The documentaries *Activist State* (2009), *San Francisco State: On Strike* (2014) and *The Turning Point* (2014), all available on YouTube, feature primary footage from the strikes as well as interviews with student activists.

TWLF strikes were highly publicized and provided Asian American activists a platform from which to demonstrate pride in Asian American identity and reject the stereotype of being politically passive or complicit with inequality and racial discrimination. TWLF galvanized a new and growing Asian American community to self-identify among other communities of color and work toward a common goal of social justice and equality. While Asian American movement organizations and leaders often focused on issues of immigration, labor practices, and racial discrimination as it affected Americans of Asian ancestry, interracial coalitions helped inspire Asian Americans to continue to demand change and equality beyond the 1970s.

Asian Americans and Educational Access

At the heart of TWLF protests was the belief that the history of racism against minorities in the United States was important to teach in public education. TWLF activism and its legacy of interracial coalition ensured that Ethnic Studies as a disciplinary field was institutionalized at universities and colleges across the nation. Though the Asian American movement supported this educational curriculum component of interracial coalitions, the history of Asian Americans and educational access differs markedly from that of Latinx Americans and African Americans (see accompanying lesson plan in Section III).

The first major case that established a place for Asian Americans in public education was *Tape v. Hurley* (1885). Eight-year old Mamie Tape was denied entry to a San Francisco elementary school based on her Chinese ancestry. Though the Supreme Court ruled in her favor and established it unconstitutional to deny an American-born child public education, the San Francisco school board eventually followed the same "separate but equal" practices of *Plessy v. Ferguson* (1896) and established the Oriental Public School both to avoid integration and to accommodate Chinese Americans, and shortly thereafter, most Asian American students. For Asian Americans in other parts of the country, educational access and integration depended largely on local practices and populations. The *Gong Lum v. Rice* (1927) decision exposed the position of Asian Americans under Jim Crow practices as firmly on the "colored" side of the color line in the South. Chinese American Martha Lum was denied entry to her hometown Rosedale white public school after her lawyers unsuccessfully argued for Chinese access to Mississippi white public schools based on Chinese Americans not being "negro" nor of mixed blood. *Gong Lum v. Rice* not only established Chinese as legally "colored," but also reaffirmed *Plessy v. Ferguson*, as Chinese American children were permitted to attend either African American schools or establish their own separate Chinese school (Kuo, 1998).

Asian Americans were subject to the same "separate but equal" policies that limited access to quality and well-funded public education for other communities of color during the early twentieth-century, but the *1965 Immigration and Nationality Act* dramatically shifted Asian American demographics. Post-1965 immigration policies gave preference to students, scientists, and highly-educated and skilled professionals from Asia to immigrate to the United States. This wave of Asian immigration helped perpetuate the *model minority* stereotype or myth which assumes the inherent educational achievement and advancement of Asians and Asian Americans (Wu, 2013). The model minority stereotype is the societal assumption that Asians and Asian Americans are culturally or genetically endowed with educational and economic success. In the classroom, the stereotype operates to obscure Asian American student learning challenges, mistreatment, and financial need. The model minority stereotype also creates one-dimensional generalizations about Asian American students, pressure for achievement or achievement-oriented competition, and implicit comparisons with other minority groups detrimental to interracial relations and coalition building (Lee, 2015).

With few racial barriers post-Civil Rights Movement to attend public schools and the assumption of educational success based on the model minority stereotype, Asian Americans gained unfettered access to educational institutions into the 1980s and 1990s. The new demographics of Asian Americans ushered in by the shift in immigration policy and the model minority stereotype obscure the decades of discrimination against Asian Americans in educational access, undermine interracial coalitions advocating for educational equality, and fails to acknowledge the continued struggle and achievement gap present within the Asian American community, most notably among the Southeast Asian refugee communities.

While the Asian American movement inspired and created an Asian American identity that is very much present and active today, the history of educational access that demonstrates a shared history of prejudice and discrimination is easily overlooked. Teaching the history of the Asian American movement, the struggles they shared, and their vision of interracial coalition uncovers the diversity and future of civil rights in the United States.

References

Daniels, R. (1971). *Concentration camps USA*. New York, NY: Holt, Rinehart and Winston.

Daniels, R. (2004). *Prisoners without trial: Japanese Americans in World War II*. New York, NY: Macmillan.

Fujino, D. C. (2005). *Heartbeat of struggle: The revolutionary life of Yuri Kochiyama*. Minneapolis, MN: University of Minnesota Press.

Gordon, L., & Okihiro, G. (2006). *Impounded: Dorothea Lange and the censored images of Japanese American Internment*. New York, NY: W. W. Norton.

Hayashi, B. M. (2004). *Democratizing the enemy: The Japanese American Internment*. Princeton, NJ: Princeton University Press.

Houston, J. W. (1973). *Farewell to Manzanar: A true story of Japanese American experience during and after the World War II Internment*. Boston, MA: Houghton Mifflin.

Kuo, J. (1998). Excluded, segregated and forgotten: A historical view of the discrimination of Chinese Americans in public schools. *Asian American Law Journal, 5*, 181–212.

Lee, E. (2003). *At America's gates: Chinese immigration during the exclusion era, 1882–1943*. Chapel Hill, NC: University of North Carolina Press.

Lee, S. J. (2015). *Unraveling the "model minority" stereotype: Listening to Asian American youth* (2nd ed.). New York, NY: Teachers College Press.

Louie, S., & Omatsu, G. (Eds.). (2001). *Asian Americans: The movement and the moment*. California, LA: University of California, Asian American Studies Center.

Maeda, D. J. (2009). *Chains of Babylon: The rise of Asian America*. Minneapolis, MN: University of Minnesota Press.

Maeda, D. J. (2015). Movement. In C. J. Schlund-Vials, L. T. Vo & K. S. Wong (Eds.), *Keywords for Asian American studies* (pp. 165–168). New York, NY: New York University Press.

Pulido, L. (2006). *Black, brown, yellow, & left: Radical activism in Los Angeles*. Berkeley, CA: University of California Press.

Roosevelt, F. D. (1942). *Executive order 9066*. Washington, DC.

Scharlin, C., & Villanueva, L. V. (2000). *Philip Vera Cruz: A personal history of Filipino immigrants and the farmworkers movement*. Seattle, WA: University of Washington Press.

Tachiki, A. (1971). *Roots: An Asian American reader*. Los Angeles, CA: University of California.

United States Commission on Wartime Relocation and Internment of Civilians. (1997). *Personal justice denied: Report of the Committee on Wartime Relocation and Internment of Civilians.* Seattle, WA: University of Washington Press and the Civil Liberties Public Education Fund.

Wei, W. (1993). *The Asian American movement.* Philadelphia, PA: Temple University Press.

Wu, E. D. (2013). *The color of success: Asian Americans and the origins of the model minority.* Princeton, NJ: Princeton University Press.

Section 2

Pedagogical Issues

8. Teaching the Long Civil Rights Movement

AARON C. BRUEWER AND JAYNE R. BEILKE

The historical narrative of the civil rights movement suffers the same fate as that of the Underground Railroad, whose major figures such as Harriet Tubman, Frederick Douglass, Levi and Catherine Coffin and others are often rendered one-dimensional. In both cases, memory and storytelling infuse a historical narrative that is often clouded by myth. Most egregious is the recent invention of the quilt code, which posits that quilts included symbols that gave directions to fugitives or signaled safe passages on their way north. As a trope, the quilt code appeals to those who know little of African American history and who reduce a complex, brutal story to a romantic rite of passage.

Social studies educators debate over how best to teach the civil rights movement—as a self-contained period beginning with Rosa Parks' refusal in 1956 to move to the back of the city bus and ending with the 1968 assassination of Dr. Martin Luther King, Jr., or as a movement equally rooted in the de facto segregation in the North that impeded Black progress in business, schools, real estate, and government. In her article entitled "The Long Civil Rights Movement and the Political Uses of the Past," historian Jacquelyn Dowd Hall argues that "the dominant narrative of the civil rights movement … distorts and suppresses as much as it reveals" (2005, p. 1233). The traditional social studies curriculum is often bounded and defined by events and personalities that present a one-dimensional, heroic view of historical occurrences and figures. A more contextual approach might include a broader study of context: for example, exploring the antecedents of the movement during the 1930s and the New Deal policies of President Franklin D. Roosevelt. The movement ranges well into the 1970s; and, one could argue, into the present. By using the "long civil rights movement" as the framework for interpreting the civil rights movement, students will better be able to evaluate its legacy and current movements protest movements.

The heroic version of Parks simply being "tired" as the explanation for her refusal to give up her seat minimizes her commitment to and involvement in the National Association for the Advancement of Colored People (NAACP). It also ignores the action, nine months earlier, of Claudette Colvin who also refused to give up her seat on a city bus. But Parks was perceived to be a mature, well-mannered individual who displayed middle-class values while Colvin was described as being confrontational. Colvin was a teenager who was a member of the NAACP Youth Council. It was rumored that she was pregnant and the NAACP leaders did not wish to have her seen as the face of the movement. The NAACP also employed this strategy when they challenged graduate school segregation before turning to secondary education in *Brown v. Board of Education*. In this case, Parks' personality was simplified—even sanctified—and therefore reduced of its complexity while Colvin's important precedent was ignored (Hoose, 2009). In the case of King, his lofty rhetoric is remembered for its hopeful, idealistic message of the iconic 1965 "I have a Dream" speech rather that his description of racism as an "American Dilemma," as noted by economist Gunnar Myrdal, rather than a regional one (Myrdal, 1944). In 1944, Myrdal's encyclopedic sociological work postulated that American liberal values were at odds with the oppression of African Americans. But King's message of economic equality and civil rights that is present in the speech is often lost. As greater attention is being paid to exploring the civil rights history of local communities, educators are gaining more access to tools that help us broaden, deepen, and lengthen the legacy of the past.

When thinking of the Civil Rights movement as existing prior to 1954 and past 1968, teachers begin to broaden and deepen students' understandings of the past. To do this in the classroom, teachers can utilize two frameworks: (1) the research of James Banks (2013) on curricular content integration, specifically his view of Transformative Curriculum, and (2) Herring, Koehler, and Mishra's (2016) Technological, Pedagogical, and Content Knowledge framework (TPACK) which builds on Shulman's (1986) notion of Pedagogical Content Knowledge by including a technological dimension. Using these frameworks allows us as teachers to step back from tradition and rethink our approach conceptually.

Reconceptualizing Social Studies Curricula

Research continues to encourage us toward engaging students in hands-on and minds-on activities in the social studies classroom, providing learners with opportunities to critically think about issues and content through the use of multicultural material and technology (Agarwal, 2011; Bigler, Shiller, & Willox, 2015; Patterson, Misco & Doppen, 2012; Loewen, 2007; Theiman, O'Brien, Preston-Grimes, & Barker, 2015). Considering a view of the civil rights movement that goes beyond a 1954–1968 timeframe, Banks' (2013) curriculum content integration framework and Herring, Mishra and Koehler's (2016) TPCK provides us with a way for social studies teachers to reflect on their practice and begin to rethink social studies curriculum in the classroom.

Concepts: Banks' Transformative Curriculum

Banks' (2013) Transformation approach to the curriculum provides a way for students to better grasp the breadth and depth of the civil rights movement, as well as understand its ongoing influence in the 21st century. This approach makes history relevant and part of a cohesive curriculum, instead of a sliver of a larger, non-inclusive narrative. As Banks explains, reforming a curriculum around a central concept such as civil rights allows learners to "view concepts, issues, events, and themes from the perspectives of diverse ethnic and cultural groups," (Banks, 2013, p. 246) in contrast to a particular voice or singular narrative. It re-configures a curriculum around major concepts or themes, breaks from a mainstream perspective, and challenges existing narratives of knowledge that perpetuate a Western and white perspective, often found in textbooks and other curricular materials prepared for teachers (Loewen, 2007). Using Banks, a teacher can engage the long civil rights movement by centering his or her entire curriculum in American History on civil rights. With this central concept as a curricular guide, all units and lessons connect backward and forward to this concept and to the NCSS Themes of Time, Continuity and Change; People, Places and Environments; Individuals, Groups and Institutions; Power, Authority and Governance; and Civic Ideals and Practices.

A curricular reconstruction using this model may take an American History II course (1900 to the Present), and place civil rights as one of its core concepts. Beginning with an analysis of the Reconstruction Amendments, students learn a narrative of the United States focused on the development of civil rights. Through the use of primary documents, Supreme Court cases, and amendment analysis, students can develop an expanded view of the movement beyond a moment frozen in time, one that stretches further back, and continues forward to the present. The course ceases to be a chronological march through time that holds events static in their moments, instead it becomes a conceptually centered educational experience for a cohesive look at the civil rights movement throughout history. This works within The Long Civil Rights Movement Thesis, where we as teachers are asked to begin to develop our units and courses to engage civil rights as a central theme and focus of conceptual learning, giving greater context and meaning to civil rights in American history.

Each of these themes utilizes the concept of civil rights to produce a counter narrative in the classroom that challenges textbooks and allows students to critically think about how rights have been expanded, and how they are currently under attack in today's American society. More specifically the struggle for civil rights did not suddenly begin in the mid 1950s, and it did not end in 1968. The history of the United States, instead of being a constant march of progress becomes a national march towards the expansion of civil rights. As rights are expanded and the definition of citizenship changes, students learn of new groups often excluded from deeper exposition in the text including Chicanos, Chinese American, and LGBTQ, all seeking the representation and rights guaranteed by the American Constitution.

Exploring the history of the United States as an investigation into the expansion of civil rights helps students engage with history as it matters today—relating current events and the American experience to its own history. Students can see the agency of individuals in context, consider their actions in context and transfer this critical thinking to today.[1] Banks conceptual approach to the curriculum provides power to teachers to unpackage standards and explore the concepts that reside within. As concepts transcend time and place, they allow for connections to be made throughout history between past and present, helping students to relate history as not just yesterday, but today and tomorrow.[2]

Digital Technology and Expanding Pedagogy through TPACK

To further the classroom reconceptualization and transformation of the curriculum, teachers can integrate technology using the Technological Pedagogical Content Knowledge (TPACK) Framework[3] (Mishra & Kohler, 2016). TPCK builds on what teachers already know—their content and their pedagogy, and asks us to consider the role of technology in content development and pedagogy. It encourages the emergence of technology integration as a natural occurrence. Starting with what teachers know, teachers can explore new opportunities afforded by technology in the classroom as they build their own technological knowledge. The idea that technology should emerge naturally from the pedagogy which itself emerges from the content is consistent with Dewey's (2009) notions on the relationship between content and pedagogy. There is no true separation of content and pedagogy—they are one and the same—one can argue as well that technology is now also part of that entity of learning. Through these frameworks, we can consider the Long Civil Rights Movement Thesis, and the content it presents which allows for an emergent inquiry focused pedagogical approach that is enhanced organically through the use of digital web based tools.

Digital Tools and Curricular Transformation

Timelines and stories are an essential element of the social studies classroom, and the affordances of digital timelines and digital stories are many. Particular to Banks Curriculum Transformation is the ability to investigate the Civil Rights movement more deeply and broadly through a curated, chronological narrative argument. To help students construct these products, there are many free programs for use on the web. Which one a teacher uses often comes down to personal preference and ease of use. The majority of modern programs focus on student learning rather than coding, resulting in a drag and drop ability that helps students focus on the content and not the tool itself. For timelines, specific programs like Timeglider and Time Toast include ways for students to engage the study of history through investigation and standard timeline depiction, however other programs like Sutori and Prezi, while not specifically timeline programs, have the capability to depict deep understandings through the use of multimedia presentations in timeline formats. For digital stories aside from iMovie, YouTube and other platform specific (i.e. designed for Mac or PC) and web programs, a digital program worth checking out is Adobe Spark.[4]

Meaningful Multimedia Timelines

Consider the timeline, long a staple of social studies classrooms. When combined with digital technology it is no longer a two-dimensional paper and pencil product. Timelines take on a new element as multimedia representations of how students understand the content and when coupled with project based inquiry are powerful ways for students to develop deeper and broader understandings of content.

Creating Digital Timelines with Time Glider and Sutori. Two recommended programs[5] are Time Glider and Sutori. Time Glider is a more traditionally oriented timeline that allows students to include dates, and give those dates weight to show a visual significance. The timeline also allows the inclusion of multimedia components (video, graphics and audio) within each selected event, giving greater depth to the students expressed understanding.

Sutori is a top to bottom scrolling timeline, which has expanded to include interactive modules that provide the ability to include quizzes and forum questions in the timeline that can generate critical thinking and expressions of understanding. Video and imagery can also be embedded within the timeline itself, as students locate or create them in their investigation of civil rights. Students' creation of a digital product that tells a particular point of view through time helps them develop perspective on history, which can lead to empathy and self-knowledge.

Time Glider provides students the opportunity to create a standard timeline, with modifications that expand the depth and scope of the content they present. Students have the ability to include images and hyperlinks to further information that provide greater context for their curated chronological argument.

In addition to a basic typed description, Time Glider allows students to include links, audio and video in addition to images, and other customizable options. Students develop a timeline that expresses what they learned. Time Glider also allows students to set the "importance" of an event on the timeline, which adjusts the size of the event on the line itself. It provides the ability to zoom in and out, seeing the big picture and specific years at the same time.

With digital technology like TimeGlider or Sutori, multiple decades can now be displayed along with multiple events, and conceptual themes transcending a single era. This allows students to build connections from year to year, decade to decade, and foreword to the present in a collaborative fashion. Beyond mere points on a line, these creations can include video, audio and text in ways that helps students construct an expression of deeper knowledge beyond a date and title. These modern timelines allow students to work within the actual "line" and present broader context, purpose and direction.

New Narratives through Digital Story Telling

Digital archives bring the three-dimensional lives of historical figures to the forefront for students, placing their images, words and lives at their fingertips. These sources can help to humanize and ground figures in a student's reality and allow students to see the humanity of historical figures. Examples of this access are the interviews between Harry Bellefonte and Martin Luther King Junior and Robert F. Kennedy, among others, during the week when Bellefonte hosted the Tonight Show. Traditional figures of the civil rights movement, King and Kennedy are humanized by their appearance on a talk show. Compared to the simplified descriptions of these men found in textbooks and in public records, students are encouraged to question how they understand these men presented not as words on a page, but as the living, breathing humans they were (Walsh, 2017).

Digital tools and access allow for the rediscovery of these moments that humanize heroes and show the multifaceted viewpoints they embodied beyond the classic decade unit and can perhaps encourage the types of stories that allow teachers and historians alike to break free from the traditional Civil Rights Movement narrative. Viewing these historical moments can spark student's interest, and help generate questions about their views, and actions jumpstarting to initiate the inquiry process. Other primary sources can be located and analyzed by students and teachers who are seeking to investigate events and people beyond the textbook narrative. From here students begin to construct new narratives they can convert into a story that expresses students' newfound perspective, empathy and understandings.

Digital Storytelling with Adobe Spark

A program that has great promise for allowing students to blend these archival files with new material in order to create a unique and personalized understanding is Adobe Spark. Adobe Spark allows the use of text and images to tell a story or generate animated videos either from scratch or using one of their templates. Using this program opens possibilities for students to make what can be described as an in-motion infographic, combining images and text to tell a story or generate animated videos with the use of templates or from scratch. As one scrolls down an Adobe Spark Page, the text, images and video change to tell a full story, as designed by students. Adobe Spark is a versatile tool that can be geared for the social studies classroom. The singular page flow allows students to mix images and words to tell a story, each blending together as you scroll the page allowing the inclusion of hyperlinks, video and slideshows of multiple images to be displayed, all curated by the students. Three video templates, "Tell What Happened" "The Heroes Journey" and "Explain an Idea" help students craft their stories and arguments with the use of the evidence they uncover in their transformed classroom. The program can accept video made by students, or edited from other works, images, sound, and text to generate a story that is owned by the student.

Implications for Classroom Practice

Technology allows civil rights heroes frozen in time to be made vibrant and moving again, as teachers engage students in the conversation and provide an environment for student inquiry and knowledge generation that can be developed through the use of digital technology rooted within constructivist pedagogy and deep teacher knowledge of content.[6] The integration of digital timelines and digital stories into a transformative American History II course are many—a teacher may have the students construct a class timeline in Prezi as they investigate civil rights through time. An example would be a timeline of constitutional amendments and laws, that can go beyond dates and brief descriptions, instead incorporating images of those who worked to bring about the changes, and the influence of the laws on their life in the United States.

As students construct their timelines, new faces and events may come to light that are of significance to the student and the course, offering opportunities for the telling of new stories to compare and contrast with what is already known. It is a chance for teacher and student to investigate history together, and discover the rich stories that lay just below the surface of words on textbook page or other print material. Following the creation of a timeline where students present a chronological argument, they may develop new questions about the figures presented, and identify questions that require deeper and more robust attention.[7] Students may utilize Adobe Spark to tell the story of this unsung member of history. The story of Rosa Parks is one example that can be more fully explored, as she is often a narrative used to support a "right way" to protest—i.e. sitting quietly on a bus (Carlson, 2003). A student with the ability to tell a digital story about her that expands their understandings of her as a member of the Civil Rights movement by providing broader context helps students to rethink what they know. Other figures and events can be explored such as Bayard Rustin who fought for not only African American rights, but also gay rights in the 1980s, Harriet Tubman's often forgotten service in the American Civil War, and the questions that abound when learning about Columbus, Thanksgiving and the Black Panthers. Students begin to form more comprehensive identities of historical figures as they create their stories. Using digital narratives, teachers can address the silent voices of historical figures that are often left out of the American textbook narrative which tends to simplify and streamline history, fulfilling Banks (2013) request to open the content and reconfigure the curriculum to be inclusive and not narrow.

Conclusion

This chapter has identified ways in which teachers can expand, enhance, and enrich the teaching of civil rights as both a concept and a movement in their classrooms. It is suggested that combining the long Civil Rights Movement

Thesis with digital technology provides opportunities for expanded context and expression for student learning. Students can make relevant and real connections with the past due to the greater context for authentic learning. As a result, narrow textbook narratives are enlarged and a more complicated historical story emerges, one with more questions and avenues for student exploration. Students who are immersed in this experience can develop comprehensive perspectives on citizenship, beyond personal to participatory. Examples of these technologies integrated with content were explored, and resources shared. The starting point is Halls' Long Civil Rights Movement Thesis, which presents a modern approach to the African American Civil Rights movement. This view brings to the classroom a more relevant and meaningful learning environment, generated from the central concept of civil rights, inspiring opportunities for greater understanding of citizenship in the current political climate. Through the utilization of digital technology, students and teachers can produce robust timeline investigations and digital story narratives that help break us free from the confines of traditional textbook narrative and thought.

Notes

1. To support the idea of reconfiguring the American history classroom, and to counter the fact that history is often mistaught (Loewen, 2009) by following the grand narrative that provides for all pieces to fit into a neat package ever moving forward, teachers can consider relevant and positive examples of successful challenges and ideas for making this idea a reality. Hawkman and Castro (2017), Au (2014), and Schultz (2010) are all excellent places to start to see what happens when you take a risk with curriculum and do something different.
2. The NCSS Theme Time, Continuity and Change is a strong constant in these investigations as are Individuals, Groups and Institutions, Power, Authority and Governance and Civic Ideals and Practices.
3. For more information TPACK and how this framework can help, see http://tpack.org/
4. Adobe Spark can be found at https://spark.adobe.com/
5. Many programs exist, including Timetoast, and Tiki-Toki, but have become pay sites instead of free. Most have free versions that allow students to make at least one free timeline, before requiring a paid subscription. Find the best free program that works for you.
6. Examples of what can be done is found with the Shoah Foundation's IWitness, where a student can utilize archives of Holocaust survivor recordings to construct their own documentaries that encircle themes selected by students. Youtube, among other video generators, gives students a chance to create, recreate and mash up their own narratives, furthering the expansion of the concept of civil rights, and questioning the existent narrative with their own voice; this is the promise of digital web 2.0 technology.

7. Teachers may draw on the inspiration of the musical Hamilton, or movies like Hidden Figures or Loving to provide examples of the importance of context and "unsung" heroes of history.

References

Agarwal, R. (2011). Negotiating visions of teaching: Teaching social studies for social justice. *Social Studies Research and Practice, 6*(3), 52–64.

Au, W., (2014) Rethinking Multicultural Education: Teaching for Racial and Social Justice, 2nd Edition. WI: Rethinking Schools.

Banks, J. (2013). *Introduction to multicultural education.* Boston, MA: Pearson.

Bigler, E., Shiller, J. T., & Willox, L. (2015). Chapter 10: The teaching of race and class in American social studies classrooms. In J. Passe & P. G. Fitchett (Eds.), *The status of the social studies: Views from the field* (pp. 53–180). Charlotte, NC: Information Age.

Carlson, D. (2003). Troubling heroes: Of Rosa Parks, multicultural education, and critical pedagogy. *Cultural Studies ↔ Critical Methodologies, 3*(1), 41–63.

Dewey, J. (2009). *Democracy and education: An introduction to the philosophy of education.* New York, NY: The New Press.

Hall, J. D. (2005). The long civil rights movement and the political uses of the past. *The Journal of American History, 91*(5), 1233–1263.

Hawkman, A. M., & Castro, A. J. (2017). The long civil rights movement: Expanding black history in the social studies classroom. *Social Education, 81*(1), 28–32.

Herring, M. C., Koehler, M. J., & Mishra, P. (2016). *Handbook of technological pedagogical content knowledge for educators.* New York, NY: Routledge.

Hoose, P. (2009). *Claudetter Colvin: Twice toward justice.* New York, NY: Farrar, Straus and Giroux.

Loewen, J. (2007). *Lies my teacher told me: Everything your American history textbook got wrong.* New York, NY: Touchstone.

Loewen, J. (2009). *Teaching what really happened: How to avoid the tyranny of textbooks and get students excited about doing history.* New York, NY: Teachers College Press.

Myrdal, G. (1944). *An American dilemma: The Negro problem and modern democracy.* New York, NY: Harper and Bros.

Patterson, N., Doppen, F., & Misco, T. (2012). Beyond personally responsible: A study of teacher conceptualizations of citizenship education. *Education, Citizenship and Social Justice, 7*(2), 191–206.

Shulman, L. (1986). Those Who Understand: Knowledge Growth in Teaching. *Educational Researcher,* 15 (2), 4–14.

Schultz, B. (2008). Spectacular Things Happen Along The Way: Lessons from an Urban Classroom. New York, NY: Teachers College Press.

Theiman, G. Y., O'Brien, J. E., Preston-Grimes, P., & Barker, T. W. (2015). Chapter 3: From the field: What social studies teachers in three states report they do in the classroom. In J. Passe & P. G. Fitchett (Eds.), *The status of the social studies: Views from the field* (pp. 41–64). Charlotte, NC: Information Age.

Walsh, J. (2017, March 3). 49 years ago, Harry Belafonte hosted the tonight show and it was amazing. *The Nation.* Retrieved from https://www.thenation.com/article/49-years-ago-harry-belafonte-hosted-the-tonight-show-and-it-was-amazing/

9. The Teaching of Lynching: Considering a Pedagogic Necessity

Bryan Gibbs

Lynching is the most difficult content to teach in social studies. It is messy and unclean, dark, and tragic and describes the worst in us. Lynching involves race, racial violence, murder, police and political complicity, fear, anger, resentment, allegations of rape, sexuality, torture, mutilation, religion, White supremacy, and the celebration of these things. In our current conservative-dominated political climate that seeks to ban Muslims, build walls, and roll back the rights of women, silences around racial violence, often at the hands of the police, have similarly been resurrected and amplified. Violence targeting individuals' race, ethnicity, gender, and sexual orientation have spiked since the November election (Bates, 2017). Prior to our current turbulence, teachers were already reticent to teach about race in general, much less address racial violence. Many made the argument that a teacher recently whispered to me before her class began, "I don't want to stir anything up … they all get along so well …" referring to the ethnically mixed students in her classroom. This reticence is far from uncommon according to recent research despite evidence of the positive impact engaging in controversial issues instruction has on student learning (Hess, 2009) and in the development of politically engaged classrooms (Hess & McAvoy, 2015).

The purpose of this chapter is to outline the varied pedagogical difficulties of teaching the fraught, sickening, and terrifying history of lynching. Ultimately this chapter argues that the history of lynching, with the above-mentioned teaching radioactivity it entails, is content that must be taught, for with an honest examination of the tragedy of lynching can come clarity of understanding through a new light shone into the darkness of our past. The National Council for Social Studies (NCSS, 1992) argues in its National Standards for Social Studies that the social studies should be taught using 10 themes.[1] Teaching lynching easily falls into six of the ten themes: Culture; Time, Continuity, and Change; People, Places, and Environments; Individual Development and Identity; Individual Groups and Institutions; and, Civic Ideals and Practices. Yet, it is rarely taught. Ross (2017) suggests a reason, writing, "Social studies is the most dangerous of all school subjects. Its danger however, is a matter of perspective" (p. xxi). This reminds me of John Lennon's quote, "War is over ... if you want it." Social studies are the same way. If we, teachers and teacher educators, want the social studies to be dangerous, to be transformative to students and schools, we can have the power to do so. A subject and discipline that ought to be fraught with controversy, complex narrative, and complicated history, social studies instead is often trimmed, reduced, obfuscated, skipped, or as another teacher recently explained to me, "gently touches upon" difficult history.

I often hear three main reasons from teachers for not teaching difficult history: "There is no time"; "The standards and the test say ..."; and "I would be fired." While valid, these reasons also involve choice. Yet, there are many ways to teach lynching within these constraints. It can be taught as part of a thematic unit that allows for exploration of multiple topics, or time can be banked to teach an entire lynching unit, and in both cases lynching can be taught while meeting standards and preparing students for tests.

The teaching of lynching must be fully engaged, well researched, and built upon a strong community with understanding of who students are and what assets they bring. The teacher must also have a sense of self, understanding what they carry with them into the classroom, along with a deep sense of the community in which they teach. Furthermore, the students must have developed a critical sensibility and a burgeoning critical consciousness within a classroom environment where enough time is given to foster a pedagogy of discussion to come to an understanding of resistance figures and movements (i.e. Ida B. Wells, W. E. B. DuBois, the Niagara Movement, the NAACP). Under these conditions, I argue that the teaching of lynching can be accomplished while fostering both understanding and empowerment.

The teaching of lynching can be critical (Apple, 2014; Kincheloe & Steinberg, 2012; Ross, 2017), culturally relevant (Ladson-Billings, 1994), culturally sustaining (Parris & Alim, 2017), and based in Critical Race Theory (Ladson-Billings, 2003; Woodson, 2016). Further, if the study of lynching comes with an action-oriented focus it can help students recognize and sharpen their agency (Gillen, 2014), gain critical civic literacy (DeVitis, 2011); learn the power of interruption and disruption (Apple, 2014); and develop into Ross's notion of "dangerous citizenship" (2017). Dangerous citizenship, in particular, allows students to fully engage in difficult content, connect personally to the world, and develop and sharpen the social, academic, and intellectual skills needed for community and societal action on behalf of themselves and others.

Lynching is, however, a pedagogical minefield. Teaching it is rife with potential pitfalls that could lead to student psychic damage. The alternative, however, is to risk student psychic damage by *not* engaging in the teaching of lynching. This is a tall task and even the strongest and most well-intentioned teacher can handle complicated issues, such as lynching, clumsily. Thoughtful pedagogical planning and classroom development is vital to teaching lynching successfully.

Lynching: A History

We often think of lynching as something from our ill, misinformed, and long ago troubled past, but in 2017 lynching is still very much amongst us. The noose as a symbol of White supremacy and racialized intimidation is used quite frequently (Stolberg & Dickerson, 2017). It has appeared hanging in front of schools and colleges, and in front of Black owned businesses. Some law enforcement officials have at times categorized the leaving of these nooses as hate speech, though not often, and many activist groups have condemned it as racist intimidation (Stolberg & Dickerson, 2017). These actions are not isolated to a post-election 2017. Just after Professor Anita Hill's 1991 testimony during the Clarence Thomas confirmation hearings, current Supreme Court Justice Thomas referred to the media investigation of Professor Hill's allegations as a "high tech lynching" (Thomas, 2008). About a decade later, an African-American man named James Byrd was walking down a lonely Texas country road when two White men in a pickup truck assaulted him, chained his feet to the back of their truck, and dragged him several miles along the asphalt until his body fell to pieces (Temple-Raston, 2003). During the Obama presidency nooses made a comeback at political rallies and quite often during the eight years of his administration, images of the president hanging from his neck by a noose emerged.

Lynching, the act of violence itself and its inherent threat has been a part of American history since African-Americans began the civil rights struggle. From 1619 on, African-Americans' resisted the violence they were forced to endure. There were small victories in escapes, a few legal victories, and some attitude changes amongst the white power structures, but lynching was always there both in reality and in threat. As African-Americans struggled to gain the promises made on paper in the 13th, 14th, and 15th Amendments lynching and other forms of violence were used to maintain white supremacy and to keep African-Americans subjugated. As the Reconstruction period ended, Jim Crow laws and practices emerged hand in hand with the acceleration of lynching. The Supreme Court's "separate but equal" decision in *Plessy v. Ferguson* (1896) did nothing to stem the tide of violence against African-Americans.

Lynching is most commonly recognized as racially charged mob violence against mostly male African-Americans, but it wasn't always this. The "Lynch Law" was developed by Charles Lynch, a Justice of the Peace in Chestnut Hill, Virginia during the period of the Revolutionary War. A rabid supporter of independence, Lynch was instrumental in developing an independent court to deal with Tories (supporters of Great Britain) and other crimes such as horse thieves. Guilty parties were apparently tied to trees then whipped. Past the colonial times, "Lynch's Law" or "Lynch Law" came to describe informal mob justice (Dray, 2002).

As the Civil War came to a close and the Reconstruction Era began, lynching became something much different. The Ku Klux Klan was formed as an extension of the Lynch Law Regulator phenomenon to "keep Blacks in their place" as African-Americans began to hold office, participate in elections, and gain ground economically. Lynching began to take on a common storyline involving allegations of rape, Christian ethics, an arrest based on little evidence with resulting violence, most often murder by hanging, often with police complicity. A mob of armed White men would storm a jail, torture, then hang the "suspect" from a tree without trial. This public murder was generally followed by a scramble for souvenirs, then a celebration in the form a picnic, barbecue, or some other type of community gathering where children were often in attendance.

To illustrate the utter horror and depravity of lynching in the post-reconstruction era, consider the story of Sam Hose as recounted by historian Philip Dray (2002). Hose, 21 years old, was new to Coweta County when he was accused of using an ax to crush the skull of white farmer Alfred Cranford, killing his infant child by slamming it to the floor, and raping Mrs. Cranford. Local newspapers were reassured that Hose—who had not been arrested, arraigned in court, or formally charged with a crime—when caught, "will be lynched ..." (p. 5).

Hose was found near his mother's home and escorted back to the scene of the crime where thousands gathered and the "victim" was asked to identify the perpetrator. Cranford's mother identified Hose as a man hired to work on their farm. Subsequently, Hose was doused with kerosene near a pyre of burning wood. He was tortured, stabbed, and had various pieces of his body cut off including fingers, ears, and genitalia before he was fully pushed into the fire. The torture, it was said, lasted at least half an hour and was witnessed by thousands, many of whom had traveled by train to attend. Though hanging and the noose are often considered synonymous with lynching, Hose and others were burned to death. In some cases, the victim was first hanged and then burned (Dray, 2002).

Ida B. Wells-Barnett, former teacher, journalist, and fearsome anti-lynching activist, hired a man named LeVin to investigate Hose's murder. The counter narrative he uncovered almost completely contradicted the prime narrative of Hose's crimes as reported in the pages of the newspapers. Asking for an advancement of wages, Hose and Cranford got into a disagreement in which Cranford pulled a gun and Hose defended himself with an ax. It was reported that Hose ran into the woods after the altercation, never seeing either Cranford's wife nor his child. The child was neither injured nor killed by Hose or anyone (Dray, 2002). LeVin's report ended with this sentence, "I made my way home thoroughly convinced that a Negro's life is a very cheap thing in Georgia" (p. 16).

While lynching most often constituted murder by hanging, victims were also tortured to death, burned alive, or shot. Initially there was a public spectacle to killing by lynching. The murderers made no attempts to hide their faces nor conceal their identities, often posing for photographs with the bodies of the victims (Brophy, 2002), which in turn were commonly made into postcards sent to friends and relatives. Other times, when the accused could not be found or resistance from the African-American community was direct (as in Tulsa, Oklahoma in 1921 and Rosewood, Florida in 1923) violence against one became violence against entire communities. In both Tulsa and Rosewood hundreds were killed and the strong African-American communities of Greenwood (the parallel community to Tulsa) and Rosewood were destroyed and abandoned (Brophy, 2002; D'Orso, 1996; Hirsch, 2002).

Though it began in the South, lynching was hardly a regional phenomenon. Lynching occurred in many regions of the country, and few areas have been immune. While African-Americans account for the majority of those innocents who were murdered, Latinx, Chinese, and Jews amongst others were also lynched at different times. Between 1877 and 1950 at least 4,000 people were lynched.[2] Lynching did begin to change in the aftermath of World War II. The "spectacle lynching," a murder performed openly before the community, disappeared and was replaced by "underground lynching" in which stealth, "secrecy and complete anonymity of perpetrator" (Dray, 2002, p. 406) were prized. Though the community generally knew the identity of the murderers, the days of picnics and photographs beneath hanging corpses had largely disappeared.

The murder of Emmett Till in 1955 illustrates how lynching violence shifted away from events like the public murder of Hose. Till, a 14-year-old Chicago native visiting family in Money, Mississippi for the summer was accused of "wolf whistling" (Branch, 1988; Metress, 2002) at Carol Bryant, the white wife of a store owner Till and his cousins were visiting. Soon after, in the dead of night, Bryan's husband Roy and his half brother J. W. Milam came for Till (Branch, 1988). Till was kidnapped, tortured, shot through the head, and had his neck wrapped in chicken wire which was then attached to the engine of a cotton gin before his body was thrown into the Tallahatchie River (Metress, 2002).

When his body was discovered, his mother, Mamie Till, had an open casket public funeral to let the world see what had been done to her son. Jett Magazine published a photograph of Till's mutilated face on its cover. Despite Till's uncle, Moses Wright, bravely standing in court, testifying to the identity of Till's murderers, both Bryant and Milam were found not guilty. The murder of Till, Wright's bravery, Mamie Till's fierceness, and Jett Magazine's decision to run the photograph are credited with beginning the modern African-American Civil Rights movement. In fact, Rosa Parks' sit in on a Montgomery Bus occurred on the very day of the Milam and Bryant verdicts.

Though not a spectacle, the murder of Emmett Till was intended to silence and intimidate and was executed as punishment for a perceived offense. This is how lynching murders continued in the post World War II era—they became shootings, bombings, beatings, and dragging behind trucks. The form had changed, the effect had not.

Teaching Lynching

Teaching lynching presents enormous difficulties and complications. The issues embodied in the teaching of lynching are often understandably avoided by teachers. Educators also need to have a deep historical knowledge of lynching. They should understand how it has changed from community spectacle to a quieter form of brutal murder where the community knows who was involved but remains mute bystanders. What becomes clear in the teaching of lynching is that the teacher needs to be incredibly thoughtful in considering the purpose and context in which lynching is presented, and the identity of who is presenting it, while acknowledging the fact that there was always resistance to lynching from within the Black community. With these considerations in mind, the following sections outline how teaching lynching can be successful through embedded pedagogies that deeply consider context while addressing student and teacher cynicism within the process.

Embedding Lynching through the Use of Essential Questions

The teaching of lynching needs to be embedded within a larger unit of instruction, one focused on racism perhaps, or resistance, or focused on the African-American struggle for civil rights. A standalone unit on the horrors of lynching could be overwhelming and severely depressing, potentially leading to cynicism. For example, the statistics first collected by Ida B. Wells-Barnett and stored at the Tuskegee Institute illustrate that 10,000 African-Americans were lynched by whites between 1865 (the close of the Civil War) and the 1890s (Dray, 2002, p. 49) are simply overwhelming. Examining the photographic evidence of lynching, replete with devastated Black bodies, celebrating whites, and children smiling for photographs can be revolting and soul decaying if not embedded within a larger context. So too can the list of the at least 40 people who were essentially lynched struggling for civil rights from 1951 to 1968 (Bullard, 1993). The list of names and violence brought against them is stunning. However, as part of a larger, carefully crafted unit, the story of lynching could lead to a deeper understanding of how the atrocities of lynching connect to people in resistance movements throughout history and their empowering struggle to gain rights and freedoms to be full humans.

One of the greatest struggles while researching this chapter was my own difficulty with the detailed depravity of humanity and victimization of innocence. I had to balance my readings on lynching with a healthy dose of the stories of Ida B. Wells-Barnett, W. E. B. DuBois, Mose Wright, Mamie Till, Bob Moses, Septima Clark, and others who stood up to the fear and intimidation created by mob violence in the face of overwhelming odds and at great personal peril. Embedding lynching in a broader curricular unit means these stories can be examined as well, not just as a healing balm for the tragedy but as examples of resistance that can be mirrored, grown, and implemented differently today. For example, a unit that could embed all this history is one focused on the history of African-Americans from 1619 to 1970 (or, 1919–1970, 1954–1970, or another set of focus years), which is taught thematically. Though such a unit focuses on the history of African-Americans chronologically, it affords a more thematic approach with a deep focus on content that provides an opportunity to examine the growth of both atrocity and resistance over time.

Using an open-ended essential question will drive an embedded unit, such as the one my teaching partner once designed: *How do we emancipate ourselves?* This question pushes students to focus on emancipation, that is, the freeing of ourselves from this history. At the same time, it asks students to examine and understand what it is that "we" need to be emancipated from. Thus, students are pushed to examine the darkness and difficulty that exists within the history of lynching with a clear sense that there was and continues to be a push forward, a struggle, and refusal to give in. The question works well historically, asking students to delve and examine content deeply. The philosophical space created by an essential question is one where discussion of the complexities of lynching's associated racism, torture, sexuality, violence, and resistance can take place.

Context and Identity Matter

Who the teacher is and what they carry with them must be considered when teaching lynching. Even as the author of this chapter, I had to consider the role of my identities when writing this chapter. I am a straight, cisgender, over-educated, married father of one with a penchant for folk-rock music, who thinks of himself as outdoorsy. I carry this identity, amongst other things, with me into my classroom. For all 16 years of my teaching, I taught in East Los Angeles, California to a majority Latinx student population in a working class/working poor neighborhood. Who I was and the context in which I taught had to be factored into the approaches that I took. I also co-taught for almost all my teaching career with a female Latina teacher who had grown up near the neighborhood in which we taught. In other words, she was similar to my students and had been similarly raised. She not only helped me better understand the context in which I taught (such as how students might respond or what parents might say) but helped me co-teach lessons on lynching as well as other complicated content. Her knowledge, voice, and experience impacted my teaching and understanding of my students profoundly.

Now, I am a professor in North Carolina. A strong, but relatively new, white teacher recently shared with me that the concept of lynching came up while teaching a novel. Sensing that students had no understanding of what it was, she planned a thoughtful two-day lesson around the generalities of lynching. Subsequently, a parent raised an objection. My prejudiced assumption was that it would be a White parent reacting to the implications that whites were to blame. I was surprised, but shouldn't have been, that the reaction came from the father of a young, Black man. He didn't want his son exposed to lynching yet and wasn't sure when he would be. The father felt his son wasn't ready for the heavy topic and the father admitted that he wasn't ready either, for the questions, the concerns, or the possible impact on his son. The young man was one of three students of color in an otherwise white classroom. The child was excused from those two days of class at the father's request. The conversation between teacher and father led to another conversation, and another, and then another. The teacher would like to see if the father will work with her to develop a short series of lessons. We shall see if it comes to pass. If it doesn't, the fact that the conversation happened, that he spoke and she listened, is of strong importance and indicative of the importance of context and identity when teaching lynching.

Utilizing Stories of Resistance to Fight the Cynic in All of Us

Though he is speaking specifically of teaching apartheid, Bill Bigelow (1985) might have the best argument for the teaching of difficult history and against student cynicism. He writes:

> True, the subject is depressing. I shared other teachers' fears that if we only paid attention to the *problems* of the world we ran the risk of contributing to our students' already substantial burden of cynicism. I wanted to leave my students with the sense that change was possible; perhaps the unit could even offer them an opportunity to play a small part in creating that change. (p. vii)

The opportunities for students to combat cynicism and recognize their own power by learning how to use it in the face of tremendous difficulty, can have a profound benefit. Bigelow (1985) continues, "Underlying each lesson is the hope and expectation that South Africa—and people in general—can change" (p. xii). He argues that racism wasn't born, violence didn't occur by divine fiat; it was taught in homes, schools, and Sunday school, on the street and in private conversations. Apartheid was in many ways similar to the system that allowed lynching to occur and which pressured those in opposition to feel outnumbered, powerless, and silent. The accusations and violence, at least some of it, could have been interrupted or disrupted or wholly prevented. Not only should resistance be taught, Bigelow argues, but the philosophies, choices, tactics, and plans of individual resistors and movements, should be analyzed, critiqued and improved upon to be put into action in the lives of students.

The post-Civil War era offers incredible stories of resistance that can be employed to combat cynicism. Ida B. Wells-Barnett stands out as a particularly powerful narrative. She became a teacher as a teenager to keep her siblings together, growing into a fierce and tremendous writer, eventually collecting the stories of lynching and pushing them onto the world stage at great risk to her life. This was also the time of W. E. B. DuBois who became the pre-eminent scholar activist (Apple, 2012) and leader of the anti-racist resistance. There are others, such as Marcus Garvey's focused and re-energized "Back to Africa" campaign and nameless other writers, editors, and strangers who hid or helped African-Americans accused of crimes evade capture and death. Additionally, there were a few members of the police who refused to surrender suspected African-Americans to the mob, but did their jobs to fully investigate the allegations. This was the time of social movements like the Niagara Movement to end lynching, out of which the National Association for the Advancement of Colored People (NAACP) was born. Lynching, well-embedded, well-taught, and focused on the resistance can lead to sadness, and rage, but hopefully it will also lead students to take action to combat the cynicism that arises out of the difficulties of our current era.

One of the difficulties in teaching the resistance to lynching and mob violence is finding the story of the less-than-famous resistor. There are many who are well known, and during the time period of 1948–1976 were well known members of the Civil Rights movement. There are others who are less well known such as Vernon Dahmer and Viola Liuzzo who despite threats of violence continued the struggle and paid with their lives. As can happen in history the stories of the atrocities are well-documented and remembered. But, the stories of the resistors, who stayed alive by maintaining their anonymity, are less well known, relatively undocumented, and absent from memory. They may have quietly led boycotts of stores owned by perpetrators, hid or warned those who were accused, donated money, or joined resistance movements and organizations. A resource guide, *Putting the Movement Back into Civil Rights Teaching* (Menkart, Murray, & View, 2004), does an excellent job of framing the movement as built by unnamed and less-than-famous individuals who worked and struggled in spite of threats, intimidation, and violence.

A way to deepen investigation of resistors is by having students investigate, examine, and critique the modes of resistance that were possible. A short unit on lynching within a larger unit could begin with examining case studies like those of Hose and Till detailed earlier in this chapter. Examining maps of lynching and perhaps a few photographs to get the larger sense of the history of lynching would lead to an understanding of how lynching evolved into the era of 1948–1976. A teacher could then ask students to brainstorm some of the ways that individuals could have resisted lynching. Students may struggle with the overwhelming topic that is lynching, and this should be acknowledged by the teacher. After students make their lists and share them with the class, the teacher could present her own list of ways that we know lynching was resisted, through newspaper articles and books (media), through the attempted passage of laws (the ill-fated anti-lynching act), the formation of resistance groups and organizing (Niagara Movement, NAACP, SNCC, SCLC and others), to individual acts of resistance (silent boycotts, warnings, hiding those accused, violence, and thousands of other small acts). Ask students to rank the resistance acts on their list beginning with the acts they believe would be most effective in ending lynching and mob violence to those acts that would be least effective. Have students share their ranked list with a partner, and follow up with a whole class discussion. It would be interesting to see what students think is most effective at the beginning of a unit focused on the essential question "How do we emancipate ourselves?" as described earlier and how students might think about it at the end of a unit.

Conclusion

The teaching of lynching is hard. I don't think I've ever written a truer or more simplistic statement. The teaching of lynching presents a myriad of pedagogical potholes and complexities. It will absolutely cause students discomfort. The teacher needs to be knowledgeable of content, mindful of students' and teacher identities, and thoughtful about how lynching is taught. Lynching should, however, be taught. In the teaching of lynching, as in the teaching of other sickening, complex, and difficult histories, lie the seeds of interruption and disruption (Apple, 2014). The purpose of social studies is to create three-dimensional, fully functioning adults prepared to engage themselves, their neighborhoods, and the world for the better. We want and need our students to be dangerous citizens (Ross, 2017)—to ask the difficult questions, push the issue, understand how to organize and mobilize, and use their multiple voices for strong and powerful movement forward. The teaching of lynching, if thoughtfully done and truthfully engaged, can lead students to the path of resistance, growth, and change.

Notes

1. https://www.socialstudies.org/standards/curriculum
2. Equal Justice Initiative https://eji.org/reports/lynching-in-america

References

Apple, M. (2012). *Can education change society?* New York, NY: Routledge.

Apple, M. (2014). *Official knowledge: Democratic education in a conservative age* (3rd ed.). New York, NY: Routledge.

Bates, L. (2017, June 5). Frequency of noose hate crimes incidents surge. *Southern Poverty Law Center*. Retrieved from https://www.splcenter.org/hatewatch/2017/06/05/frequency-noose-hate-crime-incidents-surges

Bigelow, B. (1985). *Strangers in their own land*. Milwaukee, WI: Rethinking Schools.

Branch, T. (1988). *Parting the water: America in the King Years, 1954–1963*. New York, NY: Simon and Schuster.

Brophy, A. (2002). *Reconstructing the dreamland: The Tulsa riot of 1921: Race, reparations, and reconciliation*. Oxford: Oxford University Press.

Bullard, S. (1993). *Free at last: A history of the civil rights movement and those who died in the struggle*. New York, NY: Oxford University Press.

DeVitis, J. (2011). *Critical civic literacy: A reader*. New York, NY: Peter Lang:.

D'Orso, M. (1996). *Like judgment day; The ruin and redemption of a town called Rosewood*. New York, NY: Putnam & Sons.

Dray, P. (2002). *At the hands of persons unknown: The lynching of Black America*. New York, NY: Random House.

Gillen, J. (2014). *Educating for insurgency: The roles of young people in schools of poverty*. London: AK Press.

Hess, D. (2009). *Controversy in the classroom: The democratic power of classroom discussion*. New York, NY: Routledge.

Hess, D., & McAvoy, P. (2015). *The Political classroom: Evidence and ethics in democratic education*. New York, NY: Routledge.

Hirsch, J. (2002). *Riot and remembrance: American's worse race riot and its legacy*. New York, NY: Houghton-Mifflin.

Kincheloe, J., & Steinberg, S. (2012). *Unauthorized methods: Strategies for critical teaching*. New York, NY: Routledge.

Ladson-Billings, G. (1994). *The dreamkeepers: Successful teachers of African-American children*. San Francisco, CA: Jossey-Bass.

Ladson-Billings, G. (2003). *Critical race theory perspectives on the social studies: The profession, policies, and curriculum*. New York, NY: Information Age Publishing.

Menkart, D., Murray, A., & View, J. (2004). *Putting the movement back into civil rights teaching*. New York, NY: Teaching for Change Press.

Metress, C. (2002). *The lynching of Emmitt Till: A documentary narrative*. Charlottesville, VA: University of Virginia Press.

National Council for the Social Studies (NCSS). (1992). *A vision of powerful teaching and learning in the social studies: Building social understanding and civic efficacy* [Press release]. Retrieved from http://socialstudies.org/positions/powerful

Parris, J., & Alim, H. S. (2017). *Culturally sustaining pedagogies: Teaching and learning for justice in a changing world*. New York, NY: Teachers College Press.

Ross, E. W. (2017). *Rethinking social studies: Critical pedagogy in pursuit of dangerous citizenship*. Charlotte, NC: Information Age Publishing.

Stolberg, S., & Dickerson, C. (2017, July 5). Hangman's noose, symbol of racial animus, keeps cropping up. *The New York Times*. Retrieved from https://www.nytimes.com/2017/07/05/us/nooses-hate-crimes-philadelphia-mint.html?smid=fb-nytimes&smtyp=cur

Temple-Raston, D. (2003). *A death in Texas: A story of race, murder, and a small town's struggle for redemption*. New York, NY: Holt.

Thomas, C. (2008). *My grandfather's son: A memoir*. New York, NY: Harper-Perennial.

Woodson, A. (2016). We're just ordinary people: Messianic narratives and Black youth's civic agency. *Theory & Research in Social Education, 44*(2), 184–212.

10. From the Bottom Up: Citizenship Education during the Civil Rights Movement

LaGarrett J. King and John A. Moore

No other topic in U.S. history attempts to capture what is believed to be the essence of American ideas of racial progress more than the Civil Rights Movement (CRM hereafter). Everyone from conservative politicians to television/radio pundits proclaimed that the Civil Rights era was the epitome of the egalitarian ideas set forth by White Founding Fathers of the United States. A quick search on Google Scholar and Amazon reveal hundreds of books, scholarly journal articles, and reports associated with various Civil Rights events, persons, and topics. Within the past few decades, several movies and television shows have been dedicated to the movement. Recent acclaimed movies such as Lee Daniel's *the Butler* and *Selma* as well as documentaries such as *Freedom riders* and the long-lived *Eyes on the Prize* series, not only have been influential and educative for adult viewers, but have also been turned into lesson plans for K–12 schools. John Lewis, the former Student Nonviolent Coordinating Committee (SNCC) chairperson and current U.S. representative from Georgia, has seen his profile rise again after his award winning and New York Times best seller, *The March*, a graphic novel trilogy about the Civil Rights Movement as told by Lewis, was published (Lewis, Aydin, & Powell, 2013, 2015, 2016). The CRM is a constant lexicon in society as recent social and political movements such as Black Lives Matter, the Ferguson, Missouri protests, and even the Tea Party have been compared to the civil unrest of the 1960s. Quite frankly, the Civil Rights Movement is part of the pantheon of salient historical events that have shaped United States history.

Understanding the Civil Rights Movement has been a prominent exploration in higher education research. Scholarship produced by academicians and historians have attempted to advance our knowledge of the CRM for the last four decades. Steven Lawson (1991) outlined how scholars began to understand the Civil Rights Movement. He divided CRM literature into three generations, and Sudianta Keita Cha-Jua and Clarence Lang (2007) added a fourth generation. Lawson (1991) contended that historians of the late 1960s and 1970s constructed the CRM as a political movement, complete with legislative and judicial victories. From this scholarship, we begin to understand the CRM within the Brown v. Board to Memphis framework with the movement lead by heroes such as Martin Luther King Jr. and Rosa Parks. This research also credited White liberal politicians, White northerners, and the media for its coverage of racial violence in the south. The second wave, beginning in the 1980s, consisted of looking at various social movements that defined the era. Scholarship began to recognize CRM leaders who were more local, regular, and part of the working class. This research helped us understand that the CRM was not spontaneous, but was planned and deliberate. The first and second generations of CRM research can be differentiated as being top-down and bottom-up. Understanding the CRM as top down is to favor the narratives of national organizations, government entities, and a few heroes and heroines over a bottom-up framework, which examines the movement through more grassroots and local leaders as agents of change.

The third wave of CRM scholarship began to merge top and bottom up frameworks. These historians helped us to understand the complexity and nuances of the movement. Here, the scholarship began to "identify and explain the long term structural factors underlying the movement's origins, developments, and outcomes" (Cha-Jua & Lang, 2007, p. 267). At the time, Lawson (1991) surmised that the research began to present a more holistic view of the civil rights movement by "exploring the legal, theological, and political legacies" of the ideological roots of the movement and by exploring the juxtaposition between "national institutions and local activities, moderates and radicals, whites and black, women and predecessors and contemporaries" (p. 457). The fourth wave updated the scholarship to challenge the traditional framework of the Brown v. Board and Memphis time era for civil rights to include what Jacquelyn Dowd Hall (2005) and others have deemed the long civil rights movement. Here, the 1930s and 40s seemed prominent, not only as an ideological precursor but as the first phase of the movement. Additionally, the long civil rights movement expands the CRM narrative by reimagining the CRM as a series of local struggles, integrating the CRM with Black power, and resisting the South as the only geographical space where racism and civil rights were prominent.

Civil Rights Curriculum and Teaching in K–12 Schools

Yet, we argue that with so much information out there, people, especially school aged children, know very little about the Civil Rights Movement. The problem may reside in the official K–12 history curriculum, the formal curriculum represented through textbooks, curriculum materials, state and national standards, and other formalized historical narratives. Charles Payne (2004) surmised that the official K–12 history curriculum presents Civil Rights history as followed:

> Traditionally, relationships between the races in the South were oppressive. In the 1954, the Supreme Court decided this was wrong. Inspired by the court, courageous Americans, Black and white, took protest to the street, in the form of sit-ins, bus boycotts and Freedom Rides. The protest movement, led by the brilliant and eloquent Doctor Martin Luther King, aided by a sympathetic Federal government, most notably the Kennedy brothers and a born-again Lyndon Johnson, was able to make America understand racial discrimination as a moral issue. Once Americans understood that discrimination was wrong, they quickly moved to remove racial prejudice and discrimination from American life, as evidenced by the Civil Rights Acts of 1964 and 1965. Dr. King was tragically slain in 1968. Fortunately, by that time the country had been changed for the better in some fundamental ways. The movement was a remarkable victory for all Americans. By the 1970s, Southern states where Blacks could not have voted ten years earlier were sending African Americans to Congress. Inexplicably, just as the civil rights victories were piling up, many Black Americans, under the banner of Black Power, turned their backs on American society. (p. 11)

Based on Charles Payne's (2004) summation of the Civil Rights Movement in schools, most school curriculum frameworks are frozen within the first wave of CRM scholarship. The typical Civil Rights narrative is top down, meaning that too much emphasis is placed on national leadership and institutions, legislation, and large dramatic events and not of ordinary people or everyday acts of resistance by people. The top down historical framework situates the Civil Rights movement through the Montgomery (Bus boycott) to Memphis framework, which ignores previous early periods of struggle. Top down historical frameworks usually gives historical agency to those who are white, wealthy or middle-class people, male, and educated. Payne (2007), in other work, also noted that the Black church played a large role in Civil Rights curriculum, which indicates a moral imperative that gets reduced or oversimplified as strategy for the African American community. The top-down perspective does not account for the diversity of the various Black communities and their contexts that helped shaped the ideological positioning of the movement.

Yet, in schools, the Civil Rights Movement has a major influence on social studies curriculum. Oberg research (2015) noted that the Civil Rights Movement was one of the most taught subjects by social studies teachers. Wineburg and Monte-Sano's (2008) study of 2,000 high school students' ideas on famous Americans noted that two Civil Rights icons were tops of their lists, Martin Luther King Jr. and Rosa Parks. One of the limitations of their famous American study was that students were asked to list and not indicate how they understood the historical characters. For example, Alridge's study on Martin Luther King Jr indicated that most textbooks covered the Civil Rights icon but the narratives presented were problematic. He found that Martin Luther King Jr was relegated as a messiah or superhuman figure, embodiment of the civil rights movement, and as a moderate. Using these constructs ignores King as an ordinary and radical figure with complexities and challenges who leaned on many different people and personalities to push forward the movement. Scholarship has also indicated a similar approach to how students understand Rosa Parks as a civil rights icon (Carlson, 2003).

This understanding of narrative is important to consider given that diverse perspectives within official social studies curricula are largely measured by its quantitative presence, while ignoring the qualitative aspects of narratives. Vasquez Heilig, Brown, and Brown's (2012) work speaks to the illusions of topics that are meant to teach about race and racism, yet when examining the merits of the state standards, they notice that the knowledge in which students are to learn and teachers are to teach are missing salient information that helps provide nuanced understandings. Therefore, while Civil Rights curriculum and teaching may be a prominent aspect of the social studies curriculum, the narratives are problematically constructed, which leads to miseducation (Woodson, 1933) about the complexity of the movement.

There is little proof that the majority of Civil Rights curricula provide teachers the necessary knowledge or frame to explore the nuances of the movement (Alridge, 2006; Carlson, 2003; King, 2015). Take for instance Anderson's (2013) study, *The trouble with unifying Narratives: African Americans and the Civil Rights movement in U.S. History Content Standards*, in which he analyzed nine state's standards on Civil Rights Teaching. These states were Arizona, Washington, DC, Florida, Michigan, New Jersey, South Carolina, South Dakota, Virginia, and Washington State. His purpose was to find out which states emphasized historical inquiry as an instructional strategy. Historical inquiry involves students in the process of doing history. It is suggested that students view history through multiple perspectives and use the skills closely associated with historians to investigate and manufacture history based on the historical evidence. For several decades, researchers and practitioners consider history instruction through inquiry as a best practice for teachers.

Anderson's findings indicate that Civil Rights standards tend neither to engage students in historical thinking or introduce discordant/conflict perspectives about the experiences of African Americans during the CRM. He breaks down Civil Rights teaching into three categories, contributory, progressive/exceptional, and discordant/conflict. According to Anderson (2013):

> A standard was contributory if it focused primarily on praising or reinforcing the cultural contributions of African Americans during the CRM. A standard was progressive/exceptional if it primarily focused on gradual but inevitable democratic progress on U.S. race relations or generally implied a non-conflictual historical narrative. A standard was discordant/conflict if it substantively challenged or questioned the master narrative of the U.S. as a land of inevitably expanding freedom/equality over time for African Americans. (p. 114)

The standards with majority contributory standards were Florida (72%), South Carolina (57%), and South Dakota (75%). Washington, DC (57%), Michigan (60%), and Washington State (60%) had majority progressive/exceptional standards. Arizona, New Jersey, and Virginia had a 50%–50% split between contributory and progressive/exceptional standards. As for discordant/conflict standards, Washington, DC had four (13%), while Michigan and Washington State each had one (13% and 20% respectively) (Anderson, 2013).

While it is true that K–12 history teachers are gatekeepers of what eventually happens in their classrooms, the pressures for high school teachers to teach to the test and the marginalization of social studies in elementary schools, might influence them to over rely on the official curriculum as presented by

Table 10.1 Civil Rights Movement State Standards, Anderson (2013).

Orientation	States	Percentage of CRM standards associated with Orientation
Contributory Standards	Florida	72%
	South Carolina	57%
	South Dakota	75%
Progressive/Exceptional Standards	Washington D.C	57%
	Michigan	60%
	Washington State	60%
Discordant/Conflict Standards	Arizona	50%
	New Jersey	50%
	Virginia	50%

Source: Author.

state guidelines and textbooks. Even if teachers have the requisite knowledge to move beyond the official curriculum, factors such as time constraints, testing accountability, and loss of tenure make state's guidelines as to what and how to teach more valuable. Without support, as Anderson's study proves, teachers' approach to Civil Rights teaching is more reliant on the official curricula that dictate the standardized tests.

From the Bottom-Up: What to Consider in Civil Rights Teaching

Resisting the top-down approach and enhancing the bottom-up approach to CRM curriculum and teaching is important for several reasons. First, students learn, as the Southern Poverty Law Center (2014) noted, "what it means to be active American citizens … recognize injustice … the transformative role played by thousands of ordinary individuals, as well as the importance of organization(s) for collective change" (p. 11). Second, in many ways, civil rights history is about our identity as citizens in a racial egalitarian state. The history of the Civil Rights Movement, generally, presents to students who we are as a collective nation and where we still must go in terms of racial equity and justice. What examining history from the bottom-up does is provide all students a perspective from the nation's most vulnerable. Bottom-up history instills respect for and awareness of people's lives, cultures, and traditions not typically considered important. These bottom-up perspectives, whether intentional or not, are largely silenced through school curricula. Top-down perspectives hold certain privileges, which influences a different vantage point of the world. These vantage points may become discriminatory to those who do not hold those same privileges. It has been documented that Black people who were poor, female, and gay had a different set of circumstances (even being discriminated themselves within the larger Movement) than who is typically presented as the guardians of the CRM, who are typical male, middle class, and sometimes of a lighter skin tone.

Third, intersectional identities through history are important because in order to promote citizenship within social studies curricula, students need to learn who counts as a citizen. Studies have shown that students, based on various racial, ethnic, class, and gender identities, learn history differently (Epstein, 2010; Levy, 2017; Woodson, 2016). Through top-down narratives, we receive a limited view of citizenship and ways to approach agency to achieve those citizenship rights. Building on the work of Alridge (2006), Woodson (2016) makes this point when discussing how Black students understand the concept of Civil Rights history through messianic narratives. She surmised that learning about those messiahs in the CRM, who are presented as intellectually and morally superior, has a negative influence on students' civic identities. They ultimately feel that they, as a regular person, do not possess the necessary aptitude for civic agency to make the world a more racially just state. For these students, a bottom-up approach to Civil Rights helps them recognize their own power and their opportunities to act on their desires.

Additionally, teaching the CRM from the bottom-up illustrates how grassroots agency and regular people, under the right circumstances, can provide the seeds for mass resistance. It demonstrates how new political, social, and economic spaces can emerge and prosper. It also illustrates how ordinary people's lives and culture can encompass radical consciousness and how their patterns of resistance can influence historical change. We do warn that all bottom-up history should not be presented as too celebratory, as some might be contentious to other historical events. The point here is that bottom-up perspectives presents the Movement as sophisticated and multifaceted. To be sure, we are not advocating that teachers and/or curriculum designers should disregard top-down CRM curriculum and teaching, but we advocate that diligence in expanding our conception of the CRM through bottom-up approaches provide a more democratic, more truthful, and equitable way to examine history.

What follows in subsequent sections are exemplars of how teachers and citizens can approach CRM teaching and curriculum through a bottom-up approach. We took heed of Payne's critiques of traditional Civil Rights teaching and decided to focus our lessons on aspects of citizenship education during the Civil Rights Movement. We focus on the Mississippi Freedom schools organized by Council of Federated Organizations (COFO) and Student Nonviolent Coordinating Committee (SNCC) and Citizenship schools created by Septima Clark and Bernice Robinson. The freedom schools were a collection of alternative schools. We address bottom-up citizenship education through the lens of both children and teachers.

The absence of children and the issue of education within the Civil Rights narrative are problematic for teachers who teach in k–12 schools. Messiah narratives are also problematic because young people are left out of the story. While some curricula and teachers may mention the Birmingham children's crusade of 1963 where young children marched and got sprayed with water hoses and attacked by dogs, usually the narratives presented are seen as a strategy of the adults with limited understanding of how kids saw themselves in struggle. Children are rarely looked upon as instrumental in the fight for Civil Rights.

Education can be considered "ground zero" for the civil rights activists. As stated before, the Brown decision is typically considered one of the first events associated with the modern Civil Rights Movement. This is where ideologies formed and school aged school children risked their lives as well as experienced psychological and educative psychic violence in the name of education. Here, we would like to highlight teachers and other educators who helped improve the intellectual agency of the movement. Both Freedom schools and Citizen schools were to establish the foundation of Black agents of change.

We address three Civil Rights topics through the C3 framework to exemplify how teachers can approach Payne's call to unfreeze Civil Rights Movement teaching and learning from within the first wave. The first lesson asks 3rd–5th grade elementary students to analyze and interpret a quote by Septima Clark. The second lesson helps middle level students explain why Freedom Summer Schools were organized in Mississippi during 1964. And the third lesson offers high school students an opportunity to review and assess the impact of the Freedom Summer Schools on its participants [see Lesson Plans and Resources].

References

Alridge, D. P. (2006). The limits of master narratives in history textbooks. *Teachers College Record, 108*(4), 662–686.

Anderson, C. B. (2013). The trouble with unifying narratives: African Americans and the civil rights movement in US history content standards. *The Journal of Social Studies Research, 37*(2), 111–120.

Carlson, D. (2003). Troubling heroes: Of Rosa Parks, multicultural education, and critical pedagogy. *Cultural Studies ↔ Critical Methodologies, 3*(1), 44–61

Cha-Jua, S. K., & Lang, C. (2007). The "long movement" as vampire: Temporal and spatial fallacies in recent Black freedom studies. *The Journal of African American History, 92*(2), 265–288.

Epstein, T. (2010). *Interpreting national history: Race, identity, and pedagogy in classrooms and communities.* New York, NY: Routledge.

Hall, J. D. (2005). The long civil rights movement and the political uses of the past. *The Journal of American History, 91*(4), 1233–1263.

King, L. J. (2015). Learning other people's history: Pre-service teachers' developing African American historical knowledge. *Teaching Education, 25*(4), 427–456.

Lawson, S. F. (1991). Freedom then, freedom now: The historiography of the civil rights movement. *American Historical Review, 96*(2), 456–471.

Levy, S. A. (2017). How students navigate the construction of heritage narratives. *Theory & Research in Social Education, 45*(2), 157–188.

Lewis, J., Aydin, A., & Powell, N. (2013). *March: Book one.* Marietta, GA: Top Shelf Productions.

Lewis, J., Aydin, A., & Powell, N. (2015). *March: Book two*. Marietta, GA: Top Shelf Productions.

Lewis, J., Aydin, A., & Powell, N. (2016). *March: Book three*. Marietta, GA: Top Shelf Productions.

Payne, C. (2004). Critique of the traditional narrative. In D. Menkart, A. Murray, & J. View (Eds.), *Putting the movement back into civil rights teaching* (p. 11). Washington, DC: Teaching for Change.

Payne, C. M. (2007). *I've got the light of freedom: The organizing tradition and the Mississippi freedom struggle*. Berkeley, CA: University of California Press.

Southern Poverty Law Center. (2014). *Teaching the movement 2014. The state of civil rights education in the United States*. Washington, DC: Southern Poverty Law Center.

Vasquez Heilig, J., Brown, K., & Brown, A. (2012). The illusion of inclusion: A critical race theory textual analysis of race and standards. *Harvard Educational Review, 82*(3), 403–424.

Wineburg, S., & Monte-Sano, C. (2008). "Famous Americans": The changing pantheon of American heroes. *The Journal of American History, 94*(4), 1186–1202.

Woodson, A. N. (2016). We're just ordinary people: Messianic master narratives and Black youths' civic agency. *Theory & Research in Social Education, 44*(2), 184–211.

Woodson, C. G. (1933). *The Mis-education of the Negro*. Trenton, NJ: Africa World Press.

11. *"It was never that simple": Complicating the Master-Narrative around School Desegregation*[1]

ArCasia James

Desegregation is a topic K–12 schools regularly accentuate across the country. Popular opinion holds that the 1954 *Brown v. Board of Education of Topeka, Kansas* symbolizes a shining moment in US history, inviting a sense of collective pride, American exceptionalism, and the country's willingness to right its wrongs (Loewen, 1995; Williamson, 2006). The master-narrative, a term which refers to the dominant story of American history in which idealistic, simplistic, heroic, celebratory interpretations show consistent progress toward democracy. When historians, and thus textbooks, highlight exceptional acts by exceptional individuals along racist, sexist, and classist lines (Aldridge, 2006; Cox & Stromquist, 1998; Loewen, 1995), they misinterpret school desegregation as an occasion when the country reconciled its systemic abuse of its Black citizens. In this tradition, history celebrates the desegregation of public schools, the overturning of *Plessy v. Ferguson* (1896), and delegitimization of Jim Crow.

Inside the desegregation master-narrative and beyond, textbook, curriculum, and social studies standards writers routinely illustrate a tidy, pleasant version of US history in which African Americans as individuals lack autonomy and configure sporadically and inconsequentially into the past. For example, research reveals how secondary history textbooks regularly mischaracterize US history by including incomplete explanations of the past that hinge on American exceptionalism and Anglo-centrism (Loewen, 1995), push narratives of victimization and oppression when discussing racially marginalized groups (LaSpina, 2003), and drastically downplay the significance of race, racism, and racial violence (Brown & Brown, 2010).[2] Related studies

(Anderson, 2013; Journell, 2008) evaluating multiple states' social studies standards show significant issues with their disjointed treatment of African Americans as a group, exposing how such standards prevent students from comprehending the steady presence and impact of African Americans in the US.[3] Even icons such as Mrs. Rosa Parks and Dr. Martin Luther King Jr. are commonly misrepresented in textbooks, as writers tend to dilute and warp their historical legacies by describing their impact within a framework of exceptional, individual actors, rather than through their efforts to act as part of a broad movement (Alridge, 2006; Epstein, 1994).

Within an analysis of school desegregation, this tainted version of history, as documented in numerous textbooks studies, is both untrue and problematic. Such an interpretation encourages students to believe that by banning racially separate schools and ultimately conceding that inequality was protected by the law's separate but (un)equal practices, "American history becomes a story of perpetual progress and is understood as the only appropriate way to understand the American past" (Williamson, 2006, p. 46). And though numerous White communities violently fought the ruling and devised schemes to maintain racially homogenous schools, these details are often missing from typical portrayals.

More nuanced renditions of the Civil Rights Movement (CRM) and school desegregation remain isolated in academic literature, scantly informing K–12 curricula. This estrangement affects how individuals perceive society, fostering simplified (mis)understandings of the past and present, to which this chapter responds by attempting to narrow the gap between academic literature and K–12 curricula. Specifically, this brief piece disputes the dominant desegregation narrative through the lens of an ordinary young, working class, Black woman in the Midwest,[4] Ms. Esther Evans.[5] Details of her story, as extracted through a broader oral history project, demonstrate the complex nature of desegregation, raise controversial questions about the experience, and disrupt long-standing assumptions about the process. I discuss pedagogical challenges teachers may encounter, offer ways to address both content and skills, and note the relevance of this topic to the political climate today.

Evans' counter-story joins others captured in memoirs (Beals, 1995) and research (Dingus, 2006; Fields-Smith, 2005; Horsford, 2010; Morris & Morris, 2002; Tillman, 2004), outlining the diverse feelings and reactions Black students, parents, teachers, and administrators had in response to the school desegregation mandate. These sources describe aspects of the desegregation counter-narrative, which emphasize how: some Black communities did not desire to desegregate; scores of Black teachers and administrators lost their jobs as a consequence of school desegregation; and holistic teaching and care diminished in desegregated schools. These texts work against assumptions embedded within the master-narrative that all Black people had the same goals, fought the same battles, maintained the same considerations, and used the same means to achieve their aims.

Ms. Esther Evans, who demonstrates one version of such a counter-story, was born and raised in a small, urban city in the Midwest, where she attended a segregated Black elementary school until the end of fourth grade in 1959. At that point, her mother and community activist, saw to it that Ms. Evans and her siblings attended formerly segregated white schools to live out the promise of the *Brown* decision. Ms. Evans continued her formal education in predominantly white institutions, where she currently works. Her story drives this chapter, and excerpts describing her experiences are provided in Appendix A.

Teaching Desegregation

Being aware that students often bring familiarity of the master-narrative with them into classrooms is useful because, as Jennifer Frost's (2012) and Ashley Woodson's (2017) research posits, educators can use this as a starting point for robust discussions about the complex nature of school desegregation. The use of oral histories, or bottom-up perspectives, does not necessarily provide heightened authority on significant historical events; however, when these perspectives draw on the experiences of marginalized groups, such as women, African Americans, or folks from working class backgrounds, they can help students contextualize their understanding of historical events and processes in ways that promulgating the master-narrative, or a top-down approach, does not. What I am advocating here, and more broadly beyond the desegregation discourse, is for educators to help students develop a sensitivity to and pointed curiosity about historical blind spots, such as race, gender, and class, so they develop habits that help them interrogate versions of history that silence, distort, or sanitize aspects of oppression and struggle. Neither approach advances us toward progress alone, but multiple, bottom-up insights can certainly help enrich and complicate understanding of top-down perspectives, especially those privileged in textbooks, standards, and curricula in general.

Rarely is the desegregation story told from perspectives of Black students who felt it was a mistake—from Black students who dearly loved and missed their all-Black schools. These are stories that represent the counter-narrative against the prevalent master-narrative. Memoirs like Melba Beals' (1995) of the Little Rock Nine hint at historical actors' feelings of regret, sorrow, and trauma, but overwhelmingly cast a linear trajectory of progress that valorizes

Black sacrifice, discomfort, and longsuffering. Texts like these also showcase whites as those most likely to label racial integration an error and convey Black people as those in need of better quality schools, illuminating the deficits of segregated Black schools through overgeneralization.

Historical simplification of this nature is not limited to *Brown* or desegregation, even within the context of teaching about the CRM. Teaching about this era in K–12 schools across the country has long overlooked many of the classist elements that characterized the Black freedom struggle, including the official selection of Mrs. Rosa Parks over Ms. Claudette Colvin to jumpstart the Montgomery bus boycott (Garrow, 1985; Schwartz, 2009; Theoharis, 2015).[6] This approach has also obscured gender dynamics in ways that contort the presence and function of patriarchy in Black freedom movements. The impact of selectivity and respectability on the NAACP's strategic selection of causes to adopt, taking their initial hesitation as a case in point in the Scottsboro Boys trial,[7] is another overlooked, yet significant detail (McGuire, 2004; Miller, Pennybacker, & Rosenhaft, 2001; Murray, 1967).

Although spotlighting the many excellent achievements activists secured after difficult battles for humanizing treatment, exclusively focusing on extraordinary, professional-class Black men encourages misinformed historical understanding for both teachers and students. Furthermore, educators inherit understandings of history that shape how they decide to frame and teach it. These historical inheritances often bend toward the master-narrative, which exalts dominant groups in society such as men, whites, Christians, and able-bodied, cis-heteronormative individuals. Despite teachers' race, gender, or socio-economic status, trying to challenge this is difficult work that requires unlearning, questioning, and critiquing much of what textbooks, media, the political climate, and standards emphasize as fact.

A special area of concern involves the intersection of important identities and how they are represented in historical materials and curricula, namely the treatment of low socio-economic women of Color, given the tendency to exclude, contort, or decontextualize their stories (Chick & Corle, 2016; Schocker & Woyshner, 2013). Unfortunately, this tradition distorts historical context by warping students' historical comprehension, a severe consequence for those teaching in a post-2016 election era. In response, the CRM in general, and school desegregation in particular, offers a proactive chance to help students clearly see the not-so-distant past and its personal and institutional ramifications for them today.

To curb potential apprehension or pushback and boost support from student caretakers or school administrators due to the controversial nature of this subject, educators may notify parties of the upcoming unit with a thorough explanation of objectives. Underlining the perspective's merit, how it prepares students for effective democratic citizenship and supports their growth of critical academic skills, might also be helpful. Promoting community engagement through the oral history suggestion can also aid in diffusing opposition, creating a learning community beyond school walls. Last, frequently restating the importance of weighing multiple views as a vital part of the democratic process might, too, prove advantageous.

Additionally, challenging the master-narrative through the lens of traditionally underserved, marginalized groups opens possibilities for students to craft necessary critical thinking, argumentation, and evidence evaluation skills. Examining oral histories is an apt way to work toward these goals. Ms. Evans' "outsider within" (Collins, 1986, p. S14) perspective grants atypical insight into school desegregation through the experiences of a working-class, Black girl in the Midwest. Her recollections cast an "oppositional gaze" (hooks, 2003, p. 94) that challenges the validity of the master-narrative, which can expand thinking and conversations about desegregation and its direct impact on involved students.

A Student's Perspective: An Oral History of Desegregation

The National Council on Social Studies proposes ten themes around which social studies lessons ought to contour (https://www.socialstudies.org/standards/strands). Themes two (Time, Continuity, and Change), five (Individuals, Groups, and Institutions), and ten (Civic Ideals and Practices) lend themselves most aptly to teaching desegregation through an intersectional lens as advised here. Ms. Evans' story explores how the passage of time affects historical norms, personal dispositions, and the extent to which these remain intact or shift over time. Assessing her as a person, the groups with which she identifies (e.g., Black, women, working class, northerner), and the educational institutions with which she was interacting, exemplify transformations one can witness. Her story traces the instilling of particular civic ideals that implicate the public good. Ideals that attach productive citizenship to homo-racial settings are largely unfavorable, yet within the socio-political context of the mid-twentieth century, civic principles begin to take on different meanings for both marginalized and dominant groups. Examining desegregation through such a lens helps strengthen one's ability to perceive and value counter-narratives that unsettle traditional historical thinking.

As a former middle school teacher, I have designed these discussion points and instructional materials with students aged eleven to fourteen in mind. However, the topic and counter-perspectives represented here are certainly useful for primary and high school levels alike. Indeed, modifications can be made to adjust the content appropriately so that students at any level can access the content and build skills accordingly.

The included excerpts in the appendix of this chapter from oral history interviews raise controversial questions about school desegregation during the CRM through a counter-narrative that responds to the following questions: (1) What was the condition of all-Black schools before the *Brown* ruling?; (2) How did desegregation impact Black, participating students?; (3) What did Black, participating students think about desegregation as it occurred?; (4) How do participating, Black students think about desegregation as adults?; (5) What role did regional differences play in school desegregation?; (6) What does a close look at "ordinary" people reveal about school desegregation?; (7) How did the featured participant's gender shape her experiences?; (8) How did her working class background shape her experiences?

The excerpts provided displace the model of linear social progress (Alridge, 2006; Anderson, 2013) presented in textbooks by clearly showing that Ms. Evans neither enjoyed having to desegregate, nor thought it was beneficial long term. She speaks fondly of her all-Black school and notes that she never again received the affirmation, fortification, or academic rigor she relished in her segregated school. This notion alone proves controversial since the master-narrative tends to convey the consequences of school desegregation as progressive and positive, rarely incorporating views that push back on this conceptualization. It also works against the premise that all were united in agreement and wanted similar outcomes (Alridge, 2006; Anderson, 2013).

Viewing desegregation from the perspective of a Black working class woman from the North disputes "simplistic thinking promoted through school curricula [that] actually [constitutes] a symptom of U.S. society's collective preference for convenient and unifying historical narratives" (Wills, 2005, p. 126). This dynamic interpretation teaches students to doubt simplified narratives that paint complex groups as monoliths with analogous views. Interrogating why Black people might have enjoyed segregated schools is integral to recognizing competing goals of diversity within the CRM. Further, non-violent desegregation accounts, which represent the minority, are also essential for supporting students in building healthy skepticism so they are able to identify historical inconsistencies and overgeneralizations.

Responses to this view of desegregation might lead students to question other options the US government or civil rights leaders might have created to attain justice during this era. A discussion of the meaning of equity/fairness would prove fruitful here to address distinctions between equality (e.g., everyone in need of shoes receives them.) and equity/fairness (e.g., Everyone in need of shoes receives a well-fitting pair.). Topics of this sort can also segue into examinations of the role region played and how Ms. Evans' experiences were, in large part, shaped by her occupancy in the North. Rather than study desegregation in the more familiar context of the deep South, where racism is thought to have been confined, a look from this vantage point exposes stark similarities and should help students consider the negative feelings she developed toward desegregation despite no episodes of physical violence or verbal attacks. The hope here is to unsettle presumptions about the character of racism throughout various regions across the country, inducing student-centered analysis of a more critical lens.

Depending on prior knowledge students bring with them, it might be difficult to imagine individuals refuting the benefits of desegregation because few witness overt signs of racism today. As evidence, Anderson (2013) reminds us that "the trope of linear progress on race relations in U.S. history remains a seductive framework in part because it allows Americans both to avoid acknowledging persistent social inequalities and to sit in self-congratulatory judgment of previous generations for failing to recognize the evils of racism" (p. 118). Interpretations that frame desegregation as one of many options—one that some Black students like Ms. Evans felt were not the most beneficial for Black people—work against tidy, sanitized historical depictions that could well serve students. Approaching desegregation through the lens of oppositional views is one way to work against this falsehood and connect to inequity today.

Accounts that challenge contemporary understandings of pre-*Brown*, all-Black schools, depicting them instead as positive, may incite confusion, as historical accounts typically portray all-Black schools as dilapidated buildings with few resources and dismal funding (Anderson, 1988; Walker, 2000). Remembering that in her Black school, she knew she was deeply cared about by her teachers, held to the highest academic and behavioral expectations, and developing her cultural identity, Ms. Evans recalls points that pair well with scholarship highlighting similar conclusions. She also explains how upon moving to her desegregated school, her white teachers interacted only academically with her, whereas her teachers before nurtured her more holistically. Additionally, regular occasions her teachers created for her to see herself realistically represented in Black history lessons were experiences unmatched until high school under the tutelage of another Black woman teacher. By refocusing desegregation conversations away from the structural obstacles that created barriers to achievement, and toward the accomplishments all-Black schools were able to achieve in spite of them, teachers can support students in assessing the illegitimacy of the master-narrative.

The intangible qualities, such as holistically caring teachers, rites of passage, tight school-community connections, affirmation, and safety, remain missing from K–12 curricular accounts of this historical moment (Walker, 1996, 2001). This absence discloses historical omissions that have yet to be acknowledged or reconciled, for "the way we write and understand history often tells us what we want to believe about ourselves in the present" (Williamson, 2006, p. 36) and the past. Therefore, showing students the vast diversity of perspectives and the merits of looking on from a marginalized position alternatively casts desegregation as something that was not particularly necessary.

Hitting Content and Skills: Pedagogical Suggestions

Striking an effective balance between relaying content and developing skills is ever the social studies teacher's dilemma. A fruitful way to accomplish both tasks, often simultaneously, is through both/and means, which prevent teachers from having to choose one over the other (Delpit, 1988). Teaching desegregation from an intersectional perspective enables teachers to engage students around issues raised and allows students to cultivate skills they can utilize across disciplines and grade levels. Stressing historical complexity (e.g., differing opinions, enduring inequality) to students at any level cannot be overstated, as misunderstandings of the past threaten democracy. Emphasizing heterogeneous perspectives of underserved, marginalized groups proves tremendously vital in combating the master-narrative and present injustice.

Using a textbook or credible, online source as a starting point can help students grow critical analysis skills, and it encourages them to pose generative questions about missing perspectives. Supplementing provided curricula with Ms. Evans' account can inspire social awareness in students, making them better able to see and understand cases of social injustice and their antecedents. The College, Career, & Civic Life (C3) Framework for Social Studies Standards delineates dimensions suitable for evaluating content in this way. For this set of lessons, dimension two is fitting, and dimensions one and four also provide opportunities to address essential content without sacrificing complexity.[8]

An oral history project that allows students to interview someone who was attending public schools fifty to sixty years ago is one student-centered instructional option. This gives students the chance to conduct their own oral history projects centered around school experiences and desegregation. Teachers can support students in locating a potential interviewee by familiarizing themselves with community resources and facilitating student connections appropriately. An excellent opportunity to develop listening, writing, and synthesizing skills, classes can collectively draft a set of questions. After scheduling and conducting interviews, students can transcribe key portions of them, and offer their data as a primary text to be analyzed by classmates. Generating a class set of these narratives can serve as a response to silences in textbooks, strengthen historical understanding, and directly engage Common Core Standards around key ideas and details, craft and structure, and integration of knowledge and ideas.[9]

Incorporating excerpts from texts that examine the character and quality of all-Black schools pre-segregation can also demystify assumptions (Ramsey, 2008; Walker, 1996). These texts speak to Ms. Evans' memories about her segregated Black school, which she says served her very well, fortifying and challenging her in ways unmatched by desegregated schools she later attended—details too frequently excluded from textbook presentations of schools pre-*Brown*. Textual comparison would comprise a useful lesson or unit, whereby students can identify and interrogate textbook erasures and begin to conceptualize the diversity of thought as it manifested within the CRM. This suggestion could easily hit eight social studies Common Core Standards.[10]

Toward the end of the unit, closing class discussions could predict other possible strategies or demands that might have better served Black students in light of the new information students have learned. Excerpts from texts on the history of schools, like Dunbar High School in Washington D.C., may also play an important role in problematizing notions about Black students, communities, and schools (Sowell, 1974; Stewart, 2013). Equipping students with evidence that counters prevailing interpretations empowers them to rigorously scrutinize new information, which can develop into appropriate skepticism necessary in today's digital age of media and technology.

Teachers can also design enriching, student-centered lessons around the concepts of citizenship and civic ideals from the perspective of desegregating students and their families. Speculating about their sense of belonging to the country, their race, or other salient identities they held might aid students in wrestling with the significance of *the public good*. These topics can be explored through songs, movie scenes, or in structured discussion groups by either creating original works or drawing on those readily available. Taking up these matters with students can guide how they form understandings of citizenship and its purpose historically for disparate groups, informing and encouraging their civic participation. Viewing the category as malleable over time and contingent upon the historical moment can help students develop a sensitivity to the ebb and flow of civic life in the US and its context across communities.

Last, conversations about innovative methods Black communities engaged to supplement their educational expenses historically can enhance student perception. Local governments regularly taxed Black communities to pay for educational resources they did not receive, funds given to white students (Anderson, 1988). In response, Black communities taxed themselves again to fund their educational aspirations (Anderson, 1988). These narratives contest ideas about Black apathy toward education and hard work, broaching topics about how economics shape education. Sharing these excerpts with students is one way to begin related conversations, decode racist policies, and stimulate critical, creative thinking. Additional strategies include designing opportunities for students to evaluate media portrayals or inspect various texts where they analyze facets of the master-narrative.

Connection to Today

Most, if not all, of these topics are deeply relevant in today's political climate. From textbook discrepancies (Alridge, 2006; Anderson, 2013; Loewen, 1995; Paxton, 1999; Williamson, 2006), to privatization campaigns advocating school choice (Saltman, 2014), to affirmative action debates (Carbado, Turetsky, & Purdie-Vaughns, 2016), to free speech controversies (Garnett, 2008), to re-segregation patterns across the country (Boger & Orfield, 2009; DeCuir-Gunby & Taliaferro, 2013; Fiel, 2013), these subjects all bear heavily on the past and the present simultaneously. Each of these topics could be a standalone lesson, using the provided citations as a starting point. As a closing lesson for the end of a unit, this list of topics could serve as a jigsaw activity.

Ending or beginning with the contemporary relevance of these issues can help increase student interest. Discussions targeting the current implications of school (re)segregation may help students identify direct connections between the present and past. Coaching students to regularly weigh-in on the past, speculating what might have been is also an excellent way to frame unit objectives and compelling questions. The political, social, and economic queries raised through these investigations are timely, pressing, and salient, training students to seriously consider the role of these forces in their lives.

Successful social studies educators encourage students to raise their own compelling, controversial questions: a reasonable goal since the ability to critically question embodies a fundamental attribute of the citizenship ideals social studies champions. The material and suggestions I have provided represent an attempt to assist educators in meeting such a challenge by working to instill in students the audacity to wrestle with history, rejecting the neat, linear historical narratives of progress and improvement. In pushing back on conventional wisdom that diminishes the complexity of the CRM generally, and desegregation specifically, students and teachers become more able to both problem-pose (Freire, 1970) and problem-solve—competencies of which we stand in great need.

Appendix

Oral History of Desegregation: An Interview with Esther Evans

The following excerpts were taken from an oral history interview conducted by the author in 2017. The woman being interviewed is Ms. Esther Evans, who was born in 1954 and raised in a small, urban Midwestern city. Ms. Evans attended a racially segregated elementary school from kindergarten through fourth grade as a Black student. In part due to her mother's political activism, Ms. Evans left this school to begin fifth grade at a different, newly desegregated elementary school across town in 1963.

Ms. Evans went on to attend racially desegregated schools from fifth grade on, earning bachelor's and master's degrees from a predominantly white university in her hometown. She currently works as an administrator in higher education. Her memories, as recorded below, highlight important details about her Black, segregated school, the meaning and purpose of education for her, and differences she experienced in predominately white schools.

Partial transcript:

I didn't see why [school desegregation] was necessary. I felt that we were getting a kind of experience that we as Black students needed, and it just wasn't that at the white elementary school. I think the teachers there were unfamiliar with us and our style, and we certainly were unfamiliar with theirs.

[School] was about discipline, structure, living up to expectations, knowing you are cared about, that you learn, and making sure you do that ... [In our schools] you are taught by teachers who know you, who know your style, and have a better understanding of how to deal with you culturally. And these are people you see in your neighborhood, in the church, in the grocery store. We used to see our teachers in the grocery store, at church; they were really part of our community.

Our teachers, they taught like they were our parents, and it was the same kind of expectations and I don't know what the other teachers thought of us or expected from us, quite frankly. That was the other thing, our teachers [at our all-Black school] expected great things and were not going to take any excuses for you not living up to those expectations.

I do think my grounding at [my all-Black] school ... being around my people, culturally and developing my own cultural identity with a people and not just, I think had I started out at a predominately white school, I don't think I'd be the same person.

The discipline that our students had been accustomed to [in all-Black schools] and the affection that they were able to feel from their teachers, it's just not the same thing. It's been so important to us as a people. I mean, if your mama couldn't feed you at home because they were struggling, [our teachers] were giving kids something to eat in the classroom.

I don't think I performed any worse. In fact, I almost believe that the (white) teachers may have graded higher, meaning their expectations were lower because I was a straight A student over there, and that had never happened at my former all-Black school. There, we had to work for our grades.

The white teachers only discussed school with us. It was a very academic, student-teacher relationship. That was different from [our all-Black school]. You never felt like you could talk to (the white teachers) about anything outside of school.

And I said, Ma, you know the worst thing I think that could have happened to us, you know, is school desegregation. And you know, she was the one involved. And that's what she said, "I said that it's not that we want to sit, that we're dying to sit next to white students in classrooms. But the only way we can ensure we have the resources, the same books that are being taught to those [white] students, [is to make sure] that our students would have access to [them, too]."

This guy I know from the [neighborhood] … as an adult, he would say, you know, your mom was my favorite teacher. She taught at a local, all-Black elementary school. He told me when we would go into the classroom, she would comb our hair, straight-up our shirts, and make sure we were neat and clean and groomed, and then send them to their seats. There, they would have some kind of food or snack that she would bring in for them every day.

Notes

1. The author would like to thank Lauren Birks, Jeremy Bledsoe, Chaddrick Gallaway, Autumn Griffin, Tiffany Harris, Jessica Lopez, Shayla Perkins, and Janie Samreth for their thoughtful comments on a draft of this chapter.
2. See Loewen's (1995) Appendix (p. 376) for detailed citations of the twelve textbooks he investigated.
3. Journell's (2008) study examined secondary social studies standards from California, Georgia, Indiana, New York, North Carolina, Oklahoma, South Carolina, and Virginia. Anderson's (2013) analyzed K–12 social studies standards from Arizona, Washington, DC, Florida, Michigan, South Dakota, South Carolina, New Jersey, Washington, and Virginia.
4. North and Midwest are used here interchangeably to refer to states located above the Mason-Dixon line; "north" in this context simply means not the deep South, or the former Confederacy.
5. A pseudonym is used to protect the identity of the oral history interviewee.
6. Claudette Colvin, a Black teen girl, was the first to be arrested for refusing to give up her Montgomery, Alabama, bus seat in March of 1955. However, scholars observe

that civil rights leaders saw her youth, her status as an unmarried pregnant teen, and the physical altercation that ensued as law enforcement officials ejected her from the bus as making her less suitable than Mrs. Rosa Parks, who was arrested nine months later, as a bus boycott catalyst.

7. The Scottsboro case occurred in Alabama in the 1930s, where nine young African American boys, aged thirteen to nineteen, stood falsely accused of raping two White women. The NAACP hesitated to provide legal counsel in defense of the young Black men due to the taboo, sexual nature of the case, which leaders believed could place their reputation in jeopardy as an upstanding, reputable, respectable organization, thus harming their ability to fight structural racism long term.

8. Relevant C3 Standards in dimensions one (D1.2.6–8, D1.5.6–8), two (D2. Civ.2.6–8, D2.Civ.3.6–8, D2.Civ.7.6–8, D2.Civ.10.6–8, D2.Civ.13.6–8, D2.Civ.14.6–8, D2.His.3.6–8, D2.His.4.6–8, D2.His.5.6–8, D2.His.10.6–8, D2.His.15.6–8), and four (D4.1.6–8, D4.2.6–8). https://www.socialstudies.org/c3

9. Relevant Common Core Standards (CCSS.ELA-LITERACY.RH.6–8.1, CCSS. ELA-LITERACY.RH.6–8.2, CCSS.ELA-LITERACY.RH.6–8.5, CCSS.ELA-LITER-ACY.RH.6–8.6, CCSS-ELA-LITERACY.RH.6–8.8, CCSS.ELA-LITERACY.RH.6–8.9). http://www.corestandards.org/ELA-Literacy/RH/6–8/

10. Relevant Common Core Standards (CCSS.ELA-LITERACY.RH.6–8.1, CCSS. ELA-LITERACY.RH.6–8.2, CCSS.ELA-LITERACY.RH.6–8.4, CCSS.ELA-LITER-ACY.RH.6–8.5, CCSS.ELA-LITERACY.RH.6–8.6, CCSS.ELA-LITERACY.RH.6–8.8, CCSS.ELA-LITERACY.RH.6–8.9, and CCSS.ELA-LITERACY.RH.6–8.10).

References

Alridge, D. P. (2006). The limits of master narratives in history textbooks: An analysis of representations of Martin Luther King, Jr. *Teachers College Record, 108*(4), 662.

Anderson, C. B. (2013). The trouble with unifying narratives: African Americans and the Civil Rights Movement in US history content standards. *The Journal of Social Studies Research, 37*(2), 111–120.

Anderson, J. D. (1988). *The education of Blacks in the South, 1860–1935.* Chapel Hill, NC: University of North Carolina Press.

Beals, M. (1995). *Warriors don't cry: Searing memoir of battle to integrate little rock.* New York, NY: Simon and Schuster.

Boger, J. C., & Orfield, G. (Eds.). (2009). *School resegregation: Must the South turn back?* Chapel Hill, NC: University of North Carolina Press.

Brown v. Board of Education, 347 U.S. 483 (1954).

Brown v. Board of Education, 349 U.S. 295 (1955).

Brown, A. L., & Brown, K. D. (2010). Strange fruit indeed: Interrogating contemporary textbook representations of racial violence toward African Americans. *Teachers College Record, 112*(1), 31–67.

Carbado, D. W., Turetsky, K. M., & Purdie-Vaughns, V. (2016). Privileged or mismatched: The lose-lose position of African Americans in the affirmative action debate. *UCLA Law Review Discourse, 64,* 174.

Chick, K. A., & Corle, S. (2016). Confronting gender imbalance in high school history textbooks through the C3 framework. *Social Studies Research & Practice, 11*(2), 1–16.

Collins, P. H. (1986). Learning from the outsider within: The sociological significance of Black feminist thought. *Social problems, 33*(6), s14–s32.

Cox, J., & Stromquist, S. (Eds.). (1998). *Contesting the master narrative: Essays in social history.* Iowa City, IA: University of Iowa Press.

DeCuir-Gunby, J. T., & Taliaferro, J. D. (2013). Chapter 7: The impact of school resegregation on the racial identity development of African American students. *The Resegregation of Schools: Education and Race in the Twenty-First Century, 95,* 139.

Delpit, L. (1988). The silenced dialogue: Power and pedagogy in educating other people's children. *Harvard Educational Review, 58*(3), 280–299.

Dingus, J. E. (2006). "Doing the best we could": African American teachers' counterstory on school desegregation. *The Urban Review, 38*(3), 211–233.

Epstein, T. L. (1994). Tales from two textbooks: A comparison of the civil rights movement in two secondary history textbooks. *The Social Studies, 85*(3), 121–126.

Fiel, J. E. (2013). Decomposing school resegregation: Social closure, racial imbalance, and racial isolation. *American Sociological Review, 78*(5), 828–848.

Fields-Smith, C. (2005). African American parents before and after Brown. *Journal of Curriculum & Supervision, 20*(2): 129–135.

Freire, P. ([1970] 2000). *Pedagogy of the oppressed.* New York, NY: Bloomsbury Publishing.

Frost, J. (2012). Using "master narratives" to teach history: The case of the civil rights movement. *The History Teacher, 45*(3), 437–446.

Garnett, R. W. (2008). Can there really be free speech in public schools. *Lewis & Clark Law Review, 12,* 45.

Garrow, D. J. (1985). The origins of the Montgomery Bus Boycott. *Southern Changes, 7*(5), 21–27.

hooks, b. (2003). The oppositional gaze: Black female spectators. In A. Jones (Ed.), *The feminism and visual cultural reader* (pp. 94–105). New York, NY: Routledge.

Horsford, S. D. (2010). Mixed feelings about mixed schools: Superintendents on the complex legacy of school desegregation. *Educational Administration Quarterly, 46*(3), 287–321.

Journell, W. (2008). When oppression and liberation are the only choices: The representation of African Americans within state social studies standards. *Journal of Social Studies Research, 32*(1), 40.

LaSpina, J. A. (2003). Designing diversity: Globalization, textbooks, and the story of nations. *Journal of Curriculum Studies, 35,* 667–696.

Loewen, J. W. (1995). *Lies my teacher told me: Everything your American history textbook got wrong.* New York, NY: The New Press.

McGuire, D. L. (2004). "It was like all of us had been raped": Sexual violence, community mobilization, and the African American freedom struggle. *The Journal of American History, 91*(3), 906–931.

Miller, J. A., Pennybacker, S. D., & Rosenhaft, E. (2001). Mother Ada Wright and the international campaign to free the Scottsboro Boys, 1931–1934. *The American Historical Review, 106*(2), 387–430.

Morris, V. G., & Morris, C. L. (2002). *The price they paid: Desegregation in an African American community.* New York, NY: Teachers College Press.

Murray, H. T. (1967). The NAACP versus the Communist Party: The Scottsboro Rape Cases, 1931–1932. *Phylon (1960-), 28*(3), 276–287.

Paxton, R. J. (1999). A deafening silence: History textbooks and the students who read them. *Review of Educational Research, 69*(3), 315–339.

Plessy v. Ferguson, 63. U.S. 537 (1896).

Ramsey, S. Y. (2008). *Reading, writing, and segregation: A century of Black women teachers in Nashville* (Vol. 112). Champaign, IL: University of Illinois Press.

Saltman, K. J. (2014). Neoliberalism and corporate school reform: "Failure" and "creative destruction". *Review of Education, Pedagogy, and Cultural Studies, 36*(4), 249–259.

Schocker, J. B., & Woyshner, C. (2013). Representing African American women in US history textbooks. *The Social Studies, 104*(1), 23–31.

Schwartz, B. (2009). Collective forgetting and the symbolic power of oneness: The strange apotheosis of Rosa Parks. *Social Psychology Quarterly, 72*(2), 123–142.

Sowell, T. (1974, Spring). Black excellence: The case of Dunbar high school. *The Public Interest,* 35, 3.

Stewart, A. (2013). *First class: The legacy of Dunbar, America's first Black public high school.* Chicago Review Press.

Theoharis, J. (2015). *The Rebellious Life of Mrs. Rosa Parks.* Boston, MA: Beacon Press.

Tillman, L. C. (2004). (Un) intended consequences? The impact of the Brown v. Board of Education decision on the employment status of black educators. *Education and Urban Society, 36*(3), 280–303.

Walker, V. S. (1996). *Their highest potential: An African American school community in the segregated South.* Chapel Hill, NC: University of North Carolina Press.

Walker, V. S. (2000). Valued segregated schools for African American children in the South, 1935–1969: A review of common themes and characteristics. *Review of Educational Research, 70*(3), 253–285.

Walker, V. S. (2001). African American teaching in the South: 1940–1960. *American Educational Research Journal, 38*(4), 751–779.

Williamson, J. A. (2006). A tale of two movements: The power and consequences of misremembering Brown. *Yearbook of the National Society for the Study of Education, 105*(2), 36–57.

Wills, J. S. (2005). "Some people even died": Martin Luther King, Jr, the civil rights movement and the politics of remembrance in elementary classrooms. *International Journal of Qualitative Studies in Education, 18*(1), 109–131.

Woodson, A. N. (2017). "There ain't no white people here" master narratives of the civil rights movement in the stories of urban youth. *Urban Education, 52*(3), 316–342.

12. The GI Forum, Felix Longoria and El Movimiento: *Understanding the Latina/o Civil Rights Movement through Critical Historical Inquiry*

CINTHIA S. SALINAS, AMANDA E. VICKERY, AND
NOREEN NASEEM RODRIGUEZ

For Mexican Americans, Tejanas/os, Chicanas/os or Mexicanas/os in the United States Southwest the early historical, economic and geographic narrative of their civic-ness is long and vast, stretching as far back as Mayans, Incas, and Aztecs as well as the Navajo and Apache. The story of their identities, agency and membership as citizens/noncitizens extends as far away as Spain and Mexico and includes early Spanish and French colonizers like Hernán Cortés, Álvar Nuñez Cabeza de Vaca, and Robert Cavelier de La Salle, illegal immigrants like Davy Crockett and William Travis, and American invaders like Major General Zachary Taylor (see Gonzalez, 1999; Meier & Ribera, 1972). Since 1848 under the Treaty of Guadalupe Hidalgo, Mexican Americans, Tejanas/os, Chicanas/os or Mexicanas/os have been a part of the American narrative (see Montejano, 1987). The inclusion of Puerto Ricans and Cubans, as well as Guatemalans, Nicaraguan, El Salvadorians and so forth also bring to our national story the civic-ness of other Latinas/os[1] and is essential in understanding an expansive Latinidad as well as the intra group differences of the community (see MacDonald, 2013; Menchaca, 2001; San Miguel, 2011).

However, the official school narrative in general neglects these dark histories, contested geographic spaces, and dubious exploitations of economies (see Gómez, 2007). Most often, Latinas/os are reduced to the Mexican American War, Spanish American War and Cesar Chavez (see Wills, 2001). The challenge at hand is not new since scholars (see Barton & Levstik, 2004;

Epstein, 2009; Trouillot, 1995) have long critiqued the nation-building and celebratory narrative that entails a shallow understanding of history, offers few opportunities for more advanced analysis and consequently promotes passive consumers rather than active and engaged learners (see VanSledright, 2008). For Latinas/os the problematic narrative and its construction (see Salinas, Fránquiz, & Naseem Rodriguez, 2016) is compounded by "a pattern of 'knowing but not believing'" and need for counter narratives in response to a sense of "'believing but not knowing'" (Wertsch, 2000, p. 39).

With this project we examine the challenge of the dominant narrative taught in social studies classrooms as well as reasons why teachers and their students might consider taking up the narrative of the Latina/o civil rights movement, *el movimiento,* through more critical uses of historical inquiry. We use the well documented but rarely taught case study of WWII Private Felix Longoria and the civil rights organization the G. I. Forum, led by their president Dr. Hector P. Garcia, to examine a crucial event in Latinas/os' struggle for equality. In asking the larger question, how did Latinas/os plan and engage in *el movimiento?* We consider at least two fundamental reasons why this question is often omitted from the school curriculum. First, we return to the age old argument regarding for "whom curriculum and knowledge is developed for" (see Apple 1992, 2004) and consequently encourage teachers to continuously question and pursue the curriculum as dynamic and including rather than static and excluding. Second, we acknowledge that teaching *other* histories can reveal the tensions of history vs. heritage (see Levy, 2014; Lowenthal, 1998), ethnic identity (see Halagao, 2004) as well as the challenges of teaching traumatic and/or difficult histories (see Stoddard, Marcus, & Hicks, 2014). Regardless, the onus of engaging in narratives that provide Latinas/os with portraits of their civic identity, agency and membership are essential if we are to prepare the next generation of citizens.

Attention to the Narrative

The growing availability of digitized historical archives and resulting opportunity for promoting historical inquiry has introduced distinctive instructional opportunities for classroom teachers. First, at the heart of historical inquiry is a shift away from textbooks or second hand accounts that treat teachers and students as passive consumers of historical narratives. Through historical inquiry and the use of primary sources, teachers and students may instead engage in the interpretation of the historical evidence at hand and the construction of historical narratives that are supported through their own reasoning (see Stearns, Seixas, & Wineburg, 2000). The use of historical inquiry focuses on not only historical significance and change over time, but also the nature of historical evidence asking when a primary source was produced, for whom and for what purpose. Moreover, in examining letters, journal entries, government documents, photographs and so forth, teachers and students attend to the choices, dilemmas, struggles and decisions people from the past encountered (see Seixas & Peck, 2004). Through perspective taking and a lens on agency, we can empathize with and empower those from the past by deepening our understanding of their circumstances and actions (see Barton & Levstik, 2004).

Second, the use of historical inquiry also lends itself to more deliberate attention to those narratives all too often excluded or neglected by the official school curriculum. Rather than dominant and often simplistic stories of America's progress and homogeneity, more complex narratives and in particular the histories of women and communities of color can be deliberately reclaimed through more critical uses of historical inquiry. For classroom teachers the focus on these counter narratives through critical historical inquiry include historical, geographic and economic perspectives that portray the civic identities as well as agency and membership of African Americans, Latinas/os, Asian Americans, Native Americans and women that are not traditionally included in the telling of America's story (see Salinas & Blevins, 2014; Salinas, Blevins, & Sullivan, 2012). Embedded in these narratives are the ways in which communities of color and women have participated in our democracy, demonstrated their civic commitments, and forged forth their roles as citizens. There can be little doubt that in our increasingly culturally and linguistically diverse school settings, these narratives reflect a civic identity and sense of agency and membership essential to developing an enlightened and engaged citizenry (see Westheimer & Kahne, 2004).

Finally, using critical historical inquiry as a means to teach more inclusive narratives that also reflect the civic identities, agency and membership of women and Communities of Color is well aligned with several standards based approaches. For example, the National Council for Social Studies (NCSS) includes thematic strands like (1) Culture, (2) Time, Continuity and Change, and (3) Individuals, Groups, and Institutions that promote the development of more critical applications of historical inquiries and narratives that complicate, nuance or counter commonly held understandings of history, geography and economics (see Table 12.1). Numerous other themes could also be applicable based on the teacher's instructional design.

Likewise, the College, Career, and Civic Life: C3 Framework for Social Studies Standards supports more critical applications of historical inquiries through the Inquiry Arc by (a) developing of questions and planning

Table 12.1 Sample of National Council for Social Studies Strands (NCSS).

(1) Culture: Through the study of culture and cultural diversity, learners understand how human beings create, learn, share, and adapt to culture, and appreciate the role of culture in shaping their lives and society, as well the lives and societies of others. In schools, this theme typically appears in units and courses dealing with geography, history, sociology, and anthropology, as well as multicultural topics across the curriculum.
(2) Time, Continuity, and Change: Through the study of the past and its legacy, learners examine the institutions, values, and beliefs of people in the past, acquire skills in historical inquiry and interpretation, and gain an understanding of how important historical events and developments have shaped the modern world. This theme appears in courses in history, as well as in other social studies courses for which knowledge of the past is important.
(3) Individuals, Groups, and Institutions: Institutions such as families and civic, educational, governmental, and religious organizations, exert a major influence on people's lives. This theme allows students to understand how institutions are formed, maintained, and changed, and to examine their influence. In schools, this theme typically appears in units and courses dealing with sociology, anthropology, psychology, political science, and history.

Source: NCSS Social Studies Standards (2012).

inquiries, (b) applying of disciplinary concepts and tools (c) evaluating sources and using evidence, and (d) communicating conclusions and taking informed action. Disciplinary concepts and tools standards can include Civics, Geography and History standards (Table 12.2). Again, teachers and their students can readily identify other standards.

The Challenge at Hand in Teaching El Movimiento

We contend that teachers seeking to include Latina/o perspectives through critical historical inquiry must initially confront some general challenges. First, the inclusion of other narratives requires deep content knowledge hidden away from most classroom teachers. Knowing the history of Latinas/os would for instance focus upon how the United States negated the original articles IX and X of the Treaty of Guadalupe Hidalgo (1848) granting American citizenship and property rights to those Mexicans now on the other side of the newly drawn border (Griswold del Castillo, 1996). Teachers would likely need to explore the importance of community-based organizations, *mutualistas,* that served to both sustain and acculturate new Mexican American citizens in 1800 and 1900s (Calderón, 2000; Zamora, 2000). A myriad of legal cases like *Romo v. Laird* (1925), *Mendez et al. v. Westminster* (1947),

Table 12.2 C3 Dimension 2, Applying Disciplinary Concepts and Tools.

Civics: Civic and Political Institutions	D2.Civ.2.9–12. Analyze the role of citizens in the U.S. political system, with attention to various theories of democracy, changes in Americans' participation over time, and alternative models from other countries, past and present.	D2.Civ.5.9–12. Evaluate citizens' and institutions' effectiveness in addressing social and political problems at the local, state, tribal, national, and/or international level.
Geography: Human-Environment Interaction	D2.Geo.5.9–12. Evaluate how political and economic decisions throughout time have influenced cultural and environmental characteristics of various places and regions.	
History: Change, Continuity, and Context	D2.His.1.9–12. Evaluate how historical events and developments were shaped by unique circumstances of time and place as well as broader historical contexts.	D2.His.4.9–12. Analyze complex and interacting factors that influenced the perspectives of people during different historical eras.
History: Perspectives	D2.His.4.9–12. Analyze complex and interacting factors that influenced the perspectives of people during different historical eras.	D2.His.5.9–12. Analyze how historical contexts shaped and continue to shape people's perspectives.
History: Perspectives	D2.His.6.9–12. Analyze the ways in which the perspectives of those writing history shaped the history that they produce.	

Source: C3 Framework, NCSS (2017).

Hernandez v. Texas (1954) and *Keyes v. School District No. 1, Denver* (1973) that challenged the segregation practices endured by Mexican Americans are essential in recognizing the persistence of the community (see San Miguel & Valencia, 1998). Likewise, the immeasurable contributions of civil rights organizations like the La Liga Protectora Mexicana (1917), League of United Latin Americans Citizens (1929), the Mexican American Youth Organization (1967), and the Mexican American Legal Defense Fund (1968) to name a few reflect a vibrant and active struggle for equality (see Gonzalez, 1999). However, one can begin to utilize a wealth of knowledge only after considering the distinct histories, economies and geographies of Mexican Americans living in Arizona, California, Colorado, Nevada, New Mexico, Texas, Utah and Wyoming (see Acuña, 2004).

Second, beyond the need for considerable content knowledge, teachers and students might also consider how easy it would be to reduce the history of the Mexican American community to a few key figures and events and how those figures and events might be portrayed without regard to fuller narratives. For example, often noted in the dominant narrative are the contributions of Cesar Chavez, a civil rights activist and founder of the United Farm Workers Union. The numerous schools, streets, parks and state holidays named after him are a shrine to his motto "Sí, se puede" stand on behalf of migrant farm workers. However, what is commonly missing from the grand narrative is the equal importance of the co-founder of the UFW-Dolores Huerta who actually originated the phrase, "Sí, se puede." Likewise what is also commonly missing is the importance of the Filipino Agricultural Workers Organizing Committee (AWOC) to the farm labor movement. In no way do we diminish the significance of Cesar Chavez, but teachers should question how the narrative came to ignore Dolores Huerta and the vast organization and efforts of the communities who were fundamental to a rich history of labor organization and resistance (García, 2008; Lien, 2010).

Third, historians have long argued on behalf of the "long civil rights movement" as opposed to our shortened memory that reduces or contains the struggle for equality to the 1960s and early 1970s (e.g. Hall, 2005). In noting the Treaty of Guadalupe Hidalgo (1848) we argue the struggle for equality and the civic identities, agency and membership of Mexican Americans began long before the Civil Rights Act of 1964 and 1965. Likewise in marking the Treaty of Guadalupe Hidalgo (1848), mutualistas, legal precedents, civil rights organizations and fundamental flaws in simplistic and narrow narratives, we note a more compelling timeline—creating a portrait of an engaged citizenry that "struggle[ed] to build communities, claim social rights, and become recognized as active agents in society" (Flores & Benmayor, 1997, p. 2). Consequently teaching and learning *el movimiento* reflects a long-standing resistance and claims for citizenship. Moreover, the inclusion of *el movimiento* moves teachers' and students' thinking beyond a Black/white binary that dominates our thinking regarding race and male-centric narrative that ignores the intersectionality of race and gender (Vickery, 2017).

The Longoria Affair as a Case Study of Civicness

How did Latinas/os plan and engage in *el movimiento*? For the Latina/o community there are countless cases of opposition, resistance and participation that teachers and learners can draw from to deepen their understanding of *el movimiento*. For example, as Latina/o World War II veterans returned home as heroes who had served their nation, they encountered the enduring consequences of racism and discrimination. Organizing as a community the GI Forum (1948) in Corpus Christi, Texas, the veterans, led by Dr. Hector P. Garcia, initially called for equal access to medical care but eventually began to join others in advocating for the education, economic and political rights of all Mexican Americans (García, 2002).

On June 16th 1945 Private Felix Longoria, a native of Three Rivers, Texas, died on the island of Luzon in the Philippines. In January of 1949, his wife received notice that his body had been recovered and would soon arrive in the United States. As Beatrice Longoria sought to make final arrangements for her husband's funeral, she was told by the Rice Funeral Home manager Tom. W. Kennedy that Private Longoria's family would not be able to use the chapel because Mexican Americans had never been allowed to use the space. Denied access to the chapel, the family was distraught, however almost immediately Dr. Garcia of the GI Forum was contacted as well as George Groh, writer for the local newspaper the Corpus Christi Caller-Times. While Mexican Americans had endured such acts of racism before, the act of discrimination was now targeted at a war veteran—one who had lost his life in defense of our great nation. Unexpectedly Dr. Garcia, the GI Forum and the family of Private Felix Longoria were about to launch the campaign that brought *el movimiento* to the national conscious.

Primary One: Gran Junta De Protesta

A flurry of activity immediately occurred including a hurriedly called meeting of the GI Forum (see Lesson Plans and Resources). The GI Forum meeting flyer sets the stage for what is now known as the "Longoria Affair." Though written in Spanish there are enough cognates so that teachers and students will want to ask the typical sourcing questions (e.g., What type of primary source is this? And for whom was it written and for what purpose?). The flyer will allow readers to ask what is meant by a "*Gran Junta De Protesta*" as well as where and when the *gran junta de protesta* was held. Readers might be interested in who "Dr. Hector P. Garcia, Pres." was and his contributions to this entire event. Importantly, students should be asked about the inclusion and purpose of key words that are in bolded face and/or large caps including *Gran Junta De Prostesta, negado, soldado, cruel, humillacion,* and *veteranos.* As historians would do, the larger and bolded face passage ("Cuando una casa funeraria … protestar esta injusticia") in the center of the flyer should be translated by the teacher or students since the texts present the crux of the Longoria Affair. Questions regarding the Latina/a communities' indignation and ability to organize and resist should become central to the discussion (American G. I. Forum, 1949).

At least two invaluable conversations can be yielded through interrogating the flyer. First, the flyer contains the language and agency of citizens who have been maligned, mistreated and denied their rights as American heroes some of whom gave their lives to our democracy. The injustice extends beyond the Mexican American veterans of World War II by negating the sacrifices of their families and entire communities. Secondly, the flyer is written in Spanish not because the members of the GI Forum and others from the community could not speak English or were uneducated but because it is the language of their heritage and their right to organize and protest in the language of their choice. Language should be seen as a central and inseparable element of the civic identity of Mexican American veterans and civil rights advocates.

Primary Two: The Un-American Action of the Rice Funeral Home

The night before the GI Forum *Gran Junta De Prostesta* on January 10, Dr. Garcia sent telegrams of appeal to the Texas governor, state Attorney General, a state senator, two congressman, Good Neighbor Commission, the Secretary of Defense and President Harry Truman, on behalf of the Longoria family and as the president of the GI Forum. Each of the recipients responded to one degree or another. However, Dr. Garcia wrote a more detailed letter to newly elected senator Lyndon Baines Johnson. The letter (see Lesson Plans and Resources) details the grievances regarding not only the case of Felix Longoria but also those more common events of racism and discrimination encountered by all Mexican Americans. As teachers and students examine the nature of the source, they will consider when and why the letter was written. They might then begin to ask what arguments does Dr. Garcia make and how do these claims further not only the case on behalf of Felix Longoria but also how do they further the entire *movimiento?* What becomes important again is for teachers and students to consider the exact language chosen by Dr. Garcia and if that language reveals a deliberate strategy on the part of the GI Forum as a civil rights organization.

With the GI Forum meeting flyer and letter from Dr. Garcia and the GI Forum to the Honorable Lyndon Johnson, the understanding of the Felix

Longoria Affair begins to reflect the angst the Longoria family as well as the members of the GI Forum must have experienced, as well as the symbolic import the case begins to represent. The broadening conversation might lead students to predict how LBJ will respond to Hector P. Garcia and the GI Forum's request. The historical tensions between Latinas/os and whites might prompt many teachers and students to believe that Senator Johnson will not act in support of the Longoria family and GI Forum. One might also imagine that students will consider LBJ as a politically astute Texan that will assist in hopes of his own political aspirations. Finally, perhaps some readers will consider that LBJ was a former school teacher in Cotulla, Texas, and had worked dutifully on behalf of Mexican American students and would later sign the Civil Rights Acts of 1964 and 1965.

Primary Three: LBJ Offers an Honorable Solution

LBJ's telegram response to Dr. Garcia and the GI Forum arrived as the meeting was being held on January 10 and was read to the entire group present. One can only imagine the relief if not celebration experienced that night by the Longoria family and Dr. Garcia and other members of the GI Forum. As teachers and students read the telegram as a primary source, they should note the date and the salutations as well as LBJ's signature. Most students will need to learn about telegrams and their prevalence during this time period in conveying information quickly. Considering LBJ as a leader of our nation, the students may focus on the limits of his power (e.g. "I have not authority over civilian funeral homes …") as well as the use of his power in offering two honorable solutions (e.g. "I am happy to have a part in seeing that this Texas hero is laid to rest with the honor and dignity he deserves."). Readers cannot help but also note LBJ's choice of language in rebuffing racism (e.g. "this injustice and prejudice is deplorable …") and elevating Felix Longoria and other veterans (e.g. "… where the honored dead of our nation rest …"). Teachers may take this opportunity to contrast and compare the perspectives as well as the agency of the Longoria family, the GI Forum and Dr. Garcia, and Senator Johnson. Ultimately, the inquiry begs for the larger question of how Latinas/os planned and engaged in *el movimiento?*

Understanding the Latina/o Civil Rights Movement through Critical Historical Inquiry

The story of the Felix Longoria Affair is much more complex than the reading of three primary sources can reveal. There is a cache of primary sources that could further our understandings of not only this incident but the political relationship that grew between Dr. Garcia and Lyndon Baines Johnson. However, through the short critical inquiry project outlined here, students will most likely begin to view Latinas/os as citizens that participated in defending our democracy, organized in hopes of equality and prosperity and utilized those principles of a republic to assert their rights.

Importantly, the case exemplar of the Longoria Affair becomes a means by which other narratives—even more contemporary narratives-can emerge. The enduring struggle for civic membership can be centered through the Bracero Program (1942–1964), Operation Wetback (1954), English-only movements, the Development, Relief, and Education for Alien Minors Act (DREAM ACT) (MacDonald, 2013) and the stories of civil rights activist like Emma Tenayuca, Martha Cortera and Irma Rangel (Garcia, Martinez-Ebers, Corondano, Navarro, & Jaramillo, 2008). At the heart of these narratives is controversy and trauma, difficult and dark histories and the challenge of ensuring the civic identities, agency and membership of Latinas/os who are embodied in the narratives of our social studies classrooms.[1]

Note

1. For the purpose of this project we use the term Latina/o for the broader Latinidad of Mexican Americans, Tejanas/os, Chicanas/os or Mexicanas/os, Puerto Ricans, Cubans, Guatemalans, Nicaraguan, El Salvadorians and others communities. In no way does the term "Latina/o" capture the unique and complex histories and identities of each community. When appropriate we will use more explicit identities for example in describing Puerto Ricans and Spanish Harlem.

References

Acuña, R. (2004). *Occupied America: A History of Chicanos.* Harlow, England: Pearson Longman.

American G. I. Forum. (1949) *Gran Junta de ProtestaI.* [Flyer]. Retrieved from http://omeka.tamucc.edu/items/show/4.

Apple, M. (1992). The text and cultural politics. *Educational Researcher, 21*(7), 4–11.

Apple, M. (2004). *Ideology and curriculum.* New York, NY: RoutledgeFalmer.

Barton, K., & Levstik, L. (2004). *Teaching history for the common good.* Mahwah, NJ: Lawrence Erlbaum.

Calderón, R. (2000). Unión, Paz y trabajo: Laredo's Mexican mutual aid societies, 1890s. In E. Zamora, C. Orozco, & R. Rocha (Eds.), *Mexican Americans in Texas history* (pp. 63–77). Austin, TX: Texas State Historical Association.

Epstein, T. (2009). *Interpreting national history: Race, identity, and pedagogy in classrooms and communities.* New York, NY: Routledge.

Flores, W., & Benmayor, R. (Eds.). (1997). Constructing cultural citizenship. In W. Flores & R. Benmayor (Eds.), *Latino cultural citizenship: Claiming identity, space, and rights* (pp. 1–23). Boston, MA: Beacon Press.

Garcia, I. M. (2002). *Hector P. Garcia: In relentless pursuit of justice.* Houston, TX: Arte Público Press.

García, M. T. (Ed.). (2008). *A Dolores Huerta reader.* Albuquerque, NM: UNM Press.

Garcia, S. R., Martinez-Ebers, V., Corondano, I., Navarro, S. A., & Jaramillo, P. A. (2008). *Políticas: Latina public official in Texas.* Austin, TX: University of Texas Press.

Gómez, L. E. (2007). *Manifest destinies: The making of the Mexican American race.* New York: NYU Press.

Gonzalez, M. G. (1999). *Mexicanos: A history of Mexicans in the United States.* Bloomington, IN: Indiana University Press.

Griswold del Castillo, R. (1996). The treaty of Guadalupe Hidalgo. In O. Martinez (Ed.), *U.S.-Mexico Borderlands: Historical and contemporary perspectives* (pp. 2–9). Wilmington, DE: Scholarly Resources Inc.

Halagao, P. E. (2004). Holding up the mirror: The complexity of seeing your ethnic self in history. *Theory and Research in Social Education, 32*(4), 459–483.

Hall, J. (2005). The long civil rights movement and the political uses of the past. *The Journal of American History, 91*(4), 1233–1263.

Levy, S. A. (2014). Heritage, history, and identity. *Teachers College Record, 116*(6), 1–34.

Lien, P. T. (2010). *Making of Asian America: Through political participation.* Philadelphia, PA: Temple University Press.

Lowenthal, D. (1998). *The heritage crusade and the spoils of history.* New York, NY: Cambridge University Press.

MacDonald, V. M. (2013). Demanding their rights: The Latino struggle for educational access and equity. *American Latinos and the Making of the United States: A Theme Study. Washington, DC: National Park Service, US Department of Interior.*

Meier, M. S., & Ribera, F. (1972). *Mexican Americans/American Mexicans: From conquistadors to Chicanos.* New York, NY: Hill and Wang.

Menchaca, M. (2001). *Recovering history, constructing race: The Indian, black, and white roots of Mexican Americans.* Austin, TX: University of Texas Press.

Montejano, D. (1987). *Anglos and Mexicans in the making of Texas, 1836–1986.* Austin, TX: University of Texas Press.

National Council for the Social Studies. (2010). *National Curriculum Standards for Social Studies: A Framework for Teaching, Learning and Assessment.* Silver Spring, MD: NCSS.

National Council for the Social Studies. (2017). *College, Career and Civil Life (C3) Framework for Social Studies State Standards: Guidance for Enhancing the Rigor of K-12 Civics, Economics, Geography, and History.* Silver Spring, MD.: NCSS.

Salinas, C., & Blevins, B. (2014). Critical historical inquiry: How might pre-service teachers confront master historical narratives. *Social Studies Research and Practice, 9*(3), 35–50.

Salinas, C., Blevins, B., & Sullivan, C. (2012). Critical historical thinking: When official narratives collide with *other* narratives. *Multicultural Perspectives, 14*(1), 18–27.

Salinas, C., Fránquiz, M., & Rodriguez, N. (2016). Writing Latina/o historical narratives: Narratives at the intersection of critical historical inquiry. *Urban Review, 48*(2), 264–284.

San Miguel, G. (2011). Embracing Latinidad: Beyond nationalism in the history of education. *Journal of Latinos and Education, 10*(1), 3–22.

San Miguel, G., & Valencia, R. R. (1998). From the treaty of Guadalupe Hidalgo to Hopwood: The educational plight and struggle of Mexican Americans in the southwest. *Harvard Educational Review, 68*(3), 353–412.

Seixas, P., & Peck, C. (2004). Teaching historical thinking. In A. Sears & I. Wright (Eds.), *Challenges and prospects for Canadian School Studies* (pp. 109–117). Vancouver, BC: Pacific Educational Press.

Stearns, P., Seixas, P., & Wineburg, S. (Eds.). (2000). *Knowing, teaching, and learning history: National and international perspectives.* New York, NY: New York University.

Stoddard, J. D., Marcus, A. S., & Hicks, D. (2014). The burden of historical representation: The case of/for indigenous film. *The History Teacher, 48*(1), 9–36.

Trouillot, M. (1995). *Silencing the past.* Boston, MA: Beacon Press.

VanSledright, B. A. (2008). Narratives of nation state, historical knowledge & school history education. *Review of Research in Education, 32*(1), 1–38.

Vickery, A. E. (2017). "Women know how to get things done": Narrative of an intersectional movement. *Social Studies Research and Practice, 12*(1), 31–41.

Wertsch, J. (2000). Is it possible to teach beliefs, as well as knowledge about history. In P. Sterns, P. Sexias, & S. Wineburg (Eds.), *Knowing teaching and learning history: National and international perspectives* (pp. 38–50). New York, NY: New York Press University.

Westheimer, J., & Kahne, J. (2004). What kind of citizen? The politics of education for democracy. *American Educational Research Journal, 41*(2), 237–269.

Wills, J. (2001). Missing in interaction: Diversity, narrative, and critical multicultural social studies. *Theory and Research in Social Education, 29*(1), 43–64.

Zamora, R. (2000). Mutualist and Mexicanist expression of a political culture in Texas. In E. Zamora, C. Orozco, & R. Rocha (Eds.), *Mexican Americans in Texas history* (pp. 83–101). Austin, TX: Texas State Historical Association.

Section 3

Lesson Plans and Resources

Appendix: Teaching Civil Rights Using Inquiry Design Method: Lesson Plans and Resources

All lesson plans use the Inquiry Design Model (IDM) template from the College, Career and Civic Life Framework. IDM and all inquiries published on C3. Teachers are licensed under an Attribution-ShareAlike 4.0 International (CC BY-SA 4.0) license.

Table A1: The Evolving Civil Rights Movement Jayne R. Beilke	
Compelling Question	How has the struggle for civil rights evolved, adapted and continued within the history of the United States beyond what is present in textbooks and American grand narrative?
Standards and Practices	**NCSS Strand 2:** Time Continuity and Change Social studies programs should include experiences that provide for the study of the past and its legacy. **NCSS Strand 3:** People Places and the Environment Social studies programs should include experiences that provide for the study of people, places, and environments. **NCSS Strand 5**: Individuals, Groups and Institutions Social studies programs should include experiences that provide for the study of interactions among individuals, groups, and institutions.

	NCSS Strand 6: Power Authority and Governance Social studies programs should include experiences that provide for the study of how people create, interact with, and change structures of power, authority, and governance. **NCSS Strand 10:** Civic Ideals and Practice Social studies programs should include experiences that provide for the study of the ideals, principles, and practices of citizenship in a democratic republic.
Staging the Question	Starting with some current news stories and reports (i.e., Black Lives Matter) students consider the connections to the concepts of Civil Rights, Authority, Government, Law and Society. Teachers/Students reflect on their multicultural curriculum experience, using Banks Four Typologies of Curriculum (Contributions, Additive, Transformative, Social Justice). Students identify what they know, and what they could learn more about as Teachers/Students (KWL)

Supporting Question 1	Supporting Question 2	Supporting Question 3
How has the Civil Rights Movement been presented through official textbooks and standards? (What do you think you already know about who, what, where, when and why?)	What lines of inquiry/ questions can we develop to probe these concepts deeper? (Who, What, Where, When, Why beyond the basics)	How are these concepts and struggles alive in today's society?
Formative Performance Task	**Formative Performance Task**	**Formative Performance Task**
Prezi Concept Map Creation (collaborative with other members of the class/group)	Prezi Concept Map Creation (collaborative with other members of the class/group)	Prezi Concept Map Creation (collaborative with other members of the class/group)
Featured Sources	**Featured Sources**	**Featured Sources**
Sutori.com http://timeglider.com/ Online Digital Archives and Findings Aids—Library of Congress https://www.loc.gov/collections/?q=Civil+Rights+MOvement	Presidential Libraries and Archives University Libraries and Archives	Online Museum Exhibits National Museum of African American History & Culture https://nmaahc.si.edu/

Summative Performance Task	Argument	The march for civil rights continues today due to a truncated understanding of the "civil rights movement" as a short time span and limited to African Americans.
	Extension	Students can create interactive museum displays using the Augmented Reality program Aurasma.
Taking Informed Action	Contacting local museums to develop displays that are more accurate Contacting local museums and developing digitally interactive augmented reality displays Identifying local areas of interest to provide more robust commentary and accuracy.	

Swan, Lee, and Swan, 2014

Table A2: Segregation in the United States Today Gary A. Homana			
Compelling Question	How does segregation occur in the United States today?		
Standards and Practices	CCR Anchor Standard (Maryland). Grades 11–12. Draw evidence from literary or informational texts to support analysis, reflection and research. Inquiry Standard: Analyze the major developments, controversies and consequences of the Civil Rights Movement between 1946 and 1968		
Staging the Question	What are the effects of legalized segregation (Jim Crow) in the United States		
Supporting Question 1	**Supporting Question 2**	**Supporting Question 3**	**Supporting Question 4**
What is your understanding about legalized segregation in the United States?	What was Jim Crow and what role did it play in segregation?	What role did African American communities in Baltimore play in the lives of their children?	How does life under Jim Crow compare to life for African Americans and other people of color today?
Formative Performance Task	**Formative Performance Task**	**Formative Performance Task**	**Formative Performance Task**
During class: Each student outlines responses to each of the following questions using the three-columned table: What was legal segregation? How were children and communities affected by legal segregation? What were the implications of legal segregation for learning? **In class activity** (small groups):	**Before class:** Each student explores the three sources and develops a list defining Jim Crow, where it existed and why, how it affected the lives of African Americans, and actions taken to eliminate legalized segregation. Each student also writes at least one full page in her/his reflection	**In Class:** Students watch the film, *Voices of Baltimore* paying attention to how the film participants describe their lives under legalized segregation and the role that the black communities played. Each student writes down responses in	**In Class:** The class is divided into two or four groups (depending on size). One group (or set of two groups) reads *The New Jim Crow* and the other group (or set of two groups) reads *Educating for Insurgency.* In addition, each student finds

Students engage in critical discussion about their responses to the three questions examining similarities and differences. Following the discussion they write in their reflection journal about how their thinking has changed based on the discussion and why.	journal about what they think about Jim Crow and its implications for the lives of African Americans. **In-class activity** (small groups): Students engage in critical discussion about their reactions to Jim Crow written in their reflection journals. After the discussion, each student writes in her/his reflection journal how their thinking has been challenged/changed based on the discussion and why.	her/his reflection journal then writes at least one full page analysis examining her/his initial thoughts and assumptions about life under Jim Crow in Q1, how it has changed and why, especially regarding expectations for how academic achievement, moral integrity, and responsibility to others in the community. Students also review the Louis S. Diggs website looking specifically at the overview of his books to provide context for black life in Baltimore. **In-class activity** (small/large groups): Students engage in critical discussion about their journal reflections focusing especially on the community expectations for education and academic achievement,	a newspaper article related to an issue raised in their book. Using this newspaper article, each student writes in his/her journal a critical analysis of the article topic comparing and contrasting the old Jim Crow to the article. This analysis will serve as the basis of an action component in the "Taking Informed Action" section of this lesson plan. **In-class activity** (small group discussion): Students meet in small groups based on their book chapters to discuss and begin to prepare a short multimodal presentation to the class.

		moral integrity, and responsibility to others in the community. They also explore in their groups how this differs from how they view urban communities today and why. Students return to their journals and write at least a one page analysis of their small group discussion. Next, utilizing all material and discussions to-date the entire class has a critical discussion about the three questions from supporting question one.	
Featured Sources	**Featured Sources**	**Featured Sources**	**Featured Sources**
Source A: Three-columned table **Source B:** Reflection journal	**Source A**: The Rise and Fall of Jim Crow (http://www.pbs.org/wnet/jimcrow/) **Source B**: The Jim Crow Museum of Racist Memorabilia (http://www.ferris.edu/jimcrow/index.htm) **Source C**: Jim Crow photo bank	**Source A**: *Voices of Baltimore: Life under Segregation* (film documentary available soon on the *Voices of Baltimore* website) **Source B:** Website, Louis S Diggs (http://www.louisdiggs.com/books.html)	**Source A:** Select chapter(s) from *The new Jim Crow: Mass incarceration in the Age of colorblindness.* (Alexander, 2011). See for example Chapter 5—The New Jim Crow. **Source B:** *Educating for*

	and map/sign of the Mason-Dixon Line		*insurgency: The roles of young people in schools of poverty* (Gillen, 2014). See for example Part 1, pp. 39–75. **Source C:** Select newspaper clippings.
Summative Perfor-mance Task	**Argument** **Extension**	How does segregation occur in the United States today? Develop a critical analysis that addresses this compelling question using relevant information from your research, discussions, and journal entries. Create a multimodal presentation that addresses (be sure to include a creative activity that engages the class in your presentation) the compelling question through critical analysis using relevant historical and contemporary evidence to support your views. Be sure to include how your thinking about the issue has changed and how your newspaper article relates to the compelling question.	
Taking Informed Action	**UNDERSTAND** Identify at least one way that segregation exists in American society today at the local, state or national level. Include whether or not communities are involved and how. **ASSESS** Evaluate the differing points of views on the possible causes and solutions. **ACTION** Using the newspaper article and information from your research, discussion, and journal entries analyze the issue and develop a letter to the editor, an op-ed, or a letter to the local government agency or Board of Education (depending on the focus of the article). Formulate your action plan and include three recommendations on how to address the issue.		

Table A3: Black Athletes, Anti-Racist Activism and Patriotism Christopher L. Busey		
Compelling Question	Are Black activist athletes patriots?	
Standards and Practices	**D2.Civ.5.9–12.** Evaluate citizens' and institutions' effectiveness in addressing social and political problems at the local, state, tribal, national, and/or international level. **D2.Civ.12.9–12.** Analyze how people use and challenge local, state, national, and international laws to address a variety of public issues.	
Staging the Question	Show students an image of former San Francisco 49ers QB Colin Kaepernick taking a knee during the Star-Spangled Banner. Then play a video or provide direct quotes where Kaepernick explained his motives for kneeling during the national anthem being rooted in anti-Black racism and racial violence. Then have a discussion whether students consider Colin Kaepernick's decision to kneel patriotic or unpatriotic.	
Supporting Question 1	**Supporting Question 2**	**Supporting Question 3**
How did Black athletes resist and call attention to anti-Black racism during the mid-20th century?	Should contemporary athletes demonstrate anti-racist activism or just "play ball"?	How is Black athlete activism perceived?
Formative Performance Task	**Formative Performance Task**	**Formative Performance Task**
After analyzing primary source images and videos, students will discuss whether Black athlete activism during the mid-20th century was patriotic or unpatriotic.	Develop a claim explaining whether or not they believe Black athletes should participate in forms of anti-racist activism.	Summarize resistance to Black athletes' activism from the mid-20th century until present times.
Featured Sources	**Featured Sources**	**Featured Sources**
Source A: Image from the Cleveland Summit, June 4, 1967 **Source B:** Image of Tommie Smith and John Carlos Black Power Salute at the	**Source A:** Image of Colin Kaepernick kneeling during the national anthem http://assets.nydaily-news.com/polopoly_ fs/1.2986929.1488478315!/ img/httpImage/image.	**Source A:** Brent Musberger commentary on John Carlos and Tommie Smith Black Power Salute

Summer Olympics Mexico City, Mexico **Source C:** Muhammad Ali video interview regarding his refusal to fight in Vietnam **Source D:** The Black Scholar Interviews Muhammad Ali (http://www.theblackscholar.org/memoriam-black-scholar-interviews-muhammad-ali-1970)	jpg_gen/derivatives/article_1200/49ers-panthers-football.jpg **Source B:** Video or Image of St. Louis Rams Players "Hands Up, Don't Shoot" https://www.youtube.com/watch?v=xC6tSO9Ry3I **Source C:** Image of Miami Heat Players wearing hoodies in tribute to Trayvon Martin http://a4.espncdn.com/combiner/i?img=%2Fphoto%2F2012%2F0323%2Fnba_lebron1_300.jpg&w=267	http://www.oxfordaasc.com/public/features/archive/0712/photo_essay.jsp?page=6 **Source B:** Muhammad Ali and Vietnam article by Krishnadev Calamur from The Atlantic (https://www.theatlantic.com/news/archive/2016/06/muhammad-ali-vietnam/485717/) **Source C:** The Case of Hodges vs. the N. B. A. New York Times article (http://www.nytimes.com/1996/12/25/sports/the-case-of-hodges-vs-the-nba.html)
Summative Performance Task	**Argument**	Are Black activist athlete's patriots? Construct a written or oral argument that addresses the compelling questions by drawing upon evidence from the sources.
	Extension	Create a multimedia presentation such as a video blog, podcast, or talk show where students address the compelling question.
Taking Informed Action	Identify a national journalist or commentator who disagrees with students' individual perspectives. Have students write formal articles or send videos to the journalist/commentator engaging them in discussion as their perceptions on Black activist athletes as patriots.	

Table A4: Desegregation as a Strategy ArCasia James		
Compelling Question	Was desegregation the best strategy for challenging *separate but equal, according to students?*	
Standards and Practices	NY Grade 8: 8.9a The civil rights movement began in the postwar era in response to long-standing inequalities in American society, and eventually brought about equality under the law, but slower progress on economic improvements.	
Staging the Question	List reasons a student would want to desegregate. List reasons a student would not want to desegregate.	
Supporting Question 1	**Supporting Question 2**	**Supporting Question 3**
Which issues did the *Brown* decision try to mend in schools?	How did school conditions and climates change and vary for students before and after desegregation?	How did desegregating students view the issue, the process, and the outcomes?
Formative Performance Task	**Formative Performance Task**	**Formative Performance Task**
Identify examples of *separate but unequal* in US schools.	Generate a list about the merits and costs of desegregation for students.	Based on the list and evidence, generate an argument about desegregation.
Featured Sources	**Featured Sources**	**Featured Sources**
Source A: Mississippi Public School Integration http://www.mshistorynow.mdah.ms.gov/articles/305/the-last-stand-of-massive-resistance-1970 **Source B:** *Plessy v. Ferguson, 1896 http://www.loc.gov/exhibits/brown/brown-segregation.html#obj3* **Source C:** Instances of *separate but unequal http://www.loc.gov/*	**Source A:** Mississippi Public School Integration http://www.mshistorynow.mdah.ms.gov/articles/305/the-last-stand-of-massive-resistance-1970 **Source D:** Ave Alvarado-Blackwell's oral history excerpts of school desegregation. **Source E:** George W. McLaurin Segregated to the Anteroom *http://www.loc.gov/exhibits/brown/*	**Sources A, B, C, D, E, F, G, H, I and J** **Source K:** Nathaniel Banks' chapter excerpt (Banks, 2009)

exhibits/brown/ brown-segregation. html#obj20	*brown-segregation. html#obj47* **Source F:** School Integration in Clinton, Tennessee *http:// www.loc.gov/exhibits/ brown/brown-after- math.html#obj125C* **Source G:** School Dilemma: *Dorothy Geraldine Counts http://www.loc.gov/ exhibits/brown/ brown-aftermath. html#obj125B* **Source H:** The Little Rock Nine & US Army 101st Ariborne Division *http://www.loc.gov/ exhibits/brown/ brown-aftermath. html#obj130B* **Source I:** Ruby Bridges *http://www.loc.gov/ exhibits/brown/ brown-aftermath. html#obj148* **Source J:** "Free school" in Farm- ville, Virginia *http:// www.loc.gov/exhibits/ brown/brown-after- math.html#obj203A*	
Summative Performance Task	**Argument**	Did school desegregation accomplish its goals? Con- struct a composite character monologue that blends provided perspectives from evidence on desegregation from a student's perspective.
	Extension	Record a podcast or radio pro- gram on which students who desegregated discuss their experiences and opposing views.

Taking Informed Action	**UNDERSTAND** Identify racial re-segregation trends in a particular city, noting at minimum two key players and stakeholders in addition to current students. **ASSESS** Analyze the perspective of each identified stakeholder, and specifically evaluate how the views of the two non-students compare with those of current students. Weigh the costs and benefits of each perspective. **ACTION** Locate relevant contact information, and begin a correspondence exchange with students who are currently attending a racially segregated school. After securing permission and consent, encourage students to share their views with school, district, and city leadership.

Grant, Lee, and Swan, 2014

Table A5: Septima Clark (Elementary Grades) LaGarrett J. King	
Compelling Question	*What did Septima Clark mean by her quote "The air has finally gotten to the place that we can breathe it together"?*
Standards and Practices	*Apply civic virtues and democratic principles in school settings (**D2. Civ.7.3-5**).* *Identify the beliefs, experiences, perspectives, and values that underlie their own and others' points of view about civic issues (**D2.Civ.10.3-5**).* *Explain how rules and laws change society and how people change rules and laws (**D2.Civ.12.3-5**).* *Compare life in specific historical time periods to life today (**D2. His.2.3-5**).* *Generate questions about individuals and groups who have shaped significant historical changes and continuities (**D2.His.3.3-5**).*
Staging the Question	**Provide students with the following background information about Septima Clark. Brief discussion can follow as well.** **Septima Poinsette Clark** (May 3, 1898–December 15, 1987) was an American educator and civil rights activist. Clark developed the literacy and citizenship workshops that played an important role in the drive for voting rights and civil rights for African Americans in the Civil Rights Movement. Septima Clark's work was commonly under appreciated by Southern male activists. She became known as the "Queen mother" or "Grandmother" of the Civil Rights Movement in the United States. Martin Luther King, Jr. commonly referred to Clark as "The Mother of the Movement". Clark's argument for her position in the Civil Rights Movement was one that claimed "knowledge could empower marginalized groups in ways that formal legal equality couldn't." ***The Spread of Citizenship Schools*** Clark is most famous for establishing "Citizenship Schools" teaching reading to adults throughout the Deep South, in hopes of carrying on a tradition. The creation of citizenship schools developed from Septima Clark's teaching of adult literacy courses throughout the interwar years. While the project served to increase literacy, it also served as a means to empower Black communities. Her teaching approach was very specific in making sure her students felt invested in what they were learning, so she connected the politics of the movement to the needs of the people. She was not only teaching literacy, but also citizenship rights. Clark's goals for the

schools were to provide self-pride, cultural-pride, literacy, and a sense of one's citizenship rights. She was recruiting the rural communities to get involved with the movement. Citizenship schools were frequently taught in the back room of a shop so as to elude the violence of racist whites. The teachers of citizenship schools were often people who had learned to read as adults as well, as one of the primary goals of the citizenship schools was to develop more local leaders for people's movements. Teaching people how to read helped countless Black Southerners push for the right to vote, but beyond that, it also developed leaders across the country who would help push the civil rights movement long after 1964. The citizenship schools are just one example of the empowerment strategy for developing leaders that was core to the civil rights movement in the South. The citizenship schools are also seen as a form of support to Martin Luther King, Jr. in the nonviolent Civil Rights Movement. Source: https://en.wikipedia.org/wiki/Septima_Poinsette_Clark		

Supporting Question 1	Supporting Question 2	Supporting Question 3
Do all people need air to live? In your opinion, what does Septima Clark mean by "air"?	What does "literacy" mean?	Why did Septima Clark organize citizenship schools is the South?
Formative Performance Task	**Formative Performance Task**	**Formative Performance Task**
Explain what the "air" was like for African Americans during Septima Clark's time period.	Write a brief paragraph to explain how knowing how to **read and write** can help a person know (**be aware**) if they are being treated fairly.	Explain how Clark's *Citizenship Schools* were **similar** to *General Educational Development (GED) schools* that exist today? Explain how they were **different**?
Featured Sources	**Featured Sources**	**Featured Sources**
Septima Poinsette Clark Quotes See quote number 6 http://www.azquotes.com/author/22324-Septima_Poinsette_Clark	Septima Poinsette Clark Quotes See quote number 6	Septima Poinsette Clark Quotes See quote number 6

| Summative Perfor-mance Task | Argument | Write a paragraph that explains and supports Septima Clark's quote that *"the air has finally gotten to a place that we can breathe it together"*. |
| | Extension | Create a new quote for Septima Clark that will make her quote *"the air has finally gotten to a place that we can breathe it together"*, more clearly understood. |

Table A6: Freedom Schools in Mississippi (Middle Grades) LaGarrett J. King	
Compelling Question	*Why Were Freedom Summer Schools Organized in Mississippi?*
Standards and Practices	*Distinguish the powers and responsibilities of citizens, political parties, interest groups, and the media in a variety of governmental and non-governmental contexts (**D2.Civ.1.6–8**).*
	*Describe the roles of political, civil, and economic organizations in shaping people's lives (**D2.Civ.6.6–8**).*
	*Compare historical and contemporary means of changing societies, and promoting the common good (**D2.Civ.14.6–8**).*
	*Use questions generated about individuals and groups to analyze why they, and the developments they shaped, are seen as historically significant (**D2.His.3.6–8**).*
	*Analyze multiple factors that influenced the perspectives of people during different historical eras (**D2.His.4.6–8**).*
	*Explain how and why perspectives of people have changed over time (**D2.His.5.6–8**).*
	*Analyze how people's perspectives influenced what information is available in the historical sources they created (**D2.His.6.6–8**).*
Staging the Question	Provide students with the following background information about Mississippi Freedom Schools. Brief discussion can follow as well.
	"The Mississippi Freedom Schools were developed as part of the 1964 Freedom Summer civil rights project, a massive effort that focused on voter registration drives and educating Mississippi students for social change. The Council of Federated Organizations (COFO)—an umbrella civil rights organization of activists and funds drawn from SNCC, CORE, NAACP, and SCLC—among other organizations, coordinated Freedom Summer.
	In December 1963, during planning for the upcoming Freedom Summer project, Charles Cobb proposed a network of "Freedom Schools" that would foster political participation among Mississippi elementary and high school students, in addition to offering academic courses and discussions.

	Activists organizing the Freedom Summer project accepted Cobb's proposal and in March 1964 organized a curriculum planning conference in New York under the sponsorship of the National Council of Churches. Spelman College history professor Staughton Lynd was appointed Director of the Freedom School program. *Over the course of Freedom Summer, more than 40 Freedom Schools were set up in black communities throughout Mississippi. The purpose was to try to end political displacement of African Americans by encouraging students to become active citizens and socially involved within the community. Over 3,000 African American students attended these schools in the summer of 1964. Students ranged in age from small children to the very elderly with the average approximately 15 years old. Teachers were volunteers, most of whom were college students themselves."* **SOURCE:** https://en.wikipedia.org/wiki/Freedom_Schools	
Supporting Question 1	**Supporting Question 2**	**Supporting Question 3**
What is the purpose of the Council of Federated Organizations (COFO)?	What types of activities did the Council of Federated Organizations (COFO) conduct during Freedom Summer?	Were there any fees that participants had to pay in order to participate in Freedom Summer?
Formative Performance Task	**Formative Performance Task**	**Formative Performance Task**
Based on the Civil Rights activities listed on the COFO flyer, in which activities would you liked to have participated?	What other types of Civil Rights activities could COFO have included during Freedom Summer?	Are there any free Civil Rights summer activities available in your community today? Explain your answer.
Featured Sources	**Featured Sources**	**Featured Sources**
Council of Federated Organizations (COFO) Flyer https://tinyurl.com/COFOFlyer	COFO Flyer https://tinyurl.com/COFOFlyer	COFO Flyer https://tinyurl.com/COFOFlyer

Summative Performance Task	Argument	Write at least a paragraph that discusses how the COFO Flyer helps explain why the Freedom Summer activities were helpful to people during 1964.
	Extension	Pretend you are a teacher/volunteer in one of the Freedom Summer Schools during 1964. Create an outline of Civil Rights activities you would plan for your students.
Taking Informed Action	1. What are some Civil Rights issues that need attention in our local, state, or national community today? 2. What would be some benefits/advantages and disadvantages for attending to those issues? 3. Construct a brochure/flyer that advertises summer activities that address current local, state, or national Civil Rights issues.	

Table A7: Freedom Schools in Mississippi (Secondary Lesson) LaGarrett J. King	
Compelling Question	*Did the Mississippi Freedom Summer Schools make a difference in what students learned about Civil Rights education?*
Standards and Practices	*Evaluate citizens' and institutions' effectiveness in addressing social and political problems at the local, state, tribal, national, and/or international level (**D2.Civ.5.9–12**).*
	*Evaluate social and political systems in different contexts, times, and places, that promote civic virtues and enact democratic principles. (**D2.Civ.8.9–12**).*
	*Analyze the impact and the appropriate roles of personal interests and perspectives on the application of civic virtues, democratic principles, constitutional rights, and human rights (**D2.Civ.10.9–12**).*
	*Critique the usefulness of historical sources for a specific historical inquiry based on their maker, date, place of origin, intended audience, and purpose (**D2.His.11.9–12**).*
	*Integrate evidence from multiple relevant historical sources and interpretations into a reasoned argument about the past (**D2. His.16.9–12**).*
Staging the Question	Provide students with the following background information about Mississippi Freedom Schools. Brief discussion can follow as well.
	"In the summer of 1964, forty-one Freedom Schools opened in the churches, on the back porches, and under the trees of Mississippi. The students were native Mississippians, averaging fifteen years of age, but often including small children who had not yet begun school to the elderly who had spent their lives laboring in the fields. Their teachers were volunteers, for the most part still students themselves. The task of this small group of students and teachers was daunting. They set out to replace the fear of nearly two hundred years of violent control with hope and organized action. Both students and teachers faced the possibility, and in some cases, the reality, of brutal retaliation from local whites. They had little money and few supplies. Yet the Freedom Schools set out to alter forever the state of Mississippi, the stronghold of the Southern way of life."
	Source: INTRODUCTION FREEDOM SUMMER AND THE FREEDOM SCHOOLS
	By Kathy Emery, Sylvia Braselmann and Linda Reid Gold
	http://educationanddemocracy.org/FSCfiles/A_02_Introduction.htm

Supporting Question 1	Supporting Question 2	Supporting Question 3
What was the freedom movement?	Why were students and teachers in freedom schools?	What alternatives did the freedom movement offer students and teachers?
Formative Performance Task	**Formative Performance Task**	**Formative Performance Task**
What does freedom mean to you?	Based on the Freedom School Students' work, compare and contrast regular schools in 1964 and freedom summer schools in America in 1964.	In your opinion, how could American civil rights be taught to students so that there would be no need for the Freedom Summer School movement?
Featured Sources	**Featured Sources**	**Featured Sources**
Examples of Freedom Summer School Student Work http://www.educationanddemocracy.org/FSCfiles/B_18_ExcerptsOfStudentWork.htm	Examples of Freedom Summer School Student Work http://www.education-anddemocracy.org/FSCfiles/B_18_ExcerptsOfStudentWork.htm	Examples of Freedom Summer School Student Work http://www.education-anddemocracy.org/FSCfiles/B_18_ExcerptsOfStudentWork.htm

Summative Performance Task	Argument	After reading examples of students' work from the 1964 Freedom Summer Schools, write an essay defending the content of the students' work to be appropriate in American schools in 1964?
	Extension	• Among the various examples of students' work from the 1964 Freedom Summer Schools, which student examples are similar to what students write about in American schools today? • If you were a student in a Freedom Summer School during 1964 … … what would you want to write about? … why would your topic be important?
Taking Informed Action		Based on your findings from examples of students' work in 1964 Freedom Summer Schools, write a letter to your Congressional representative explaining how conditions for African Americans have improved and/or remained the same today

Table A8: Interracial Alliances during the Civil Rights Movement Noreen N. Rodriguez		
Compelling Question	How does Yuri Kochiyama personify interracial alliances during the Civil Rights Movement?	
Standards and Practices	Dimension 3, Evaluating Sources and Using Evidence Dimension 4, Communicating Conclusions and Taking Informed Action Grades 6–8, 9–12	
Staging the Question	Discuss how various racial groups may have interacted with and influenced each other during the Civil Rights Movement.	
Supporting Question 1	**Supporting Question 2**	**Supporting Question 3**
How did Japanese American incarceration during World War II affect how Asian Americans, and Yuri Kochiyama specifically, understood their racial positioning in U.S. society?	How did Yuri Kochiyama's heightened activism result in the use of her Japanese name, Yuri, rather than her previously used American name, Mary, when she was 48 years old?	How did Yuri Kochiyama's relationship with Malcolm X influence her activism?
Formative Performance Task	**Formative Performance Task**	**Formative Performance Task**
Review the language of Executive Order 9066 to determine which groups were targeted. Then compare this information to the populations that were incarcerated by the War Removal Authority and explain.	Yuri Kochiyama changed her name from Mary to Yuri in 1969 after joining the Republic of New Afrika (RNA). Briefly research the RNA and consider how the organization-in addition to Kochiyama's earlier activism-might have influenced her decision to use her Japanese name.	Read the transcript of a 1972 interview with Yuri Kochiyama and compare and contrast Kochiyama's activism before and after meeting Malcolm X in 1963.

Featured Sources	Featured Sources	Featured Sources
Executive Order 9066 Video excerpts of an interview with Yuri Kochiyama at Densho Project Video interview with Yuri Kochiyama at Democracy Now (introduction begins at 27:40, ends at 37:50)	*Yuri Kochiyama: Passion for Justice* (documentary) http://tinyurl.com/PassionforJustice Biographical paper about Yuri Kochiyama written by her granddaughter, Maya http://tinyurl.com/KochihamaBio	Interview from May 19, 1972 **http://tinyurl.com/KochiyumaInterview** Life Magazine photos of Malcolm X's death (graphic) http://time.com/3880035/yuri-kochiyama-at-malcolm-xs-side-when-he-died-is-dead-at-93/ Video interview at Democracy Now (start at 39:00) http://tinyurl.com/KochiyamaRemembers
Summative Performance Task	Argument	Students will write an essay that cites at least four events, organizations and/or individuals that influenced Yuri Kochiyama's life of activism
	Extension	Students' essays may be transformed into podcasts, videos, or other multimedia presentations that include primary sources. Supplementary reading can include excerpts from Kochiyama's autobiography, *Passing It On: A Memoir*, her biography by Diane C. Fujino, *Heartbeat of Struggle*, or the lyrics (with profanity removed) from Blue Scholar's song "Yuri Kochiyama" (https://genius.com/Blue-scholars-yuri-kochiyama-lyrics). Short video by Asian Americans Advancing Justice (https://zinnedproject.org/2016/05/yuri-kochiyama-was-born/) includes multiple interviews with Yuri Kochiyama.

Taking Informed Action	How have seemingly different ethno-racial and religious groups worked in solidarity in the last decade for specific political purposes and/or issues? How have Asian Americans continued to move forward the activism that was born in the late 1960s and 1970s with contemporary issues such as affirmative action, voting rights, and media representation?

Table A9: Asian Americans and School Segregation Noreen N. Rodriguez		
Compelling Question	Did Asian Americans experience segregation in school?	
Standards and Practices	Dimension 2, Change, Continuity, and Context; Dimension 2, Perspectives Grades 3–5, 6–8	
Staging the Question	Discuss the various rationales for segregation in public schools.	
Supporting Question 1	**Supporting Question 2**	**Supporting Question 3**
How did different racial groups experience segregation in schools?	How did *Gong Lum v. Rice* affect the racial designation of Asian Americans?	What arguments were used to defend the exclusion of Asian Americans from White public schools?
Formative Performance Task	**Formative Performance Task**	**Formative Performance Task**
Compare and contrast the school experiences of Sylvia Mendez, Ruby Bridges, and Mamie Tape.	Describe how the 14th Amendment was applied to Asian American schoolchildren in the *Gong Lum v. Rice* case.	Compare the arguments used in *Tape v. Hurley* and *Gong Lum v. Rice* to explain how the segregation of Asian American children in public schools was justified.
Featured Sources	**Featured Sources**	**Featured Sources**
• Ruby Bridges Goes to School • *Mendez v. Westminster:* Desegregating California's Schools • AAPI Civil Rights Heroes: Mamie Tape	• *Gong Lum v. Rice* decision • *Gong Lum v. Rice* summary	• Beyond Black and White: API Students and School Desegregation • *Tape v. Hurley* decision

Summative Performance Task	Argument	Students will write an essay that explains the various arguments behind the segregation of Asian American children in public schools.
	Extension	Students' essays may be transformed into podcasts, videos, or other multimedia presentations that include primary sources. Supplementary read alouds/book clubs for elementary students may include *Separate is Never Equal* (Tonatiuh, 2014), *The Story of Ruby Bridges* (Cole, 1995), *Ruby Bridges Goes to School* (Bridges, 2000), and *Sylvia and Aki* (Conkling, 2011).
Taking Informed Action	Are schools more or less segregated now than they were in the 1960s after *Brown v. Board of Education?* Students can research statistics of public schools across the U.S., taking into account differences in urban, suburban, and rural schools and looking at different racial groups.	

Table A10: Examining the Chicano Movement Ellen Bigler	
Compelling Question	Background: How and why did the Chicano Movement differ from the black civil rights movement? In what ways were they similar? (This assumes that students have studied the black civil rights movement—New York State Social Studies Framework Key Ideas 11.10a). **Compelling Question: Should both the Chicano and the black civil rights movements be included in depth in U.S. History classrooms? Why or why not?**
Inquiry Standard (New York State Social Studies Framework Key Ideas)	11.10 SOCIAL AND ECONOMIC CHANGE/DOMESTIC ISSUES (1945–present): Racial, gender, and socioeconomic inequalities were addressed by individuals, groups, and organizations. b. Students will trace the following efforts in terms of issues/goals, key individuals and groups, and successes/limitations: Brown Power (Chicano) movement (e.g., Cesar Chavez, United Farm Workers)
Staging the Question	Should students and their communities have a say in what is taught in high schools? Should states determine what is taught in high schools? (Examination of current Arizona ban on ethnic studies classes in public schools compared to California's new requirement for an ethnic studies class for graduation, see for example http://www.houstonchronicle.com/opinion/out-look/article/Diaz-Mexican-American-studies-are-path-to-suc-cess-6222889.php)

Supporting Question 1	Supporting Question 2	Supporting Question 3
What problems did Mexican Americans face in the United States from their incorporation into the U.S. into the 1960s?	What key individuals and organizations challenged the status quo for Mexican Americans? What approaches did they use?	How and why did Chicano communities join in the struggles for change? How did the arts play a role in inspiring action?
Formative Performance Task	**Formative Performance Task**	**Formative Performance Task**
How did the U.S. justify taking over half of Mexico? What were the effects for the U.S.? For Mexico? How did Mexicans in the U.S. become second class citizens?	After viewing Episode 5, list the following: What issues confronted Mexican Americans in the 1960s and 1970s? What were their responses?	The two videos document how everyday people took up the struggle for change in two different communities, East Los Angeles and Barrio Logan California.

What were the challenges for Mexican Americans? How did Mexican Americans push back against the unfair treatment in each of the following instances (jigsaw): • Pecan Shellers' work conditions • Longoria Affair • Sylvia Mendez' treatment in school • (Zoot Suit Riots time permitting)	What events and individuals are most memorable? Why? Compare notes with a partner.	What were the various reasons for their getting involved in each of these communities? What form did their involvement take? (In the video *Chicano Park*, the famous takeover of the park and the interviews with community members who respond to aspects of the Chicano Movement can be closely examined. "Involvement" ranges from cooking food for the marchers to producing art that has important political messages. Students will need advance preparation to understand the context.)
Featured Sources	**Featured Sources**	**Featured Sources**
(Review Mexican American War results as needed using PBS *Latinos* excerpts. Links to listed in **resources.** https://ri.pbslearningmedia.org/resource/51745c4f-f181-45a9-8feb-638537950dc0/the-mexican-american-war/#.WVwDc1GQzIW **Pecan Shellers Strike** http://www.apwu.org/labor-history-articles/pecan-shellers%E2%80%99-strike-sparked-hispanic-workers%E2%80%99-movement	Latino Americans: Episode 5, Prejudice and Pride (available for download on iTunes or on PBS for members) http://www.pbs.org/video/2365076196/ *Who Is a Chicano? And What Is It the Chicanos Want?* Ruben Salazar, Los Angeles Times 2/6/1970, p. 235. http://publishing.cdlib.org/ucpressebooks/view?docId=ft-058002v2&chunk.id=d0e7791&toc.depth=1&toc.id=d0e6486&brand=ucpress	**Blowouts** **Short version:** https://www.youtube.com/watch?v=FG-1pZOFX6xo **-OR-** **Long version:** https://www.youtube.com/watch?v=xY6cytReBm8 **Chicano Park** https://www.youtube.com/watch?v=hXw-ZLo8hrp4

Longoria
https://vimeo.
  com/98575791
 	
Mendez
http://latinousa.
  org/2016/03/11/
  no-mexicans-al-
  lowed-school-segrega-
  tion-in-the-southwest/
 	
Zoot Suit Riots
http://www.mercurynews.
  com/2013/06/04/zoot-
  suit-riots-sailors-vs-pachu-
  cos-a-turning-point-for-la-
  tino-culture-in-california/		

Summative Performance Task	**Argument**	Develop a list of similarities and differences between the two movements, considering struggles, responses, and goals. Construct an argument (e.g., detailed outline, poster, essay) that addresses the compelling question of whether both warrant in-depth inclusion in U.S. history classrooms, using relevant information from your research, or whether the African American experience is adequate.
	Extension	Examine the requirements for social studies and available electives in both urban and suburban schools in your region. Are there different requirements? How could that work to advantage or disadvantage student groups?
Taking Informed Action		Identify a contemporary concern in your own community or school that you would like to see improved. Evaluate competing claims from various perspectives for addressing or not addressing the issue. Propose an action that you believe would be effective and likely to accomplish your objectives. Cite information from what you have learned studying the civil rights movement in the U.S.

 C3 TEACHERS

Grant, Lee, and Swan, 2014

Resources

The list of resources provided is not intended to be an exhaustive list, but rather to point to materials pertinent to the chapters in this volume.

NCSS Standards and C3 Framework

National Council for the Social Studies Standards and C3 Framework

An abbreviation version of the standards is available for free on the website. Teachers can also purchase a copy of the standards that includes sample lessons and activities aligned with the NCSS standards. Two additional books on the C3 Framework are also available for purchase.
https://www.socialstudies.org/standards

C3 Teachers

C3 Teachers provides information on conducting inquiry and access to full lesson plans developed using the Inquiry Design Model (IDM). Teachers can use the IDM generator to modify existing lessons or create new ones. Although the site requires a log-in, all materials are free of charge.
http://www.c3teachers.org/

Understanding the Inquiry Design Model

Grant, S. G., Swan, K., & Lee, J. (2017). *Inquiry-based practice in social studies education: Understanding the inquiry design model.* Taylor & Francis.

Common Core State Standards

The Social Studies standards are a sub-topic within the English/Language Arts Standards
http://www.corestandards.org/ELA-Literacy/

African American Civil Rights Movement

Books/Print

Borstelmann, T. (2001). *The cold war and the color line: American race relations in the global arena.* Cambridge: Harvard University Press.
Dudziak, M. L. (2000). *Cold war civil rights: Race and the image of American democracy.* Princeton, NJ: Princeton University Press.
Levy, P. J. (1998). *The civil rights movement.* Westport, CT: Greenwood Press.
Lewis, J. (1998). *Walking with the wind: A memoir of the movement.* New York, NY: Simon and Schuster.

Menkart, D., Murray, A. D., & View, J. L. (Eds.). (2004). *Putting the movement back into civil rights teaching: A resource guide for classrooms.* Washington, DC: Teaching for Change.

Sturkey, W., & Hale, J. N. (Eds.). (2015). *To write in the light of freedom: The newspapers of the 1964 Mississippi Freedom Schools.* Jackson, MI: University Press of Mississippi.

Graphic Novels

Based upon John Lewis' experiences in the Civil Rights Movement, the three volume graphic novel tells the story of marches and their impact on the movement.

Lewis, J., Aydin, A., & Powell, N. (2013). *March: Book one.* Marietta, GA: Top Shelf Productions.

Lewis, J., Aydin, A., & Powell, N. (2013). *March: Book two.* Marietta, GA: Top Shelf Productions.

Lewis, J., Aydin, A., & Powell, N. (2013). *March: Three.* Marietta, GA: Top Shelf Productions.

Museums and Archives

The Civil Rights Digital Library
This digital library provides access to a number of digital collections that include unedited news film from WSB (Atlanta) and WALB (Albany, GA); the archives of the Walter J. Brown Media Awards. Teachers have access to a number of resources, including the Freedom on Film. http://crdl.usg. edu./?Welcome

Diggs-Johnson Museum
Small museum located in the Cherry Hill African Union Methodist Protestant Church in Granite Maryland.
http://diggsjohnsonmuseum.com/

Library of Congress Digital Collections

Two collections may be of interest to educators (1) the Civil Rights History Project which includes multiple oral history interviews; and (2) Cartoon Drawings: Herblock Collection which collects the civil rights political cartoons drawn by Herbert L. Block.
https://www.loc.gov/collections/?q=Civil+Rights+Movement

Maryland State Archives and the University of Maryland College Park
A Guide to the History of Slavery in Maryland includes primary sources, a timeline, and a narrative of the history of slavery in Maryland.
http://msa.maryland.gov/msa/intromsa/pdf/slavery_pamphlet.pdf

National Archives
The National Archives house numerous primary sources related to the
Civil Rights movement collected from the Office of Education, Census Bureau,
Social Security Administration, Department of Health, Education and Welfare,
and the Equal Employment Opportunity Commission, among others.
https://www.archives.gov/research/electronic-records/civil-rights.html

National Museum of African American History and Culture
The Smithsonian's newest museum opened in 2016 in Washington, D.C. The
museum website includes online collections and exhibits useful for planning
units on a wide variety of topics related to African American History.
https://nmaahc.si.edu/

Multimedia and Websites

Carter Center for K–12 Black History Education
The center conducts and disseminates research on the teaching K–12 Black
History as as designing curricula for use by teachers and districts.

Education and Democracy
The website includes access to the Freedom School Curriculum including a
Master Index and .pdf file of the entire curriculum. http://educationandde-
mocracy.org/ED_FSC.html

Facing History, Facing Ourselves is dedicated to teaching students about
hatred and bigotry. In addition to materials on race in U.S. history, teachers
can find resources related to immigration, antisemitism and the Holocaust,
human rights, and genocide. https://www.facinghistory.org/

Interactive Map: University of Washington
Interactive maps of social movements in the U.S. including the NAACP,
SNCC, CORE, Black Panther Party, and Civil Rights Congress
http://depts.washington.edu/moves/

National Association for the Advancement of Colored People (NAACP)
Official website of the NAACP includes a brief history of the organization.
http://www.naacp.org/oldest-and-boldest/

SNCC Digital Gateway
The Student Non-Violent Coordinating Committee website provides educators access to an interactive timeline, audio files from oral history interviews

(including Septima Clark), as well as other primary and secondary sources related to the history of the Civil Rights movement and the organization. https://snccdigital.org/

Teaching Tolerance Film Kits
All film kits from Teaching Tolerance are available to educators free of charge and include a teacher's guide. Titles include: *Selma Bridge to the Ballot Mighty Times: The Children's March America's Civil Rights Movement: A Time for Justice*
https://www.tolerance.org/classroom-resources/film-kits

The Rise and Fall of Jim Crow
Documentary and companion website from PBS. Teachers can find lessons plans, tools and activities, an interactive map, and primary source documents. http://www.pbs.org/wnet/jimcrow/

Voices of Baltimore
Life under Segregation Documentary film based on oral history interviews of individuals involved in the desegregation of public schools in Maryland. The film and companion teacher's guide are forthcoming.

Chicano Civil Rights Movement

Books/Print

Meier, M. S., & Revera, F. (1994). *The Chicanos: A history of Mexican Americans.* New York, NY: Hill & Wange Publishers.
Montoya, M., & Stavans, I. (2016). *Chicano movement for beginners.* Danbury, CT: For Beginners.
Valdez, L. (2011). *Zoot suit and other plays.* San Juan Bautista, CA: El Teatro Campesino.

Multimedia and Websites Activist State

Documentary on the San Francisco State strike in 1968.
https://www.youtube.com/watch?v=aoPmb-9ctGc

American Experience: Zoot Suits
Film documenting the zoot suit phenomena and the zoot suits riots. Includes a teacher's guide to the film. https://shop.pbs.org/american-experience-zoot-suit-riots-dvd-av-item/product/AMER7405

Chicano Park
Documentary of the creation of Chicano Park in San Diego, CA.
https://www.youtube.com/watch?v=hXwZLo8hrp4

Delores Huerta Foundation
Overview of Huerta's role in founding the UFW http://doloreshuerta.org/
dolores-huerta/

Interactive Map: University of Washington
Interactive maps of social movements in the U.S. including the United Farm
Workers, MeChA, Raza Unida Party, Chicano Newspapers, Brown Berets,
and LULAC
http://depts.washington.edu/moves/

NPR Online: Before "Brown v. Board"
Interview with Sylvia Mendez who integrated an all-white school in the Westminster District of California in the 1940s.
http://www.npr.org/sections/codeswitch/2014/05/16/312555636/
before-brown-v-board-mendez-fought-californias-segregated-schools

Ruben Salazar Man in the Middle
Documentary by Phillip Rodriguez examining the life and death of journalist
Rube Salazar.
http://www.pbs.org/program/ruben-salazar-man-middle/

The Delano Manongs
A short film produced by PBS/WGBH on the Delano Grape Strike of 1965
and the creation of the United Farm Workers. http://www.pbs.org/video/
kvie-viewfinder-delano-manongs/

GI Forum Flyer
Flyer announcing the *Gran Junta de Protesta*, after the death of Private Longoria during World War II. https://tamuccgarcia.omeka.net/items/show/57

The Great Wall in Los Angeles
History of The Great Wall murals including teaching materials from the Social
and Public Art Resource Center (SPARC)

The Lemon Grove Incident
Explores the story of the 1931 desegregation court ruling in a case about a California school that barred Mexican-Americans. Includes the film: The Lemon Grove Incident and other related materials compiled by the Zinn Education Project.
https://zinnedproject.org/materials/the-lemon-grove-incident/

Movimiento Estudiantil Chicano de Aztlan
Official website of M.E.CH.A.
http://www.chicanxdeaztlan.org/

The Turning Point: The San Francisco State Strike of 1968
Documentary includes primary new footage of the strike and interviews with participants.
https://www.youtube.com/watch?v=Qd6-P3kHRBY

Walkout in Crystal City
Overview of the student walk in Crystal City, Texas compiled by Teaching Tolerance.
https://www.tolerance.org/magazine/spring-2009/walkout-in-crystal-city

Who Is a Chicano? And What Is It Chicanos Want?
Article written by Ruben Salazar for the Los Angeles Times in 1970.
https://forchicanachicanostudies.wikispaces.com/file/view/Ruben+Salazar.pdf

Viva La Causa
Documentary of the Chicano movement from Teaching Tolerance provided free of charge to educators. Includes a teacher's guide.
https://www.tolerance.org/classroom-resources/film-kits/viva-la-causa

Museums and Archives

Bracero History Archive
Archives of primary sources documents and teaching resources covering the Bracero Program, 1942–1964
http://braceroarchive.org/

Farmworker Movement Documentation Project/Wayne State University
https://libraries.ucsd.edu/farmworkermovement/category/commentary/ufw-photoswayne-state-archives/

Handbook of Texas
Provides a brief history of the Mexican American Youth Organization founded in 1967.
https://tshaonline.org/handbook/online/articles/wem01

Library of Congress
Educators can access newspapers, photos, film and video covering a wide range of topics related to Latina/o history in the U.S. https://www.loc.gov/

National Park Service
Provides an overview Latina/o heritage in the United States.
https://www.nps.gov/subjects/tellingallamericansstories/americanlatino-heritage.htm

Pomona College Department of Theatres and Dance
The Zoot Suit Discovery Guide provides background materials, primary source documents, and a teacher's guide to examining the zoot suit era.
http://research.pomona.edu/zootsuit/

San Diego Mexican & Chicano History
Website maintained by the Sand Diego State University includes a section on Chicano Activism. http://aztlan.sdsu.edu/chicanohistory/

United States House of Representative: History, Art and Archives
Overview of Operation Wetback including photos and links to relevant sources.
http://history.house.gov/Exhibitions-and-Publications/HAIC/Historical-Essays/Separate-Interests/Depression-War-Civil-Rights/

Asian American Civil Rights Movement

Books/Print Materials

For Teachers

Chen, E. W., & Omatsu, G. (2006). *Teaching about Asian Pacific Americans: Effective activities, strategies, and assignments for classrooms and communities.* Lanham, MD: Rowman & Littlefield.
Fujino, D. C. (2005). *Heartbeat of struggle: The revolutionary life of Yuri Kochiyama.* Minneapolis, MN: University of Minnesota Press.
Lee, E. (2015). *The making of Asian America.* New York, NY: Simon & Schuster.

Louie, S., & Omatsu, G. (2001). *Asian Americans: The movement and the moment*. Los Angeles, CA: University of California Los Angeles Asian American Studies Center Press.

Maeda, D. J. (2011). *Rethinking the Asian American movement*. New York, NY: Routledge.

McWilliams, C. (1939). *Factories in the field*. Berkeley, CA: University of California Press.

Schlund-Vials, C. J., Wong, K. S., & Chang, J. O. (Eds.). (2017). *Asian America: A primary source reader*. New Haven, CT: Yale University Press.

Tachiki, A. (1971). *Roots: An Asian American reader*. Los Angeles, CA: Continental Graphics.

Takaki, R. (1983). *Pau Hana: Plantation life and labor in Hawaii, 1835–1920*. Honolulu, HI: University of Hawaii Press.

Takaki, R. (1989). *Strangers from a different shore*. San Francisco, CA: Back Bay Books.

Yang Murray, A. (2000). *What did the internment of Japanese Americans mean?* Boston, MA: Bedford/St. Martin's.

For Students
Picture Books
James, H. F., & Loh, V. S. (2013). *Paper Son: Lee's journey to America*. Ann Arbor, MI: Sleeping Bear Press.

Lee, M. (2006). *Landed*. New York, NY: Frances Foster Books.

Robles, A. D. (2006). *Lakas and the Makibaka hotel*. San Francisco, CA: Children's Book Press.

Uchida, Y. (1996). *The Bracelet*. New York, NY: Puffin.

Yin. (2001). *Coolies*. New York, NY: Philomel.

Chapter Books/Novels
Atkins, L., & Yogi, S. (2017). *Fred Korematsu speaks up*. Berkeley, CA: Heyday.

Conkling, W. (2011). *Sylvia and Aki*. Berkeley, CA: Tricycle Press.

Denenberg, B. (1999). *The Journal of Ben Uchida: Citizen 13559, Mirror Lake Internment Camp*. New York, NY: Scholastic.

Faulkner, M. (2014). *Gaijin: American prisoner of war*. New York, NY: Hyperion/Disney.

Rhodes, J. P. (2013). *Sugar*. New York, NY: Little, Brown & Company.

Sepahban, L. (2016). *Paper wishes*. New York, NY: Farrar Straus Giroux.

Yep, L. (2001). *Staking a claim*. New York, NY: Scholastic.

Young Adult Nonfiction
Braun, E. (2006). *Cesar Chavez: Fighting for farmworkers*. Mankato, MN: Capstone Press.

Freedman, R. (2014). *Angel Island*. New York, NY: Clarion.

Oppenheim, J. (2006). *Dear Miss Breed: True stories of the Japanese American incarceration during World War II and a librarian who made a difference*. New York, NY: Scholastic.

Museums and Archives

University of California at Berkeley's Asian American Studies
http://eslibrary.berkeley.edu/asian-american-studies-collection

Library of Congress
Photo collections of internment camps taken by Ansel Adams and Dorothea
Lang
http://www.loc.gov/pictures/collection/manz
https://www.nps.gov/manz/learn/photosmultimedia/dorothea-lange-
gallery.htm

San Jose Japanese American Museum
Includes online exhibitions on internment and Japanese-American history as
well as teaching resources.
http://www.jamsj.org/

Chinese Historical Society of America Museum
Online exhibitions chronicling the history of Chinese Americans.
https://chsa.org/

Angel Island Immigration Station Foundation
Angel Island is the Ellis Island of the West. Run by the National Park Service
the foundation website provides information on the history of the station and
the people who passed through its gates. https://www.aiisf.org/

University of California at Berkeley's Asian American Studies collection
http://eslibrary.berkeley.edu/asian-american-studies-collection

South Asian American Digital Archive
Archival collection includes photos, correspondence, lecture transcripts and
event pamphlets related to the life of Bhagat Singh Thind
https://www.saada.org/collection/bhagat-singh-thind-materials

Korematsu Institute
Collection of materials related to Japanese American internment and Fred T.
Korematsu's Supreme Court petition.
http://www.korematsuinstitute.org

San Francisco State University Collections
Documents and commentary on the Third World Liberation Front Strike at
SFSU
https://diva.sfsu.edu/collections/strike/7105

New York State Historical Society Museum and Library
Primary and secondary sources, video, and educational resources for teaching
Chinese American exclusion.
http://chineseamerican.nyhistory.org/we-have-always-lived-as-americans/

Websites and Digital Media

Densho
Collection of oral history interviews centered on Japanese American internment during World War II
https://www.densho.org

Zinn Education: Yuri Kochiyama Was Born
Overview of Kochiyama's work on behalf of Asian Americans, includes video clips from the documentary Asian Americans Advancing Justice, and links to other sources.
https://zinnedproject.org/2016/05/yuri-kochiyama-was-born/

Contributors

Jayne R. Beilke received her doctorate in History of American Education from Indiana University—Bloomington. She is a professor of social foundations and multicultural education at Ball State University. Her research interests are African American educational history and critical multicultural education. She is currently researching the reaction and resistance to the 1869 Indiana School Law, which established segregated schooling throughout the state.

Ellen Bigler entered public school teaching through National Teacher Corps, where she worked in an upstate New York urban school setting and earned her M.A.T. in secondary social studies education. She subsequently taught Social Studies in New York for 13 years before leaving to pursue graduate work in cultural anthropology. Ellen served as consultant for the New York State K–12 curriculum project Latinos in the USA: Yesterday, Today and Tomorrow, and has led teacher training sessions on diversity-related issues. She is the author of American Conversations: Puerto Ricans, White Ethnics, and Multicultural Education, and her publications include "Hispanics/Latinos" in the Anthropology text Race and Ethnicity: The United States and the World. Ellen holds a joint appointment in Educational Studies and Anthropology at Rhode Island College (RIC), where she prepares secondary social studies teachers and teaches courses.

Whitney G. Blankenship earned her Ph.D. at the University of Texas at Austin in the fall of 2010 in Social Studies Education. Prior to her move to higher education, Dr. Blankenship taught history and social studies at the secondary level for seventeen years. She joined the faculty of Rhode Island College in the fall of 2012 where she currently teaches in the Departments of Educational Studies and History. Her research interests include curriculum history, the integration of technology into the social studies, and place-based education.

Aaron C. Bruewer began his educational career in Ohio in 2002, graduating Miami University, Oxford and teaching six years of high school social studies before returning to Miami and earning his Masters in Teaching Political Science. He then continued his education at Ball State University earning a Doctorate in Educational Studies with a dissertation that focused on the first year phenomenological experience of social studies teachers. His focus is on ways to improve the curricular experience of K–12 students and teachers in social studies by encouraging teacher candidates to utilize philosophy, technology and multicultural education in meaningful and authentic ways—allowing students to reflectively enquire and experience a Deweyan democratic life in the classroom.

Christopher L. Busey is currently an assistant professor at the University of Florida in the School of Teaching and Learning. He began his career at Evans High School in Orland, FL where he taught world and U.S. history, global studies, and AP U.S. Government. After a brief stint teaching in New York City he completed his doctoral studies in Social Studies education in 2013 at the University of Florida. His research and teaching focuses on preparing teachers to work with culturally diverse population as well as implanting a meaningful and powerful educational experience.

Robert Cvornyek is a professor in the History Department at Rhode Island College where he specializes in sports history. He received his Ph.D. in History from Columbia University. He has written extensively on the intersection of race, sports, and cultural expression and, recently, edited the autobiography of baseball hall-of-famer Effa Manley. He served as co-curator and principal scholar for an exhibit at the Museum of African American History in Boston titled "The Color of Baseball in Boston: A History of Black Teams, the Players, and a Sporting Community." Robert also co-directs the program "It Don't Mean a Thing If It Ain't Got That Swing: Baseball, Jazz, and Black Cultural Expression."

Kristen E. Duncan is an Assistant Professor of Curriculum & Instruction at Texas State University. She earned her Ph.D. in Educational Theory & Practice at the University of Georgia, and her research focuses largely on the ways Black teachers help students navigate systems of White supremacy. Her research has appeared in *Social Education, Bank Street Occasional Papers Series*, and other journals and edited books.

Chaddrick Gallaway is a PhD student in Education Policy, Organization, and Leadership Department at the University of Illinois, Urbana-Champaign. He attended the University of Michigan as an undergraduate student and was a special education case manager in New Orleans, LA. In the spring of 2017, he earned his M.Ed from University of Illinois, Urbana-Champaign.

Chaddrick's research interest include intergroup dialogue, community colleges, racial climate on higher education campuses, Black women's roles during the Civil Rights Movement, Critical Race Theory, the sociology of education, diversity, equity and inclusion practices in the Preschool-Graduate institutions. He is currently a research assistant for The Office of Community College Research and Leadership as well as a University Council of Education Administration Barbara Jackson Scholar.

Bryan Gibbs taught social studies in East Los Angeles, California for 16 years. He is currently an Assistant Professor of Education at the University of North Carolina at Chapel Hill.

Gary A. Homana is an Assistant Professor in the Department of Elementary Education at Towson University where he teaches courses in urban education and ethics, education and change. His research interests include the social organization of classrooms and schools and their connection to community. He is particularly interested in the intersection of civic engagement, service-learning, school climate, and communities of practice for improved teaching and learning. He has been in involved in several national research studies and projects including the National Commission on Service-Learning, chaired by Senator John Glenn. Dr. Homana served as special assistant in education to Maryland's Governor where he was involved in numerous education initiatives including a statewide education program serving 6,000 at-risk youth and adolescents. He began his career as a music therapist working with autistic children in Boston.

ArCasia James is a PhD student in the Education Policy, Organization, and Leadership Department at the University of Illinois, Urbana-Champaign. She earned her BA from the University of Texas, Austin and taught social studies and literature domestically and abroad, subsequently completing her MSEd from the University of Pennsylvania. Her research interests include oral history, student narratives of school desegregation, the historic role of philanthropy in constructing Black educational and schooling practices, social studies curriculum, Critical Race Theory, and Black Feminisms. She is an Illinois Distinguished Fellow, a University Council of Education Administration Barbara Jackson Scholar, and a member of Phi Kappa Phi Honor Society.

LaGarrett J. King is an Assistant Professor of Social Studies Education. He received his Ph.D. from the University of Texas at Austin after an eight-year teaching career in Georgia and Texas. His primary research interest examines how Black history is interpreted and taught in schools and society. He also researches critical theories of race, teacher education, and curriculum history. Dr. King has received two early career scholar awards for the Critical Issues in Curriculum and Cultural studies special interest group of the American Educational Research Association and the College and University Faculty Assembly of the National Council for the Social Studies. He has also been published in scholarly journals such as *Theory and Research in Social Education, Race, Ethnicity, and Education, Journal of Negro History, and Teaching Education.*

Paul D. Mencke received a PhD in Cultural Studies and Social Thought in Education from Washington State University, and currently teaches in the Curriculum and Instruction Department at Texas State University. As a social justice educator he is most passionate about moving critical theory into practice in settings such as "Open Mic Fridays" at a local high school, and as a facilitator at a summer camp for elementary and middle school students.

John A. Moore is a Professor in the School of Teacher Education at Western Kentucky University. Dr. Moore is also a former President of the National Council for the Social Studies (2012–2013). His research interests are Pre-service Social Studies Teachers' Expectations of Student Teaching and Internship, The Teaching Profession and Civic Engagement in the Classroom, Multicultural Curriculum Development, Middle Level Education, Pre-service Teacher Reflection on Teaching. He can be reached john.moore@wku.edu

Phonsia Nie is a historian who specializes in 20th century U.S. history, Asian American history, and comparative race relations. She holds a PhD from Northwestern University in History and currently is an adjunct professor at the University of Texas Austin's Center for Asian American Studies.

Noreen Naseem Rodriguez is an assistant professor of elementary social studies at Iowa State University. She was a bilingual elementary teacher for nine years in Austin, Texas and studies how the pedagogy of Asian American and Latinx teachers is influenced by their cultural identities and understandings of citizenship.

Cinthia S. Salinas is a professor in Social Studies Education in the Department of Curriculum and Instruction in the College of Education at the University of Texas at Austin. An affiliate faculty member in the Bilingual/Bicultural and the Cultural Studies in Education program areas, her research focus includes more critical understandings of historical inquiry in elementary bilingual and secondary education late arrival immigrant ESL and bilingual classroom settings as well as broader understandings of citizenship. Her work also exams social studies teachers' use of histories that are essential to the civic identifies, agency and membership of Latinas/os.

Amanda E. Vickery is an Assistant Professor of Teacher Preparation at the Mary Lou Fulton Teachers College at Arizona State University. She teaches undergraduate and graduate courses in elementary social studies methods.

Her research focuses on how Black women teachers utilize experiential and community knowledge to reconceptualize the construct of citizenship. Her scholarship has been published in *Theory and Research in Social Education, Urban Education, Journal of Social Studies Research, Gender and Education, The High School Journal, Social Studies Research and Practice,* and *The International Journal of Multicultural Education.* Dr. Vickery is active in the social studies community and currently serves as Chair of the Scholars of Color Faculty Forum of the College and University Faculty Assembly (CUFA) of the National Council for the Social Studies (NCSS) and also serves as the Elections Chair on the CUFA Executive Board. She is a former middle school social studies teacher in Pflugerville, Texas.

Index

TEACHING CRITICAL THEMES IN AMERICAN HISTORY

Caroline R. Pryor, Jason Stacey,
Erik Alexander, Charlotte Johnson,
and James Mitchell
General Editors

In the United States, the Common Core Standards, the C3 Framework for Social Studies Standards (NCSS), and the 10 themes of the National Curriculum Standards (NCS/NCSS) each pose challenges for teachers preparing to teach skills, content, and critical issues of American history. The problem for many middle and secondary teachers is that textbooks do not contain sufficient primary source documents and varied secondary literature linked to these standards. The volumes in the Teaching Critical Themes in American His-tory fill this need by providing teachers with history content, pedagogical strategies, and teaching resources. The series is organized around key problems/issues in American history so that teachers can select which critical topics upon which they might want to concentrate.

Middle and Secondary pre-and in-service educators will find the books in this series essential for developing and implementing American history and social studies curriculum in diverse and complex classrooms. Teachers will find the books in this series valuable as they search for methodologies and material that will help them address the Common Core Standards in the social sciences and his-tory. Community College history instructors can also find the books in this series helpful as supplementary texts in their U.S. history survey courses. The practical—not to mention exciting—implementation of perspectives offered in each title is a key feature of this series.

This series will address topics such as the formation of the American Republic, the problem of slavery in America, causes of the Civil War, emancipation and reconstruction, America's response to industrialization, the New Deal, the fight for Civil Rights, and more. The Series Editors invite proposals for edited volumes in American history and social studies, along with articles and lesson plans for both the topics above, and other topics of the series.

For additional information about this series or for the submission of manuscripts, please contact any of the series editors.

Caroline R. Pryor | Jason Stacey
capryor@siue.edu | jstacy@siue.edu
Erik Alexander | Charlotte Johnson | James Mitchell
eralexa@siue.edu | shypoke09@gmail.com | MitchellCSUEB@aol.com

To order other books in this series, please contact our Customer Service Department: (800) 770-LANG (within the U.S.), (212) 647-7706 (outside the U.S.), or (212) 647-7707 (FAX). Or browse online by series at www.peterlang.com.